Personal Computing

**Communicating
With the
IBM PC Series**

1988   0 471 91667 6

**IBM PC
Upgraders Manual**

1988   0 471 63177 9

**DOS Productivity
Tips & Tricks**

1988   0 471 60895 5

**IBM PS/2
User's
Reference Manual**

1990   0 471 62150 1

Reference

**The Complete
Modem
Reference**

1991 0 471 52911 7

**Data and Computer
Communications:
Terms, Definitions
and Abbreviations**

1989   0 471 92066 5

NOW AVAILABLE

Save time and avoid keyboarding errors . . . . All major programs listed in this book are available on disk for your IBM PC or compatibles.

Order the program disk today from your computer store, bookseller, or by using the appropriate tear-off order card below (see over for details).

Please send me .... copies of **Held: Practical Network Design Techniques** Program Disk at $115 each plus my local sales tax.
ISBN (0 471 92942 5)

☐   Payment enclosed (Wiley pays postage and handling on prepaid orders)

☐ Bill me

☐ Charge my   Am Ex   Visa   MC   (Circle one)
    (Postage and handling will be added on bill and charge orders)

CARD NUMBER ⬚⬚⬚⬚⬚⬚⬚⬚⬚⬚⬚⬚⬚⬚⬚⬚ Exp. date ....

NAME ....

ADDRESS ....

....

CITY/STATE/ZIP ....

SIGNATURE ....
(Order invalid without signature)

Please send me .... copies of **Held: Practical Network Design Techniques** Program Disk at £51.75 each (including VAT)
ISBN (0 471 92942 5)

Orders for one disk only — please add £1.50 to cover postage.
Two or more disks — postage free.

☐   Remittance enclosed £ .... (payable to John Wiley & Sons Ltd)

☐   Please charge this order to my credit card (all orders subject to credit approval).
    Delete as necessary: AMERICAN EXPRESS, DINERS CLUB, BARCLAYCARD/VISA, ACCESS/MASTERCARD

    CARD NUMBER ⬚⬚⬚⬚⬚⬚⬚⬚⬚⬚⬚⬚⬚⬚⬚⬚

    Expiry date ....

☐   Please send me an invoice for prepayment.

NAME ....

ADDRESS ....

....

OFFICIAL ORDER NUMBER .... **SIGNATURE** ....
Please keep me informed of new books in my subject area which is

....

Order your disk from Wiley:

In the United States: John Wiley & Sons Inc, using the order card
                          below to NJ.

In the United Kingdom,   John Wiley & Sons Ltd, using the order card
Europe and the rest of   below to Bognor Regis.
the world:

Customer Service Department
John Wiley & Sons Limited
Distribution Centre
Shripney Road
Bognor Regis
Sussex PO22 9SA
England

■ PRACTICAL
NETWORK
DESIGN
TECHNIQUES

PRACTICAL NETWORK DESIGN TECHNIQUES

GILBERT HELD

4-Degree Consulting,
Macon, Georgia, USA

JOHN WILEY & SONS

Chichester • New York • Brisbane • Toronto • Singapore

Copyright © 1991 by John Wiley & Sons Ltd.
Baffins Lane, Chichester
West Sussex PO19 1UD, England

Other Wiley Editorial Offices

John Wiley & Sons, Inc., 605 Third Avenue,
New York, NY 10158-0012, USA

Jacaranda Wiley Ltd, G.P.O. Box 859, Brisbane,
Queensland 4001, Australia

John Wiley & Sons (Canada) Ltd, 22 Worcester Road,
Rexdale, Ontario M9W 1L1, Canada

John Wiley & Sons (SEA) Pte Ltd, 37 Jalan Pemimpin #05-04,
Block B, Union Industrial Building, Singapore 2057

Library of Congress Cataloging-in-Publication Data:

Held, Gilbert, 1943–
    Practical network design techniques / Gilbert Held.
       p.   cm.
    Includes index.
    ISBN 0 471 92938 7
    1. Data transmission systems.   2. Computer networks.   I. Title.
TK5105.H428   1991
004.6—dc20   90-49505

British Library Cataloguing in Publication Data:

Held, Gilbert *1943–*
    Practical network design techniques.
    1. Computer systems. Networks. Data transmission. Design &
    analysis
    I. Title
    004.65

    ISBN 0 471 92938 7

Printed in Great Britain by Courier International Ltd, Tiptree, Essex

CONTENTS

171749

4   Multiplexing and Line Sharing Equipment   65

PREFACE

One of many tasks associated with managing a nationwide data communications network is the training of employees. Although there are many fine schools and seminar companies that teach a variety of data communications related topics, conspicuous by its absence is a course or seminar that provides a practical guide to the design of networks. Recognizing this void, I originally developed a series of short monographs and lecture notes that I used as a basis to disseminate information to readers of a communications journal in the form of articles as well as to conduct informal lectures for employees covering a variety of network design techniques. Since the monographs and notes formed a foundation for writing this book, a discussion of the rationale behind the selection and presentation of material for the previously mentioned articles and lectures is warranted.

In developing the material to include in my articles and lectures, I had to first answer two key questions—what subjects in network design to cover and then how to present each subject. Although both questions at first appeared simple to resolve, in actuality I spent a considerable amount of time answering both to my satisfaction based upon journal readership and employee requirements to learn practical network design techniques.

Due to the tremendous growth in different types of networks and network structures based upon the introduction of new equipment and facilities, it is highly doubtful if any one book could ever be all-encompassing. Thus, one key decision criteria I faced was what subject areas to cover. Later, in writing this book I faced a similar decision criteria in determining the topics to include in print. In resolving both decision criterias I biased the subject areas upon which to focus upon topics relevant to the majority of persons involved in the field of data communications. Thus, such key problems as where to locate multiplexers, how many ports should multiplexers and concentrators have to service a given terminal population, how does one route a multidrop line to optimize its cost, and what type of line facilities should be used under different networking conditions were selected as subject areas to cover.

The second decision criteria I faced was how to present each subject area. Network design is perhaps the most mathematically rich of all areas in the field of data communications. Since my articles and lectures were presented to persons with a wide range of mathematical backgrounds, I initially developed a series of articles and lecture notes which emphasized the theory and practice of network design techniques without losing readers and students to 'mathphobia.' When I sat down to plot the development of the book you are reading, I realized I would be writing for a wider audience. Although I have included the relevant mathematics behind the design techniques presented in this book, I have also enumerated the basis for resolving each network design problem presented in this book. Furthermore, I have incorporated numerous Basic language programs and program segments as well as a few Lotus 1-2-3 models to illustrate how many network design problems can be automated if the reader desires to put theory to practice as a data communications practitioner.

The coding of both program segments and Basic programs are explained in this book to enable readers to use them as is, or to modify them for a specific requirement. In addition, a convenience diskette is available from the publisher at a nominal cost to facilitate the use of each program. Although a Microsoft Quick-Basic compiler was used by the author, standard Basic language statements were normally used to facilitate the conversion of programs for use with other Basic compilers and interpreters. The reader is referred to the response card included in this book for information concerning the ordering of the convenience diskette.

This book can be used by college students as a text to obtain an understanding of the major types of network design problems and their solution as well as a reference book for the data communications practitioner. To maximize the use of this book, I have included a large number of practical networking problems and their solution as well as examples of methods to perform economic comparisons between different communications services throughout this book. As always, I look forward to the comments of readers concerning the material in this book and also encourage you to send me your requests for the inclusion of additional network design problems you may wish to see in a second edition.

Gilbert Held
Macon, Georgia

ACKNOWLEDGEMENTS

The development of a book in many ways is similar in scope to the winning season of a sports team—success is dependent upon the effort of many individuals. The publication of this book is no exception. Thus, I would like to personally thank my publishers, Mr Ian McIntosh and Ms Ann-Marie Franks, for their effort in backing this project as well as coordinating the numerous steps required to convert a manuscript into the book you are reading. Concerning the original manuscript, once again I would like to thank Mrs Carol Ferrell for taking my handwritten notes and roughly sketched diagrams and converting them into a professional manuscript that my editors and proofreaders could work with. Lastly, I would like to thank my family for their understanding as I turned several rooms in our house into offices as I drafted and revised my notes and developed the Basic programs contained in this book.

INTRODUCTION

Network design can be considered as both a science and an art. The scientific foundation for network design is based upon mathematics that provide the applicable tools for solving such problems as where to locate data concentration equipment and how to route a multidrop line to minimize the cost associated with a circuit configured to connect multiple network locations onto a common transmission facility. The art associated with network design involves one having knowledge of the capabilities of different types of communications equipment and how such capabilities can be used to develop a variety of network configurations.

In this book we will focus the majority of our attention upon the scientific aspect of network design, using mathematical models to illustrate important networking concepts as well as to solve many common network design problems. Although we will also examine the capabilities and limitations of several types of data communications equipment, our coverage of the 'art' side to network design will not be as comprehensive as our examination of the 'scientific' aspect to network design. For additional information covering the operation, utilization, and constraints and limitations of over 25 specific types of data communications networking devices, the reader is referred to the book *Data Communications Networking Devices 2nd Edition* (John Wiley, Chichester, 1989). The information presented in that book will provide readers with a detailed understanding of the characteristics of communications equipment that can be used to develop an insight into the 'art' portion of network design.

1.1 RATIONALE

Although the title of this book references network design, its rationale is more inclusive than simply focusing on that topic. We will examine cost and performance issues that, while falling under the network design umbrella, can also be used by network analysts and designers as tools and techniques to follow to optimize existing networks with respect to their cost and/or performance. In several instances we will examine reports generated by communications equipment to obtain an understanding of how different report elements can be used to tailor the cost or performance of a network segment. While the large disparity between the use of different types of communications equipment in different networks may result in the examination of report parameters not being applicable to some readers, the concept concerning the use of equipment reports should be applicable to all readers.

1.2 BOOK OVERVIEW

In Chapter 2 we will focus our attention upon the transmission characteristics of batch and interactive transmissions systems. After examining the characteristics of each system we will develop several models that can be used to predict performance as well as to provide readers with a foundation for understanding key communications concepts.

To obtain a firm understanding of the economics associated with different types of communications facilities we will examine the cost associated with the use of several types of analog and digital circuits and switched network facilities in Chapter 3. In this chapter we will use tariffs that were in effect in early 1990. While the use of those tariffs illustrates several economic tradeoff concepts, readers are cautioned to obtain the latest tariff for each line facility under consideration to insure the validity of their economic analysis.

Since two of the most commonly utilized types of communications equipment are multiplexers and line sharing devices, we will examine their use in Chapter 4. In this chapter we will examine the economics associated with the use of the previously mentioned equipment as well as their operational characteristics and constraints associated with their use. In Chapter 5 we will examine the use of graph theory to solve equipment location problems, such as determining the location to install a remote multiplexer based upon the geographical distribution of terminals.

Due to the importance of multidrop lines we will continue our use of graph theory in Chapter 6, examining the application of this area of mathematics to developing an optimally routed multidrop line. In Chapter 7 we will use another area of mathematics originally developed for telephone traffic engineering to determine the appropriate number of ports for different types of data concentration equipment. The process covered in this chapter is more formally known as equipment sizing and can also be applied to determine the number of lines to install at a rotary.

2

TRANSMISSION CHARACTERISTICS

In this chapter we will examine the characteristics of batch and interactive transmission as all communications applications can be placed into one of these two categories. To accomplish this we will first review the constraints associated with the development of communications applications and the relationship of those constraints to each transmission category. Next, we will develop several models that will be used to project performance. Although we will limit our modeling to one protocol, its creation and exercise will provide readers with a foundation for developing similar models for other transmission protocols.

2.1 COMMUNICATIONS CONSTRAINTS

The development of communications based applications which are the foundation of our modern society involves many tradeoffs in terms of the use of different types of communications facilities, types of terminal devices, hours of operation and other constraints. Two of the key constraints associated with the development of communications applications are throughput and response time.

2.1.1 Throughput

Throughput is a measurement of the transmission of a quantity of data per unit of time, such as the number of records, block or print lines transmitted during a predefined interval. Throughput is normally associated with batch systems where the transmission of a large volume of data to a distant location occurs for processing, file updating or printing. As this is typically an extension of batch processing and since it occurs remotely from a data center, the device transmission is from or to is referred to as a remote batch or remote job entry device.

In most batch transmission systems, a group of data representing a record, block or print line is transmitted as an entity. Its receipt at its destination must be acknowledged when using many protocols prior to the next grouping of data being transmitted. Figure 2.1 illustrates the operation of a batch transmission system by time, with the waiting time indicated by shaded areas. Since throughput depends upon the waiting time for acknowledgements of previously transmitted data, one method used to increase throughput is to transmit more data prior to requiring an acknowledgement.

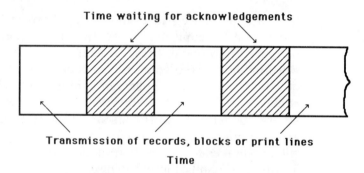

Figure 2.1   Batch transmission and throughput

$$\text{Throughput} = \frac{\text{Total records, blocks or print lines}}{\text{Total transmission time}}$$

2.1.2 Response time

Response time is associated with communications where two entities interact with one another, such as a terminal user entering queries into a computer system. Here each individual transaction or query elicits a response and the time taken to receive the response is of prime importance.

Response time can be defined as the time between a query being transmitted and the receipt of the first character of the response to the query. Figure 2.2 illustrates interactive transmission response time.

The optimum response time for an application is dependent upon the type of application. For example, a program that updates an

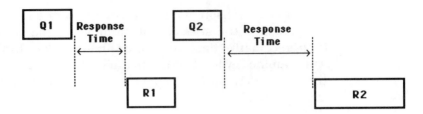

Figure 2.2 Interactive transmission response time

inventory could have a slower response time than an employee badge reader or an airline reservation system. The reason for this is that an employee entering information from a bill of lading or other data which is used to update a firm's inventory would probably find a 5 or 10 second response time to be satisfactory. For a badge reader system where a large number of workers arrive and leave during a short period of time, queues would probably develop if the response time was similar. With regard to airline reservation systems, many potential customers require a large amount of information concerning discount prices, alternate flights and time schedules. If the airline reservation clerk experienced a slow response time in scrolling through many screens of information to answer a customer query, the cumulative effect of a 5 second response time could result in the customer hanging up in disgust and calling a competitor. For other interactive communication applications, such as automated teller machines, competitive advertising has almost made slow response an issue involving the violation of a user's fundamental rights. In certain locations, it is quite common today to see banks battling against one another in advertisements over which has the fastest teller machines; yet another example of the use of communications to gain a competitive position.

2.2 INFORMATION TRANSFER RATE

Although it is common for many persons to express interest in the data transmission rate of a communications application, a reliance upon this rate can be misleading. In actuality, it is more important that analysts and designers should focus their attention upon the transfer rate of information in bits (TRIB). This rate, which is normally measured in bits per second (bps), similar to a data transmission rate, concerns the rate of flow of actual informative data. In comparison, a data transmission rate is the rate that bits flow across a transmission medium where the bits can represent both informative data and control information. In this section we will examine several factors that affect the TRIB which will provide the foundation for developing several transmission models later in this chapter.

2.2.1 Delay time

When data is transmitted between terminals, a terminal and a computer, or two computers, several delay factors may be encountered which cumulatively affect the information transfer rate. Data transmitted over a transmission medium must be converted into an acceptable format for that medium. When digital data is transmitted over analog telephone lines, modems must be employed to convert the digital pulses of the business machine into a modulated signal acceptable for transmission on the analog telephone circuit. The time between the first bit entering the modem and the first modulated signal produced by the device is known as the modem's internal delay time. Since two such devices are required for a point-to-point circuit, the total modem internal delay time encountered during a transmission sequence equals twice the modem's internal delay time. Such times can range from a few to 10 or more milliseconds. Even when transmission occurs on an all-digital facility, other equipment delay times will affect the information transfer rate. Here Data Service Units (DSUs) used for transmission at data rates up to 56/64 kbps or Channel Service Units (CSUs) used for T-carrier transmission at 1.544 Mbps will require some time to convert unipolar digital signals into bipolar digital signals.

A second delay encountered on a circuit is a function of the distance between points to be connected and is known as the circuit or propagation delay time. This is the time required for the signal to be propagated or transferred down the line to the distant end. Propagation delay time can be approximated by equating 1 millisecond to every 150 circuit miles and adding 12 milliseconds to the total.

2.2.2 Other delay factors

Once data is received at the distant end it must be acted upon, resulting in a processing delay which is a function of the computer or terminal employed as well as the quantity of transmitted data which must be acted upon. Processing delay time can range from a few milliseconds where a simple error check is performed to determine if the transmitted data was received correctly to many seconds where a search of a data base must occur in response to a transmitted query. Each time the direction of transmission changes in a typical half-duplex protocol, control signals at the associated modem to computer and modem to terminal interface change. The time required to switch control signals to change the direction of transmission is known as line turnaround time and can result in delays of up to 250 or more milliseconds, depending upon the transmission protocol employed.

We can denote the effect of the previously mentioned delays upon the information transfer rate by modeling the BISYNC communications protocol and a few of its derivatives. Although the resulting models are primarily applicable to batch transmission, the differences between the half- and full-duplex models will illustrate the advantages of the latter and similar gains can be expected from full-duplex transmission based upon the use of protocols that support this method of data transmission.

2.3 BISYNC COMMUNICATIONS PROTOCOL MODELS

One of the most commonly employed transmission protocols is the Binary Synchronous Communications (BISYNC) communications control structure. This line control structure was introduced in 1966 by International Business Machine Corporation and is used for transmission by many medium- and high-speed devices to include terminal and computer systems. BISYNC provides a set of rules which govern the synchronous transmission of binary-coded data. While this protocol can be used with a variety of transmission codes, it is normally limited to a half-duplex transmission mode and requires the acknowledgement of the receipt of every block of transmitted data. In an evolutionary process, a number of synchronous protocols have been developed to supplement or serve as a replacement to BISYNC, the most prominent being the High Level Data Link Control (HDLC) protocol defined by the International Standard Organization (ISO).

The key difference between BISYNC and HDLC protocols is that BISYNC is a half-duplex, character-oriented transmission control structure while HDLC is a bit-oriented, full-duplex transmission control structure. We can investigate the efficiency of these basic transmission control structures and the effect of different delays upon their information transfer efficiency. To do so, an examination of some typical error control procedures is first required.

2.3.1 Error control

The most commonly employed error control procedure is known as automatic request for repeat (ARQ). In this type of control procedure, upon detection of an error a request is made by the receiving station to the sending station to retransmit the message. Two types of ARQ procedures have been developed: 'stop and wait ARQ' and 'go back n ARQ', which is sometimes called continuous ARQ.

'Stop and wait ARQ' is a simple type of error control procedure. Here the transmitting station stops at the end of each block and waits for a reply from the receiving terminal pertaining to the block's accuracy (ACK) or error (NAK) prior to transmitting the next block. This type of error control procedure is illustrated in Figure 2.3. Here the time between transmitted blocks is referred to as dead time which acts to reduce the effective data rate on the circuit. When the transmission mode is half duplex, the circuit must be turned around twice for each block transmitted, once to receive the reply (ACK or NAK) and once again to resume transmitting. These line turnarounds, as well as such factors as the propagation delay time, station message processing time, and the modem internal delay time, all contribute to what is shown as the cumulative delay factors.

When the 'go back n ARQ' type of error control procedure is employed, the dead time can be substantially reduced to the point where it may be insignificant. One way to implement this type of error control procedure is by the utilization of a simultaneous reverse channel for acknowledgement signaling as illustrated in Figure 2.4. In this type of operating mode, the receiving station sends back an ACK or NAK response on the reverse channel for each transmitted block. If the primary channel operates at a much higher data rate than the reverse channel, many blocks may have been received prior to the transmitting station receiving the NAK in response to a block at the receiving station being found in error. The number of blocks one may go back to request a retransmission, n, is a function of the block size and buffer area available in the business machines and terminals at the transmitting and receiving stations, the ratio of the data transfer rates of the primary and reverse channels, and the processing time required to compute the block check character and transmit an acknowledgement. For the

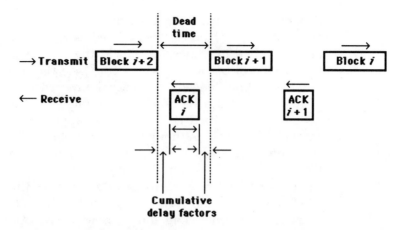

Figure 2.3 Stop and wait ARQ. In this type of error control procedure, the receiver transmits an acknowledgement after each block. This can result in a significant amount of cumulative delay time between data blocks

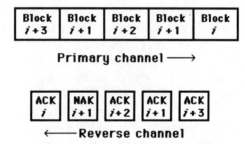

Figure 2.4 Go back n ARQ. In a 'go back n ARQ' error control procedure, the transmitter continuously sends messages until the receiver detects an error. The receiver then transmits a negative acknowledgement on the reverse channel and the transmitter retransmits the block received in error. Some versions of this technique require blocks sent before the error indication was encountered to be retransmitted in addition to the block received in error

latter, this time is shown as small gaps between the ACK and NAK blocks in Figure 2.4.

2.3.2 Half-duplex throughput model

When a message block is transmitted in the BISYNC control structure, a number of control characters are contained in that block in addition to the message text. If the variable C is assigned to represent the number of control characters per block and the variable D is used to represent the number of data characters, then the total block length is $C + D$. If the data transfer rate expressed in bps is denoted as T_R and the number of bits per character is denoted as B_C, then the transmission time for one character is equal to B_C/T_R which can be denoted as T_C. Since $D + C$ characters are contained in a message block, the time required to transmit the block will become $T_C * (D + C)$. Once the block is received, it must be acknowledged. To do so, the receiving station is required to first compute a block check character (BCC) and compare it with the transmitted BCC character appended to the end of the transmitted block. Although the BCC character is computed as the data is received, a comparison is performed after the entire block has been received and only then can an acknowledgement be transmitted. The time to check the transmitted and computed BCC characters and form and transmit the acknowledgement is known as the processing and acknowledgement time (T_{PA}).

When transmission is half duplex, the line turnaround time (T_L) required to reverse the transmission direction of the line must be added. Normally, this time includes the Request-to-Send/Clear-to-Send (RTS/CTS) modem delay time as well as each of the modems' internal delay time. For the acknowledgement to reach its destination, it must propagate down the circuit and this propagation delay time, denoted as T_p, must also be considered. If the acknowledgement message contains A characters then, when transmitted on the primary channel, $A * B_C/T_R$ seconds are required to send the acknowledgement.

Once the original transmitting station receives the acknowledgement it must determine if it is required to retransmit the previously sent message block. This time is similar to the processing and acknowledgement time previously discussed. To transmit either a new message block or repeat the previously sent message block, the line must be turned around again and the message block will require time to propagate down the line to the receiving station. Thus, the total time to transmit a message block and receive an acknowledgement, denoted as T_B, becomes

$$T_B = T_C * (D + C) + 2 * (T_{PA} + T_L + T_P) + (A * B_C/T_R)$$

Since efficiency is the data transfer rate divided by the theoretical data transfer rate, the transmission control structure efficiency (E_{TCS}) becomes:

$$E_{TCS} = \frac{B_C * D * (1 - P)}{T_R * T_B}$$

where P is the probability that one or more bits in the block are in error, causing a retransmission to occur.

Although the preceding is a measurement of the transmission

control structure efficiency, it does not consider the data code efficiency which is the ratio of information bits to total bits per character. When the data code efficiency is included, we obtain a more accurate measurement of the information transfer efficiency. We can call this ratio the Information Transfer Ratio (ITR) which will provide us with a measurement of the protocol's information transfer efficiency. This results in

$$\text{ITR} = \frac{B_{\text{IC}} * E_{\text{TCS}}}{B_{\text{C}}} = \frac{B_{\text{IC}} * D * (1 - P)}{T_{\text{R}} * T_{\text{B}}}$$

where,

ITR = information transfer ratio
B_{IC} = Information bits per character
B_{C} = total bits per character
D = data characters per message block
A = characters in the acknowledgement message
C = Control characters per message block
T_{R} = data transfer rate (bps)
T_{C} = transmission time per character ($B_{\text{C}}/T_{\text{R}}$)
T_{PA} = processing and acknowledgement time
T_{L} = line turnaround time
T_{P} = propagation delay time
P = probability of one or more errors in block

From the preceding, the information transfer ratio provides us with a more accurate measurement of the efficiency of the transmission control structure.

Computation examples

We will assume that our data transmission rate is 4800 bps and that we will transmit information using a BISYNC transmission control structure employing a 'stop and wait ARQ' error control procedure. Furthermore, let us assume the following parameters:

A = 4 characters per acknowledgement
B_{IC} = 8 bits per character
B_{C} = 8 bits per character
D = 80 data characters per block
C = 10 control characters per block
T_{R} = 4800 bps
T_{C} = 8/4800 = 0.001 66 seconds per character
T_{PA} = 20 milliseconds = 0.02 seconds
T_{L} = 100 milliseconds = 0.10 seconds
T_{P} = 30 milliseconds = 0.03 seconds
P = 0.01

Then

$$ITR = \frac{8 * 80 * (1 - 0.01)}{4800 * [0.001\,66 * (80 + 10) + 2 * (0.02 + 0.03 + 0.1) + (4 * 8/4800)]}$$

$$= 0.289\,05$$

Since the transfer rate of information in bits (TRIB) is equal to the product of the data transfer rate and the efficiency of the line discipline or protocol which we have denoted as the information transfer ratio, we obtain

$$TRIB = ITR * T_R = 0.289\,05 * 4800 = 1387 \text{ bps}$$

For the preceding example, approximately 29% of the data transfer rate (1387/4800) is effectively used.

Let us now examine the effect of doubling the text size to 160 characters while the remaining parameters except P continue as before. Since the block size has doubled, P approximately doubles, resulting in the ITR becoming

$$ITR = \frac{8 * 160 * (1 - 0.02)}{4800 * [0.001\,66 * (160 + 10) + 2 * (0.02 + 0.03 + 0.1) + (4 * 8/4800)]}$$

$$= 0.442\,94$$

With an ITR of 0.442 94 the TRIB now becomes

$$TRIB = ITR * T_R = 0.442\,94 * 4800 = 2156 \text{ bps}$$

Here, doubling the block size raises the percentage of the data transfer rate effectively used to 44.92% from approximately 29%.

To assist in the tabulation of ITRs for increasing block sizes, a computer program was written using Microsoft QuickBasic. Figure 2.5 contains a program listing of the file named BISYNC.BAS contained on the program disk readers of this book can optionally purchase. This program uses the previously assumed transmission control structure parameters to compute the information transfer ratio as the block size was varied from 80 to 3200 characters in increments of 80 characters. Table 2.1 contains the results obtained from the execution of the BISYNC.BAS program. In examining this table you will note that the ITR increases as the block size increases until a block size of 1040 characters is reached. Thereafter, the ITR decreases as the block size increases. This indicates that as the block size increases with a constant error rate, a certain point is reached where the time required to retransmit

```
REM BISYNC PROGRAM TO COMPUTE INFORMATION TRANSFER RATIO
DIM ITR(120), D(120)
A = 4'characters per acknowledgement
BIC = 8 'information bits per character
BC = 8  'total bits per character
D = 80' data characters per block
C = 10'control characters per block
TR = 4800'transmission rate in bits per second (bps)
TC = BC / TR'transmission time per character
TPA = .02 'processing and acknowledgement time in seconds (200 milliseconds)
TL = .1 'line turnaround time in seconds (100 milliseconds)
TP = .03' propagation dely time in seconds (30 milliseconds)
REM vary the block size from 40 to 2400 characters by 40
CLS
K = 1'initialize array pointer
FOR J = 1 TO 3
READ P
DATA .01,.0064,.00
IP = P
FOR D = 80 TO 3200 STEP 80
ITR = (BIC * D * (1 - P)) / (TR * (D + C) + 2 * (TPA + TL + TP) + (A * BC / TR)))
ITR(K) = ITR
D(K) = D
K = K + 1    'increment array pointer
P = P + IP   'increment probability of bit error
NEXT D
NEXT J
OPEN "BISYNC.WK1" FOR OUTPUT AS #1
FOR K = 1 TO 40
PRINT #1, D(K); ";"; ITR(K); ";"; ITR(K + 40); ";"; ITR(K + 80)
NEXT K
END
```

Figure 2.5   BISYNC.BAS program listing

a long block every so often due to one or more bits in the block being received in error negates the efficiencies obtained by the enlargement of the block size. For the parameters used in the previously constructed model the optimum block size is 1024 characters.

In actuality, a bit error rate of 1×10^{-5} or better is usually experienced on dial-up switched network facilities. Since the initial block size in the BISYNC.BAS program is 80 characters, this equates to a transmission of 640 data bits. Thus, a more realistic measurement of the ITR could be obtained by setting the probability of a bit error in a block (P) to 0.0064 in the program and incrementing that probability by 0.0064 for each block increase of 80 characters or 640 data bits. Table 2.2 contains the results obtained by modifying the BISYNC.BAS program as previously discussed. Note that the optimum block size has increased to 1360 characters.

Table 2.1 Information transfer ratio versus block size. (Probability of block error = 0.01.)

ITR	Block Size	ITR	Block Size
0.289 05	80	0.708 22	1680
0.442 94	160	0.702 56	1760
0.536 41	240	0.696 56	1840
0.597 67	320	0.690 26	1920
0.639 73	400	0.683 68	2000
0.669 44	480	0.676 87	2080
0.690 72	560	0.669 84	2160
0.706 00	640	0.662 61	2240
0.716 85	720	0.655 21	2320
0.724 35	800	0.647 65	2400
0.729 24	880	0.639 94	2480
0.732 06	960	0.632 10	2560
0.733 23	1040	0.624 14	2640
0.733 03	1120	0.616 06	2720
0.731 71	1200	0.607 88	2800
0.729 44	1280	0.599 61	2880
0.726 38	1360	0.591 25	2960
0.722 64	1440	0.582 81	3040
0.718 32	1520	0.574 29	3120
0.713 49	1600	0.565 70	3200

Table 2.2 Information transfer ratio versus block size. (Probability of block error = 0.0064.)

ITR	Block Size	ITR	Block Size
0.290 10	80	0.775 99	1680
0.446 19	160	0.773 90	1760
0.542 38	240	0.771 46	1840
0.606 63	320	0.768 73	1920
0.651 85	400	0.765 72	2000
0.684 82	480	0.762 48	2080
0.709 43	560	0.759 03	2160
0.728 10	640	0.755 38	2240
0.742 37	720	0.751 55	2320
0.753 32	800	0.747 57	2400
0.761 68	880	0.743 44	2480
0.768 00	960	0.739 18	2560
0.772 67	1040	0.734 80	2640
0.775 99	1120	0.730 31	2720
0.778 19	1200	0.725 72	2800
0.779 46	1280	0.721 03	2880
0.779 94	1360	0.716 26	2960
0.779 75	1440	0.711 40	3040
0.778 98	1520	0.706 47	3120
0.777 70	1600	0.701 47	3200

Block size versus error rate

A comparison of the data contained in Tables 2.1 and 2.2 illustrates an important concept that warrants elaboration as this concept has been applied to a variety of transmission systems to include the Microcom Networking Protocol (MNP) used in many modems. This concept is that an optimum block size is inversely proportional to the error rate. That is, a lower error rate results in a larger optimum block size, while a higher error rate results in a lower optimum block size.

Under one of the classes of the MNP protocol interactive data is assembled into packets for transmission. The size of these packets is adaptive and is based indirectly upon the line error rate. We say the adaptive packets are based indirectly upon the line error rate because the protocol counts negative acknowledgements in place of performing a bit error rate test that would preclude the transmission of data. In this instance Microcom took advantage of the fact that the error rate can vary considerably over the switched telephone network. Thus, when a lower error rate occurs the protocol places more data into a block or packet, while a higher error rate results in the protocol reducing the size of the packet.

To obtain another view of the relationship between protocol efficiency, block size, and error rate the previously constructed Basic program was executed using a value of 0 for P. This is the ideal situation where a continuously increasing block size produces additional efficiencies. Table 2.3 lists the ITR as a function of the block size when the probability of an error occurring is set to zero. While the ITR will approach a value of unity, it will do so at an extremely large block size which would be impractical to effect due to finite buffer sizes in computers.

In Figure 2.6 the ITR was plotted as a function of block size for the 0.01 and 0.0064 probability of error conditions as well as the error-free condition. The top line represents a zero probability of error which approaches unity as the block size increases. Since an error-free line is not something a data transmission network designer or analyst can expect, there will always exist a maximum block size beyond which line efficiency will decrease as indicated by the middle and lower curves in Figure 2.6. We can take advantage of this known phenomenon by either adjusting the block size of batch transmission to correspond to average line conditions or we can employ an adaptive protocol similar to the previously described MNP protocol. Regardless of the method used, it is important to understand that, in many instances, software default settings supplied with a vendor's product may be designed for 'average' line

Table 2.3 Information transfer ratio versus block size. (Probability of block error = 0.0.)

ITR	Block Size	ITR	Block Size
0.291 97	80	0.896 48	1680
0.451 98	160	0.900 72	1760
0.553 00	240	0.904 62	1840
0.622 57	320	0.908 23	1920
0.673 40	400	0.911 58	2000
0.712 17	480	0.914 69	2080
0.742 71	560	0.917 59	2160
0.767 39	640	0.920 30	2240
0.787 75	720	0.922 83	2320
0.804 83	800	0.925 21	2400
0.819 37	880	0.927 45	2480
0.831 89	960	0.929 56	2560
0.842 79	1040	0.931 55	2640
0.852 36	1120	0.933 42	2720
0.860 83	1200	0.935 20	2800
0.868 39	1280	0.936 89	2880
0.875 16	1360	0.938 49	2960
0.881 27	1440	0.940 01	3040
0.886 81	1520	0.941 46	3120
0.891 86	1600	0.942 84	3200

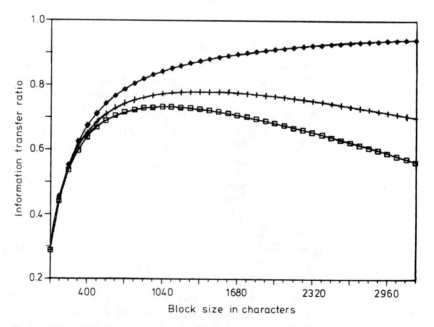

Figure 2.6 ITR plotted against block size (□ 0.01 probability of error, + 0.0064 probability of error, ◇ error free blocks)

conditions. As such, they may be far from optimum for the facilities used by your organization and a little effort and/or experimentation in changing the default settings may significantly increase the transmission efficiency of the product.

Now that we have examined how the size of a data block or packet can be altered to improve communication efficiency, let us focus our attention upon the effect of varying the protocol. Let us first examine the use of a return or secondary channel to transmit acknowledgements and then investigate the efficiency obtained from the use of a full-duplex protocol.

2.3.3 Return channel model

A return or secondary channel is built into many synchronous modems and provides a mechanism for the transmission of acknowledgements in one direction while data flows in the opposite direction. The use of this return channel eliminates the necessity of line turnarounds; however, transmission is still half duplex when a 'stop and wait ARQ' error control procedure is used, since an acknowledgement is only transmitted after each received message block is processed.

When the message block is sent to the receiving station, both propagation delay and processing delay are encountered. When the acknowledgement is returned, one additional propagation delay and processing delay results. In addition to these delays, one must also consider the time required to transmit the acknowledgement message. If A denotes the length in characters of the acknowledgement message and T_S is the reverse channel data rate in bps, then the transmission time for the acknowledgement becomes $(A * B_C)/T_S$. The total delay time due to the propagation and processing as well as the acknowledgement transmission time becomes

$$2 * (T_{PA} + T_P) + \frac{A * B_C}{T_S}$$

Thus, the information transfer ratio becomes

$$ITR = \frac{B_{IC} * D_1 * (1 - P)}{T_R * [T_C * (D + C) + 2 * (T_{PA} + T_P) + A * B_C/T_S]}$$

Let us examine the effect of this modified transmission procedure on the previous example where data was packed 80 characters per block. Let us assume that a 75 bps reverse channel is available and our acknowledgement message comprises four 8-bit characters. Then

$$ITR = \frac{8 * 80 * (1 - 0.01)}{4800 * [0.001\,66 * (80 + 10) + 2 * (0.02 + 0.03) + 4 * 8/75]} = 0.1953$$

Note that the ITR actually decreased. This was caused by the slowness of the reverse channel where it took $0.4266 * (4 * 8/75)$ seconds to transmit an acknowledgement. In comparison, the two line turnarounds that were eliminated only required 0.2 seconds when the acknowledgement was sent at 4800 bps on the primary channel. This modified procedure is basically effective when the line turnaround time exceeds the transmission time of the acknowledgement on the return channel. This situation normally occurs when the primary data transfer rate is 2400 bps or less. Thus, for a reverse channel to be efficient you should ensure that

$$\frac{A * B_C}{T_S} < 2 * T_L$$

2.3.4 Full-duplex model

A much greater throughput efficiency with the 'stop and wait ARQ' error control procedure can be obtained when a full-duplex mode of transmission is employed. Although this requires a four-wire circuit or modems that split a communications channel into two separate paths by frequency, the modems and line do not have to be reversed. This permits an acknowledgement to be transmitted at the same data rate as the message block but in the reverse direction without the line turnaround. Thus, the information transfer ratio becomes

$$ITR = \frac{B_{IC} * D * (1 - P)}{T_R * [T_C * (D + C) + 2 * (T_{PA} + T_P)]}$$

Again, returning to the original 80-character block example, we obtain

$$ITR = \frac{8 * 80 * (1 - 0.01)}{4800 * [0.001\,66 * (80 + 10) + 2 * (0.02 + 0.03)]} = 0.528$$

Note that the ability to simultaneously transmit data blocks in one direction and acknowledgements in the opposite direction raised the ITR from 0.289 05 to 0.528. Although the preceding model execution indicates that a full-duplex protocol can be much more efficient than a half-duplex protocol it is also important to understand that the overall efficiency is highly related to the size of the data blocks being transmitted. As an example, an interactive protocol in which the data block size averaged 20 characters would have an ITR of 0.22 when transmission was full duplex. Although this would be considerably higher than a half-duplex protocol in which the ITR would be 0.0925 with a block size of 20 characters, it is still relatively inefficient. This also explains why multiplexers or control units that gather and process data from several sources into a larger data block prior to transmission increase the efficiency of transmission.

In concluding this chapter, let us examine a variation of the previous model to examine the effect of a 'go back n ARQ' error control procedure. This error control procedure is employed in some non-standard BISYNC protocols and is a popular option supported by HDLC. Under a 'go back n ARQ' error control procedure only the block received in error is retransmitted. Here, the information transfer ratio becomes

$$\text{ITR} = \frac{B_{IC} * D(1 - P)}{T_R * [T_C * (D + C)]}$$

Again, substituting values from the original example we obtain

$$\text{ITR} = \frac{8 * 80 * (1 - 0.01)}{4800 * [0.001\,66 * (80 + 10)]} = 0.8835$$

This is obviously the most efficient technique since the line turn-around is eliminated and the processing and acknowledgement time (T_{PA}) and propagation delay time (T_P) in each direction are nullified due to simultaneous message block transmission and acknowledgement response. Based upon the preceding it becomes quite clear why a full-duplex transmission protocol that supports selective rejection is the most efficient method of data transmission.

3

LINE FACILITIES AND ECONOMIC TRADEOFFS

One of the most common problems facing network analysts and designers involves the selection of an appropriate line facility to satisfy the data transmission requirements of their organization. In this chapter we will examine the three basic types of line connections you can consider to support the transmission requirements of your organization. Using this information as a base, we will then examine several types of analog and digital transmission facilities as well as hybrid analog line facilities, including FX and WATS. Since tariffs, like taxes, constantly change, we will employ a set of rate schedules that were current when this book was written to illustrate the economic tradeoffs associated with different comparisons between two or more line facilities. While the rate schedules presented in this chapter may be similar to future tariffs, readers are cautioned that they should contact communications carriers to determine the actual tariffs in effect when they perform their economic analysis. Regardless of the actual tariffs in effect when your analysis is performed, the methods used in performing the economic comparisons presented in this chapter can be used as a guide for your analysis.

3.1 LINE CONNECTIONS

Three basic types of line connections are available to connect terminal devices to computer or to other terminals: dedicated, switched, and leased lines.

3.1.1 Dedicated line

A dedicated line is similar to a leased line in that the terminal is always connected to the device on the distant end, transmission always occurs on the same path, and, if required, the line can be easily tuned to increase transmission performance.

The key difference between a dedicated and a leased line is that a dedicated line refers to a transmission medium internal to a user's facility, where the customer has the right of way for cable laying, whereas a leased line provides an interconnection between separate facilities. The term facility is usually employed to denote a building, office, or industrial plant. Dedicated lines are also refered to as direct connect lines and normally link a terminal or business machine on a direct path through the facility to another terminal or computer located at that facility. The dedicated line can be a wire conductor installed by the employees of a company or by the computer manufacturer's personnel.

Normally, the only cost associated with a dedicated line in addition to its installation cost is the cost of the cable required to connect the devices that are to communicate with one another. Thus, the cost associated with a dedicated line can be considered as a one-time charge. In addition, once installed the dedicated line can be expected to have no associated recurring cost except maintenance, which may occur randomly in time. In comparison, facilities obtained from communications carriers normally have both one-time and recurring costs. The one-time cost is for the installation of the facility. The recurring cost can include a small monthly access line fee as well as a varying charge based upon minutes of use for communications over the switched telephone network. For a leased line, the recurring cost can include a monthly fee for line conditioning as well as the monthly cost of the portions of the line furnished by local exchange and interexchange carriers. The relationship between local exchange and interexchange carriers will be described when we examine leased lines in this section.

3.1.2 Leased line

A leased line is commonly called a private line and is obtained from a communications company to provide a transmission medium between two facilities which could be in separate buildings in one city or in distant cities. In addition to a one-time installation charge, the communications carrier will normally bill the user on a monthly basis for the leased line, with the cost of the line usually based upon the distance between the locations to be connected.

Until 1984, prior to AT&T's divestiture, the computation of the cost of a leased line was fairly simple as there were only two types of tariffs to consider in the United States—interstate and intrastate. Interstate tariffs were filed by AT&T and other common carriers, such as MCI and US Sprint, with the Federal Communications Commission. Intrastate tariffs were filed by Bell and independent operating companies with the public utility commissions of the states they operated in.

Although the distinction between interstate and intrastate survived divestiture, a new tariff criteria was added. This criteria considers whether or not a service is located within the local areas served by the divested local operating companies. These areas are called local access and transport areas, or LATAs, and essentially correspond to the metropolitan statistical areas defined by the US Commerce Department.

When a service is entirely within a LATA, it is an intra-LATA service, while a service linking two or more LATAs is known as an inter-LATA service. Since LATAs can cross state boundaries or reside entirely within a state there are both interstate and intrastate tariffs for inter- and intra-LATA service.

Within each LATA are interface points called points of presence (POPs) that are by law the only locations where interexchange carriers (IEC) can receive and deliver traffic. Thus, to establish a service between LATAs the local exchange carrier (LEC) facilities can be used to provide a connection to a selected IEC's POP. Once an IEC is selected, they will route their service to a POP at the destination LATA where the same or a different LEC provides a connection from the POP to the customer's distant premises.

Since many LATAs cross state boundaries while other LATAs are located entirely within a state, users have to contend with up to six types of tariffs in place of two prior to divestiture. Today there are inter-LATA, intra-LATA, and LATA access tariffs for both interstate and intrastate. To further add to the options available for user consideration, by law, users have the option to bypass the LEC and construct their own connection to the nearest central office of an interexchange carrier.

To illustrate the cost components of a leased line consider Figure 3.1 that illustrates the relationship between the LECs and a IEC. The POP or interface points where the IEC is connected to the LEC is normally a building housing facilities of both the IEC and LEC.

Users can select one of two methods to establish a leased

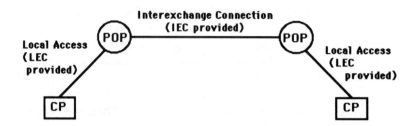

Figure 3.1 Leased line components. Unless the local exchange carrier is bypassed, a leased line will consist of two relatively short access lines provided by the same or different local exchange carriers and a line from the interexchange carrier used to connect each access line at a point of presence. (POP point of presence, IEC interexchange carrier, LEC local exchange carrier, CP customer premises)

line by ordering a transport circuit, which is also known as a baseline service, and a total-service circuit. When a transport service is ordered, the leased line is obtained from the IEC as a connection between the two distant central offices of that carrier, with the user responsible for coordinating with the LEC for the local connections at each end. Under this arrangement the user is responsible for ordering, maintaining, and testing the entire end-to-end connection as well as for overseeing the actual installation. When this occurs, the user will receive bills from each LEC for local access to the POP as well as from the IEC for the long-distance circuit.

Under the total-service concept, the IEC has end-to-end responsibility for ordering, installing, servicing, and billing, as well as for any maintenance. The IEC will coordinate the installation of the local access lines to the POP with each LEC. Normally, the IEC adds a small surcharge for the extra service and bills the user directly for both access lines and the IEC circuit on one bill.

The availability of a particular type of service depends upon both the LEC and IEC. In some instances, the LEC may not provide a service that the IEC offers. One example would be fractional T1, where an LEC might require the user to obtain a T1 access line to an FT1 facility. Similarly, not every IEC service may be available at each POP.

3.1.3 Switched line

A switched line, often referred to as a dial-up line, permits contact with all parties having access to the public switched telephone network (PSTN). If the operator of a terminal device wants access to a computer, he or she dials the telephone number of a telephone which is connected to the computer. In using switched or dial-up transmission, telephone company switching centers establish a connection between the dialing party and the dialed party. After the connection has been set up, the terminal and the computer conduct their communications. When communications have been completed, the switching centers disconnect the path that was established for the connection and restore all paths used so they become available for other connections.

The cost of a call on the PSTN is based upon many factors which include the time of day when the call was made, the distance between called and calling parties, the duration of the call, and whether or not operator assistance was required in placing the call. Direct dial calls made from a residence or business telephone without operator assistance are billed at a lower rate than calls requiring operator assistance. In addition, most telephone companies have three categories of rates: 'day', 'evening', and 'night and weekend'. Calls made between 8 a.m. and 5 p.m. Monday to Friday are normally billed at a 'day' rate, while calls between 5 p.m. and 11 p.m. on weekdays are usually billed at an 'evening' rate, which reflects a discount of approximately 33% over the 'day' rate. The last rate category, 'night and weekend', is applicable to calls made between 10 p.m. and 8 a.m. on weekdays as well as anytime on weekends and holidays. Calls during this rate period are usually discounted 50% from the 'day' rate.

Table 3.1 contains a sample PSTN rate table which is included for illustrative purposes but which should not be used by readers for determining the actual cost of a PSTN call as the cost of intrastate calls by state and interstate calls vary. In addition, the cost of using different communications carriers to place a call between similar locations will typically vary from vendor to vendor and

Table 3.1 Sample PSTN rate table (cost per minute in cents).

| | Rate Category | | | | | |
| | Day | | Evening | | Night and weekend | |
Mileage between locations	First minute	Each additional minute	First minute	Each additional minute	First minute	Each additional minute
1–100	0.31	0.19	0.23	0.15	0.15	0.10
101–200	0.35	0.23	0.26	0.18	0.17	0.12
201–400	0.48	0.30	0.36	0.23	0.24	0.15

readers should obtain a current state or interstate schedule from the vendor they plan to use in order to determine or project the cost of using PSTN facilities.

3.2 LEASED VERSUS SWITCHED FACILITY ANALYSIS

Cost, speed of transmission, and degradation of transmission are the primary factors used in the selection process between leased and switched lines.

As an example of the economics associated with comparing the cost of PSTN and leased line usage, assume a personal computer located 50 miles from a mainframe has a requirement to communicate between 8 a.m. and 5 p.m. with the mainframe once each business day for a period of 30 minutes. Using the data in Table 3.1, each call would cost $0.31 * 1 + 0.19 * 29$ or $5.82. Assuming there are 22 working days each month, the monthly PSTN cost for communications between the PC and the mainframe would be $5.82 * 22$ or $128.04. If the monthly cost of a leased line between the two locations was $450, it is obviously less expensive to use the PSTN for communications. Suppose the communications application lengthened in duration to 2 hours per day. Then, from Table 3.1, the cost per call would become $0.31 * 1 + 0.19 * 119$ or $22.92. Again assuming 22 working days per month, the monthly PSTN charge would increase to $504.24, making the leased line more economical.

Thus, if data communications requirements to a computer involve occasional random contact from a number of terminals at different locations, and each call is of short duration, dial-up service is normally employed. If a large amount of transmission occurs between a computer and a few terminals, leased lines are usually installed between the terminal and the computer.

Since a leased line is fixed as to its routing, it can be conditioned to reduce errors in transmission as well as permit ease in determining the location of error conditions since its routing is known. Normally, switched circuits are used for transmission at speeds up to 9600 bits per second (bps); however, in certain situations data rates as high as 19 200 bps are achievable when transmission on the PSTN occurs through telephone company offices equipped with modern electronic switches.

Some of the limiting factors involved in determining the type of line to use for transmission between terminal devices and computers are listed in Table 3.2.

Table 3.2 Line selection guide.

Line type	Distance between transmission points	Speed of transmission	Use of transmission
Dedicated (direct connect)	Local	Limited by conductor	Short or long duration
Switched (dial-up)	Limited by telephone access availability	Normally less than 9600 bps	Short duration transmission
Leased (private)	Limited by telephone company availability	Limited by type of facility	Long duration or many short duration calls

3.2.1 Servicing additional terminals

Now let us assume that instead of one terminal there are four terminals, each requiring 30 minutes of access per day to the distant mainframe. As previously computed, the monthly cost of using the public switched network would be $128.04 per terminal or $512.16 for four terminals, each having a daily transmission requirement of 30 minutes. However, if each terminal device were to use a separate line the relationship between the total switched network cost and leased line cost would remain the same, negating any rationale for comparing the cost of the transmission cost of individual terminals using the PSTN to the cost of providing communications via multiple leased lines. Fortunately, communications equipment manufacturers have developed a variety of products that can be employed to share the use of a leased line among terminal devices. These products include a variety of multiplexers, data concentrators, and line sharing devices whose operation and utilization are described in subsequent chapters in this book.

3.2.2 Line sharing economics

To illustrate the potential advantages associated with the use of line sharing devices, let us examine how a multiplexer could be used to share the use of a leased line among many terminal devices and the economics associated with its use.

Figure 3.2 illustrates two methods by which a multiplexer system could be used to enable four terminal devices to share the use of a common leased line. In the top portion of Figure 3.2, it is assumed that each terminal device is within close proximity

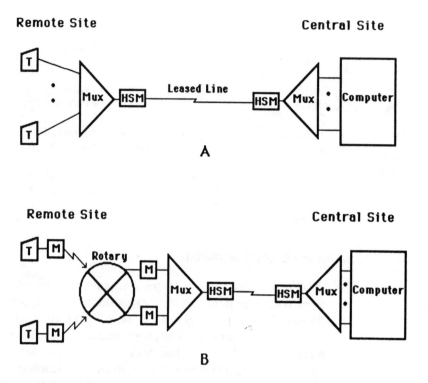

Figure 3.2 Using multiplexers to share a leased line (A.) Directly connecting terminals. (B.) Using the PSTN to access the remote multiplexer (T terminal, M modem, HSM high-speed modem, MUX = multiplexer)

to the multiplexer, enabling each device to be directly cabled to the multiplexer at the remote site. In the lower portion of Figure 3.2, a diametrically opposite situation is assumed. Here the terminals are assumed to be dispersed within the same or different buildings and accessing the multiplexer is via local PSTN calls. Not shown, but perhaps obvious, are a variety of configurations representing combinations of directly connected terminals and terminals accessing the multiplexer via the PSTN.

Now that we have reviewed the basic use of multiplexers to share the transmission capability of a leased line among a number of data sources, let us focus our attention upon the economics of their use. This will allow us to observe that, in many instances, the cost of a leased line may represent only a small portion of the cost of using a leased line.

In examining Figure 3.2A note that both a pair of high-speed modems and multiplexers is required when transmission occurs over an analog leased line. If a digital leased line was used the modems would be replaced by Digital Service Units (DSUs);

however, their costs would also have to be considered in your economic analysis in place of the cost of modems.

Since the cost of cabling is a one-time charge while leased lines are billed monthly, without considering whether or not you will purchase or lease modems and multiplexers you will still have to determine how to proportion one-time costs into a monthly basis to be able to obtain a comparison to monthly PSTN usage. To do so most organizations will first attempt to determine a realistic system life for any hardware purchased and then divide the system life in months into any one-time costs to obtain an equivalent monthly cost. While this method ignores the cost of money when making an initial one-time expenditure, it represents a fairly accurate method during periods of low to moderate interest rates for a system life under four years. Since the system life of most communications equipment is typically three years or less, we will use this method and ignore the cost of money in the economic analysis performed in this chapter.

In comparing the cost of the network configuration illustrated in Figure 3.2A to the use of the PSTN shown in Figure 3.2B, let us make several cost assumptions. First, let us assume that four terminals will be cabled directly to the multiplexer at the remote site and the cables cost $25 per terminal. Next, let us assume that the multiplexers cost $1000 per unit and each high-speed modem costs $500 while the leased line has a $1500 installation charge and a $450 monthly recurring cost. If we assume a three-year (36-month) system life, the cost of the directly connected system illustrated in Figure 3.2A as computed in Table 3.3 is $20 800. Dividing that cost by the 36-month system life results in a monthly cost of $578.

Prior to computing the system cost associated with using the PSTN to access the remote multiplexer illustrated in Figure 3.2B, let us note the differences between that network configuration and the network configuration illustrated in Figure 3.2A. In Figure 3.2B, the use of the PSTN requires each terminal to have an access line to dial a modem connected to the multiplexer. Similarly, each dial-in line at the multiplexer also requires a PSTN access line. Thus, if no contention is designed into the system, $2 * T$ access lines will be required where T equals the number of terminals to be serviced. This is because when terminals communicate over the PSTN, modems will be required for each terminal and each dial-in line as illustrated in Figure 3.2B.

In analyzing the economics associated with the multiplexer configuration illustrated in Figure 3.2B the cabling costs associated with Figure 3.2A have been replaced by the cost of eight access lines and eight modems. Otherwise the cost of the multiplexers, high-

Table 3.3 System life and monthly cost computation directly connected terminals.

	One-time cost	Monthly recurring cost
Terminal cabling 4 @ $25	$ 100	
Multiplexers 2 @ $1000	2000	
High-speed modems 2 @ $500	1000	
Leased line	1500	$450
	$4600	$450
System life cost computation		
One time	$ 4600	
Recurring $450 * 36 months	16 200	
System life cost	$20 800	

Monthly cost $\dfrac{\$20\,800}{36} = \$578$

speed modems, and leased line remains the same. Assuming the installation cost of each access line is $50 and their monthly cost is $25, while the cost of the modems connected to the terminals and dial-in lines at the multiplexer are $300 per unit, Table 3.4 analyzes the system life and monthly cost of the PSTN multiplexer configuration. As indicated in Table 3.4, the monthly cost of a

Table 3.4 System life and monthly cost computation using the PSTN to access the multiplexer.

	One-time cost	Monthly recurring cost
Access lines	$ 400	$200
Modems		
Low speed 8 @ $300	2400	
High speed 2 @ $500	1000	
Multiplexers 2 @ $1000	2000	
Leased line	1500	450
	$7300	$650
System life cost computation		
One time	$ 7300	
Recurring $650 * 36 months	23 400	
System life cost	$30 700	

Monthly cost $\dfrac{\$30\,700}{36} = \$853$

multiplexed leased line system using the PSTN to access the remote multiplexer is $853 when one-time costs are amortized over the 36-month system life.

A comparison of the monthly cost of the configurations illustrated in Figure 3.2A and 3.2B illustrates an important communications concept. Whenever possible, it is normally economically advantageous to bypass the PSTN when multiplexing data sources that can be directly cabled to a device. Of course, when terminals are widely dispersed within a geographical area you cannot directly cable those devices to the multiplexer. However, as the number of terminals to be serviced increases it becomes possible to economize upon costs by limiting the number of dial-in access lines and modems at the remote multiplexer. This process is known as sizing the multiplexer and is explained in detail in Chapter 6.

Until now we have simply computed the PSTN cost without considering the total cost associated with using that facility to access a distant computer. Now let us expand upon the PSTN cost by treating that access method as a system and examine its various cost components.

Figure 3.3 illustrates the typical method by which terminal devices would use the PSTN to access remote computational facilities. Note that this configuration is very similar to the remote site configuration previously illustrated in Figure 3.2B, with the multiplexer replaced by the computer while the requirement for a pair of high-speed modems is eliminated since no leased line is required.

Assuming that long-distance calls will be required to access the computer from each terminal location you will want to examine the rate schedule of several communications carriers, such as AT&T, MCI, and US Sprint. Table 3.5 contains the rate schedule for AT&T

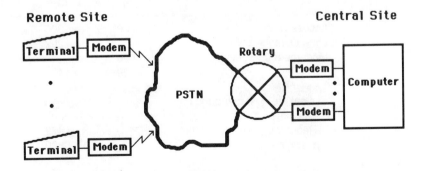

Figure 3.3 PSTN access to remote computer

Table 3.5 AT&T long distance service rate schedule tariff FCC No. 1 effective 11-29-89 direct-dialed station-to-station usage.

Rate mileage	Day		Evening		Night and weekend	
	Initial minute ($)	Additional minute ($)	Initial minute ($)	Additional minute ($)	Initial minute ($)	Additional minute ($)
1–10	0.1800	0.1700	0.1206	0.1139	0.1000	0.0975
11–22	0.2100	0.2000	0.1407	0.1340	0.1130	0.1100
23–55	0.2300	0.2200	0.1541	0.1474	0.1200	0.1200
56–124	0.2300	0.2200	0.1541	0.1474	0.1200	0.1200
125–292	0.2300	0.2300	0.1541	0.1541	0.1215	0.1215
293–430	0.2400	0.2300	0.1608	0.1541	0.1250	0.1225
431–925	0.2400	0.2400	0.1608	0.1608	0.1300	0.1260
926–1910	0.2500	0.2500	0.1675	0.1675	0.1325	0.1300
1911–3000	0.2500	0.2500	0.1675	0.1675	0.1350	0.1325
3001–4250	0.3100	0.3000	0.2077	0.2010	0.1650	0.1600
4251–5750	0.3300	0.3200	0.2211	0.2144	0.1750	0.1700

long-distance service that was in effect in early 1990 and which we will use to determine the cost of long-distance calls in the following analysis.

Table 3.6 indicates the PSTN system life and monthly cost comparison based upon the assumption that each terminal user requires an average of 10, 30, and 60 minutes of daily transmission to the remote computer 22 days per month. Assuming there is one call per day and the terminals are located 200 miles from

Table 3.6 PSTN system life and monthly cost computation.

	One-time cost ($)	Monthly recurring cost		
		10 min/ day ($)	30 min/ day ($)	60 min/ day ($)
Access lines	400	200	200	200
Long distance calls		202	607	1214
Modems 8 @ $300	2400			
	2800	402	807	1414
System life cost computation				
One time		2800	2800	2800
Recurring (monthly ∗ 36)		14472	29052	50904
System life cost		20800	31852	53704
Monthly cost (system life/36)		480	885	1492

the computer center, from Table 3.5 the initial minute and each additional minute cost $0.23. Thus, 1 hour of transmission would cost $13.80 and the monthly cost for 1 hour of transmission per day would be $13.80/hour * 1 hour/day * 22 days/month or $303.60. Note that the cost computations in Table 3.6 assume that access lines are required for each terminal as well as four access lines at the computer site. This results in a one-time cost of $400 and a monthly recurring cost of $200 based upon our previous assumption that the installation cost of an access line is $50 while their monthly cost is $25.

Based upon the previous assumptions, the use of the PSTN 10 minutes per day is more economical than using multiplexers, regardless of the method terminals employ to access the multiplexer system. As the average duration of PSTN usage increases the cost of PSTN usage increases. This results in an average PSTN daily usage of 30 minutes per day exceeding the cost of both methods of accessing a multiplexer system. Note that the monthly cost difference between PSTN usage 30 minutes per day ($885) and the use of a multiplexer where access is gained via the PSTN ($853) is essentially insignificant. In this situation you would probably prefer to continue using the PSTN to determine an average cost over a period of months prior to purchasing equipment necessary to install a multiplexer system and become committed to a leased line. However, if you observed or estimated an average of 60 minutes of PSTN usage per terminal the cost differences would now be of a sufficient magnitude to justify the use of a multiplexing system regardless of whether or not there could be some small variance in the average terminal daily transmission figure.

3.2.3 Concepts to consider

A review of the PSTN monthly costs based upon an average transmission of 10, 30, and 60 minutes per day illustrates several important concepts. First, even a minimal PSTN usage can have a substantial monthly cost due to the repeating cost of access lines and the amortization of one-time costs, such as the installation of access lines and the cost of modems. Secondly, the cost of PSTN usage is not actually uniform. As indicated in our example, the cost for 30 minutes per day of transmission is less than twice the cost of using the PSTN 20 minutes per day, while the cost for an average transmission of 60 minutes per day is approximately three times the cost associated with an average transmission of 10 minutes per day. The primary reasons for the non-uniform cost relationship include the one-time costs that are not based upon usage and the monthly access line fees that are also billed regardless of PSTN usage.

Although actual economic computations are no substitute for generalizations, we can summarize several economic concepts with respect to the use of the PSTN versus the use of leased lines. First, as the number of terminals accessing a computer facility and their transmission duration increase their cumulative monthly PSTN costs will increase. This is illustrated by curve C in Figure 3.4 which provides a general comparison of the costs of using the PSTN as opposed to multiplexing data sources onto a leased line. When transmission time is minimal the cost associated with the use of the PSTN is minimized; however, there is always an access charge and there may be one-time charges that form a base to which the cost of the calls build upon. Secondly, as the duration of communications increase long-distance PSTN charges will proportionally increase. Thus, both the number of data sources and the duration of their transmission will govern the majority of the costs associated with the use of PSTN facilities as both the number of data sources and their transmission duration increase.

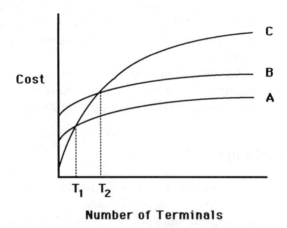

Figure 3.4 PSTN plotted against multiplexed leased line Costs. Curve A Data concentration with directly cabled terminals, Curve B PSTN access to data concentrator, Curve C PSTN access to remote computer

With regard to the use of multiplexers or other types of data concentration devices located at a remote site, we previously noted that direct cabling will be less expensive than PSTN access to a data concentration device. Curve A in Figure 3.4 represents the cost of data concentration when data sources are directly cabled to the data concentration device. This curve is relatively flat, with the increase in cost associated with an increasing number of terminals serviced by the data concentrator resulting from the additional one-time cabling cost for each terminal. Of course, a point will be reached where the multiplexer and high-speed modems may have to be replaced by devices with a higher capacity. While the cost for the expansion of multiplexers or the acquisition of higher speed modems is not shown in Figure 3.4, its effect would be to raise the curve at T_n, where T_n indicates the number of terminals that requires either servicing by large capacity multiplexers or the use of higher speed modems or both.

Curve B in Figure 3.4 represents the generalized cost of providing PSTN access to a data concentration device. Note that this curve is always higher than curve A and will similarly jump to a new height at T_n.

Two other general observations are warranted concerning Figure 3.4, which are the breakeven points labeled T_1 and T_2. T_1 represents the number of terminals whose total switched network system cost equals the cost of multiplexing or data concentration when terminals are directly cabled to a data concentration device. In general, this breakeven point occurs far quicker than T_2, which represents the breakeven point between using the PSTN and using a data concentration device where access to the device is via the PSTN.

Until now we have simply assumed a fixed monthly cost for a leased line. To provide readers with an indication of how the cost of an analog leased line varies by mileage AT&T's analog private line rate schedule that was in effect in early 1990 is reproduced in Table 3.7. The reader should note that the mileage band charges contained in Table 3.7 are only applicable to the mileage between the central offices serving each customer location. As such they do not include the cost of the local access from a subscriber's premises to an AT&T central office where the AT&T point of presence is located. The reader should also note that the central office monthly connection charge is per central office while the nonrecurring charge represents the one-time cost for connecting the local access line to AT&T's central office.

To illustrate the computation of interoffice channel charges, let us assume the mileage between offices was 1832. From Table 3.7 the fixed monthly charge would be $324.24 while the monthly charge per mile is $0.32. Thus, the monthly cost of a 1832 mile interoffice channel would be $324.24 + 1832 miles $* $0.32/mile or $910.48.

Table 3.7 AT&T analog leased line rate schedule (Tariff FCC No. 9 Effective 1/5/89).

Interoffice channel		
	Monthly Charge	
Mileage band	Fixed ($)	Per mile ($)
1–50	72.98	2.84
51–100	149.28	1.31
101–500	229.28	0.51
501–1000	324.24	0.32
1000+	324.24	0.32

Central office connection	
Monthly charge ($)	Nonrecurring charge ($)
16.40	196

3.3 ADDITIONAL ANALOG FACILITIES TO CONSIDER

There are several additional types of analog facilities offered by communications carriers readers may wish to consider. Two of the most common facilities are WATS and FX. Each of these facilities has its own set of characteristics and rate structure and requires an analytic study to determine which type or types of service should be utilized to provide an optimum cost-effective service for the user. In this section we will examine the operation and utilization of WATS and FX facilities and compare and contrast their use to PSTN and leased line facilities. In doing so we will assume certain costs associated with each service for comparison purposes; however, readers are again cautioned that they should contact their communications carrier to determine the actual cost of each service they are considering.

3.3.1 WATS

Introduced by AT&T for interstate use in 1961, wide area telephone service (WATS) is now offered by several communications carriers, including MCI and US Sprint. Its scope of coverage has been extended from the continental United States to Hawaii, Alaska, Puerto Rico, the US Virgin Islands, and Europe, as well as selected Pacific and Asian countries.

Wide area telephone service (WATS) may be obtained in two

different forms, each designed for a particular type of communications requirement. Outward WATS is used when a specific location requires placing a large number of outgoing calls to geographically distributed locations. Inward WATS service provides the reverse capability, permitting a number of geographically distributed locations to communicate with a common facility.

Calls on WATS are initiated in the same manner as a call placed on the public switched telephone network. However, instead of being charged on an individual call basis, the user of WATS facilities normally pays a flat rate per block of communications hours per month occurring during weekday, evening, and night and weekend time periods. Over the past few years, AT&T and other communications carriers have introduced a variety of WATS plans small businesses, as well as large volume users, can consider. Some of these plans, such as AT&T'S PRO WATS bill outward calls based upon the mileage to the called location, the time of day and an initial 30-second period as well as 6-second increments. Table 3.8 contains the AT&T PRO WATS Tariff No. 1 that was effective in early 1990.

Table 3.8 AT&T PRO WATS tariff intramainland and mainland to Hawaii and Alaska—dial station rates.

Rate mileage	Initial 30 second or fraction			Each additional 6 seconds or fraction		
	Day ($)	Evening ($)	Night ($)	Day ($)	Evening ($)	Night ($)
0–55	0.0960	0.0655	0.0485	0.0192	0.0131	0.0097
56–292	0.1080	0.0740	0.0565	0.0216	0.0148	0.0113
293–430	0.1155	0.0795	0.0600	0.0231	0.0159	0.0120
431–925	0.1195	0.0825	0.0640	0.0239	0.0165	0.0128
926–1910	0.1245	0.0855	0.0665	0.0249	0.0171	0.0133
1911–3000	0.1245	0.0855	0.0665	0.0249	0.0171	0.0133
3001–4250	0.1505	0.1035	0.0805	0.0301	0.0207	0.0161
4251–5750	0.1605	0.1105	0.0860	0.0321	0.0221	0.0172

In addition to the tariffs listed in Table 3.8, you must consider the cost of the WATS access line as well as volume discounts provided based upon usage volume. In general, PRO WATS provides at least a 10% discount in comparison to the use of the PSTN, and organizations with large outdial requirements may experience a 15% discount over the cost of using the switched network.

A voice-band trunk called an access line is provided to the WATS users. This line links the facility to a telephone company central office. Other than cost considerations and certain geographical calling restrictions which are a function of the service area of the WATS line, the user may place as many calls as desired on this trunk if the service is outward WATS or receive as many calls as desired if the service is inward.

For data communications users outward WATS, such as AT&T's PRO WATS, is normally used to provide communications between a central computer facility and geographically dispersed terminal devices that can be polled. In this type of communications environment the central computer will use an auto-dial unit during the evening or nighttime when rates are low to poll each terminal. Left powered on, the terminal will have an auto-answer modem and respond to the poll by transmitting previously batched data traffic to the computer for processing. Once all remote locations are polled and any required processing is completed the central computer may again dial each terminal, transmitting the processed data to its appropriate destination.

Since access lines and modems would be required for PSTN communications, the only difference in cost between outward WATS and the use of the PSTN involves the higher access line costs associated with WATS and its usage costs which, as previously explained, are 10 to 15% below the cost of using the PSTN. In general, PSTN long-distance usage exceeding $150 per month is the breakeven point between outward WATS and PSTN usage, with WATS providing a 10 to 15% savings over PSTN as the monthly cost of PSTN usage increases over $150.

Inward WATS, the well known '800' area code, permits remotely located personnel to call your facility toll-free from the service area provided by the particular inward WATS-type of service selected. The charge for WATS is a function of the service area. This can be intrastate WATS, a group of states bordering the user's state where the user's main facility is located, a grouping of distant states, or International WATS which extends inbound 800 service to the United States from selected overseas locations. Another service very similar to WATS is AT&T's 800 READYLINE[SM] service. This service is essentially similar to WATS, however, calls can originate or be directed to an existing telephone in place of the access line required for WATS service.

Figure 3.5 illustrates the AT&T WATS service area one for the state of Georgia. If this service area is selected and a user in Georgia requires inward WATS service, he or she will pay for toll-free calls originating in the states surrounding Georgia—Florida, Alabama, Mississippi, Tennessee, Kentucky, South Carolina, and North Carolina. Similarly, if outward WATS service is selected for

Figure 3.5   AT&T WATS service area one for an access line located in Georgia

service area one, a person in Georgia connected to the WATS access line will be able to dial all telephones in the states previously mentioned.

The states comprising a service area vary based upon the state in which the WATS access line is installed. Thus, the states in service area one when an access line is in New York would obviously differ from the states in a WATS service area one when the access line is in Georgia. Fortunately, AT&T publishes a comprehensive book which includes 50 maps of the United States, illustrating the composition of the service areas for each state. Similarly, a time-of-day rate schedule for each state based upon state service areas is also published by AT&T.

To illustrate the cost of inward WATS, we will examine the cost elements associated with AT&T's 800 service. Table 3.9 contains the 800 service rate schedule in effect in early 1990. The service areas numbered 1 to 6 refer to increasing bands of states surrounding the state the user is located in. Not shown are installation and access line charges as well as a service group charge and usage discounts that vary from 5% for charges exceeding $50 in a month to 15% for charges exceeding $1350 in a month. Concerning the service group charge, its fee of $20 per month per 800 number or band grouping is for the rotary that

Table 3.9 AT&T 800 service rate schedule.

Service Area	Per Hour of Use		
	Business day ($)	Night/evening ($)	Weekend ($)
1	13.42	11.06	8.90
2	13.88	11.43	8.92
3	14.11	11.61	9.35
4	14.55	11.99	9.65
5	14.79	12.18	9.80
6	16.15	13.30	10.70

automatically transfers calls to the next access line if the first access line is busy.

For cost comparison purposes let us assume that we want to service four geographically distributed terminals that will gain access to a computer system via the use of 800 service. Let us commence our analysis using four access lines and one hour per day of transmission similar to our previous PSTN economic analysis.

Figure 3.6 illustrates the use of 800 service to satisfy the communications requirements of four terminal users. Let us also assume each terminal will be serviced with a separate WATS access line, assuring the elimination of contention. Using a WATS access line charge of $267 and a recurring access line fee of $37 per month we can compute the cost for four terminals located in service area one outside of Georgia using 800 service to access a computer in that state. Table 3.10 indicates the system life and monthly cost computation to service the previously described transmission requirements via inward WATS. As indicated in Table 3.10, the expected monthly cost would be $1446, which is slightly less than the cost of using the PSTN one hour per day as computed in Table 3.6. Although the breakeven transmission time between

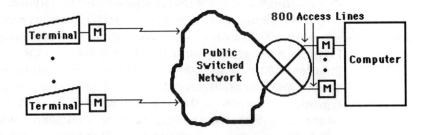

Figure 3.6 Using 800 service (M = modem)

Table 3.10 800 service system cost computation.

	One-time cost ($)	Monthly recurring cost ($)
Terminal access lines	200	100
WATS access lines	267	148
Service group		20
Low speed modems 8 @ $300	2400	
WATS usage 22 hrs/mo $* 4 * 13.42^{(1)}$		1098
	2867	1366
System life cost computation		
One time	2867	
Recurring $1466 $*$ 36 months	49176	
System life cost	52043	
Monthly cost	$\dfrac{52043}{36} = 1446$	

$^{(1)}$ Amounts in excess of $350, up to $1350, are reduced by 10%.

PSTN and 800 service will vary based upon access line charges, PSTN and WATS tariffs in effect, and average daily transmission duration, in general, savings from 800 service begin to accrue when daily transmission exceeds one hour per day. Thereafter, as transmission increases beyond one hour per day, 800 service will provide additional savings over the use of the PSTN.

3.3.2 FX

Foreign exchange (FX) service may provide a method of transmission from a group of terminal devices remotely located from a central computer facility at less than the cost of direct distance dialing. An FX line can be viewed as a hybrid combination of a leased line and public switched telephone network access.

Figure 3.7 illustrates the major components of a foreign exchange line and their relationship to one another. The access line is the local loop routed from the subscriber's premises to the serving telephone company's central office. The leased line connects the central office serving the end-user to a distant central office at which a connection to the PSTN occurs. That distant office is known as the foreign exchange, resulting in the name used to describe this hybrid combination of leased line and PSTN access line.

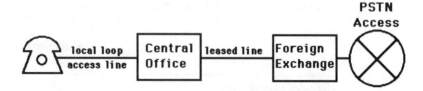

Figure 3.7 Foreign exchange line components. The foreign exchange line combines the use of a leased line and switched network access. When the local telephone is placed in an offhook condition a dial tone from the foreign exchange is received

The FX line can be used for both call origination and call reception. When the local telephone is placed off-hook, the subscriber receives a dial tone from the foreign exchange. Then, long-distance calls to the foreign exchange area can be made as local calls; however, the total cost of FX service will include the monthly cost of the access line to the central office, the leased line between the central office and the foreign exchange, as well as a monthly charge from the operating company providing the interconnection to the PSTN at the foreign exchange. The last charge can range from a flat monthly fee to a flat fee plus a usage charge, typically ranging between $0.05 and $0.10 per minute of use.

When used for call reception an FX line permits end-users to dial a local number to obtain long-distance toll-free communications. Figure 3.8 illustrates how an FX line could be used to service a number of terminal users located at a remote site. In this example, each terminal user would dial a local number associated with the foreign exchange and obtain a long-distance connection to the central site via a local call.

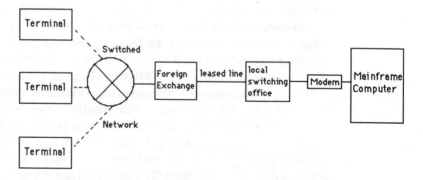

Figure 3.8 Foreign exchange (FX) service. A foreign exchange line permits many terminal devices to use the facility on a scheduled or on a contention basis

The use of an FX line permits the elimination of long-distance charges that would be incurred by users directly dialing the distant computer facility. Since only one person at a time may use the FX line, normally only groups of users whose usage can be scheduled are suitable for FX utilization—if you wish to install a single FX line. Otherwise, you can consider installing additional FX lines to reduce or eliminate potential contention between a number of remote terminal users and the number of FX lines available for connection to the central site computer.

The major difference between an FX line and a leased line is that any terminal dialing the FX line provides the second modem required for the transmission of data over the line; whereas a leased line used for data transmission normally has a fixed modem attached at both ends of the circuit.

Economics of use

The primary use of an FX line is to provide toll-free calls to or from a relatively small geographical area serviced by a foreign exchange. As such, its economics of utilization should be compared to the use of the switched telephone network and WATS.

To provide readers with an understanding of the economics associated with the use of FX lines, let us make some assumptions concerning the cost of the various components of this type of circuit. First, let us assume that the access line billed by the local operating company has an installation cost of $50 and a monthly recurring cost of $25. Next, let us assume that the leased line portion of the FX line has an installation cost of $200 and a monthly recurring cost of $450. Let us also assume that the open end of the FX line maintained by a distant operating company has an installation cost of $50, a monthly recurring cost of $25, and a usage cost of $0.08 per minute. Lastly, let us assume that the modem used by a terminal user and the modem connected to the closed end of the FX line each cost $300 and the system life of the line will be 36 months. Based upon the preceding assumptions, Table 3.11 summarizes the system life computations for an average transmission of 1 hour per day, 22 business days per month.

An analysis of the costs associated with the use of the FX line contained in Table 3.11 illustrates several important concepts concerning the economics associated with the use of a foreign exchange line. First, the recurring costs over the system life will normally substantially exceed the one-time cost to establish this type of communications system. Secondly, for a low volume of

Table 3.11 FX line system life cost computation.

	One-time cost ($)	Monthly recurring cost ($)
Closed end access line	50	25
Leased line	200	450
Open end		
Access line	50	25
Usage (60 * 22 * 0.08 * 1)		106
Modems 2 @ $300	600	—
	900	606
System life cost computation		
One time	900	
Recurring $606 * 36 months	21 816	
System life cost	22716	
Monthly cost	$\dfrac{22\,716}{36} = 631$	

transmission the cost per minute of an FX line will substantially exceed the cost of using the PSTN or WATS. This can be seen by dividing the monthly recurring cost of $606 by the 1320 minutes of transmission per month (60 * 22) which results in a per minute recurring cost of approximately $0.46. Only when a substantial volume of transmission is carried by an FX line will its cost per minute decrease to where it will be cost effective with PSTN and WATS. As an example of this consider the economics associated with increasing the transmission over the FX line to a daily average of 5 hours or 300 minutes. If this occurs, the monthly recurring cost would increase to $1028, resulting in a decrease in the per minute cost to approximately $0.16 per minute per month.

Since the per minute cost of an FX line will normally exceed the cost of using the PSTN or WATS, a reasonable question to ask is why use this line facility for data transmission? In comparison to PSTN usage, FX allows toll-free access. Thus, an organization installing an FX line could provide the access number for its customers to use without requiring the customer to make long-distance calls or collect calls that could not be accepted by a computer connected to a PSTN access line. In comparison to WATS, an FX line can be used for both incoming and outgoing calls whereas some WATS lines are restricted to either incoming or outgoing calls. Thus, a group of FX lines under certain circumstances may provide a more efficient data transmission mechanism than the use of groups of inward and outward WATS lines.

3.4 DIGITAL FACILITIES

In addition to analog service, numerous digital service offerings have been implemented by communications carriers over the last decade. Using a digital service, data is transmitted from source to destination in digital form without the necessity of converting the signal into an analog form for transmission over analog facilities as is the case when modems are used for data transmission.

3.4.1 AT&T offerings

In the United States, AT&T offers several digital transmission facilities under the Accunet^{SM} Digital Service service mark. Dataphone® Digital Service was the charter member of the Accunet family and is deployed in over 100 major metropolitan cities in the United States as well as having an interconnection to Canada's digital network. Dataphone Digital Service operates at synchronous data transfer rates of 2.4, 4.8, 9.6, 19.2, and 56 kilobits per second (kbps), providing users of this service with dedicated, two-way simultaneous transmission capability.

Originally all AT&T digital offerings were leased line services where a digital leased line is similar to a leased analog line in that it is dedicated for full-time use to one customer. In the late 1980s, AT&T introduced its Accunet Switched 56 service, a dial-up 56 kbps digital data transmission service. This service enables users to maintain a dial-up backup for previously installed 56 kbps AT&T Dataphone Digital Services leased lines. In addition, this service can be used to supplement existing services during peak transmission periods or for applications that only require a minimal amount of transmission time per day since the service is billed on a per minute basis.

Two other offerings from AT&T are Accunet T1.5 Service and Accunet Spectrum of Digital Services (ASDS). Accunet T1.5 Service is a high capacity 1.544 megabit per minute (Mbps) terrestrial digital service which permits 24 voice-grade channels or a mixture of voice and data to be transmitted in digital form. This service is only obtainable as a leased line and is more commonly known as a T1 channel or circuit.

Accunet Spectrum of Digital Services provides end-to-end single channel digital transmission at data rates ranging from 56 or 64 kbps up to 768 kbps in 64 kbps increments. Due to this transmission structure ASDS is also commonly referred to as a 'fractional' T1 or 'FT1' service.

3.4.2 European offerings

In Europe, a number of countries have established digital transmission facilities. One example of such offerings is British Telecom's KiloStream service. KiloStream provides synchronous data transmission at 2.4, 4.8, 9.6, 48, and 64 kbps and is very similar to AT&T's Dataphone Digital Service. Each KiloStream circuit is terminated by British Telecom with a network terminating unit (NTU), which is the digital equivalent of the modem required on an analog circuit.

DSUs

A digital service unit (DSU) provides a standard interface to a digital transmission service and handles such functions as signal translation, regeneration, reformatting, and timing. The DSU is designed to operate at one of five speeds: 2.4, 4.8, 9.6, 19.2, and 56 kbps. The transmitting portion of the DSU processes the customer's signal into bipolar pulses suitable for transmission over the digital facility. The receiving portion of the DSU is used both to extract timing information and to regenerate mark and space information from the received bipolar signal. A second interface arrangement for AT&T's Dataphone Digital Service is called a channel service unit (CSU) and is provided by the communication carrier to those customers who wish to perform the signal processing to and from the bipolar line, as well as to retime and regenerate the incoming line signals through the utilization of their own equipment.

As data is transmitted over digital facilities, the signal is regenerated by the communications carrier numerous times prior to its arrival at its destination. In general, digital service gives data communications users improved performance and reliability when compared to analog service, owing to the nature of digital transmission and the design of digital networks. This improved performance and reliability is due to the fact that digital signals are regenerated whereas, when analog signals are amplified, any distortion to the analog signal is also amplified.

Although digital service is offered in many locations, for those locations outside the serving area of a digital facility the user will have to employ analog devices as an extension in order to interface to the digital facility. The utilization of digital service via an analog extension is illustrated in Figure 3.9. As depicted in Figure 3.9, if the closest city to the terminal located in city 2

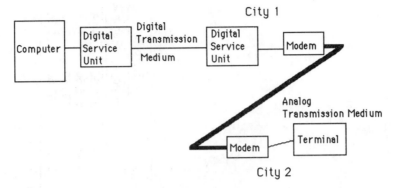

Figure 3.9 Analog extension to digital service. Although data are transmitted in digital form from the computer to city 1, they must be modulated by the modem at that location for transmission over the analog extension

that offers digital service is city 1, then to use digital service to communicate with the computer an analog extension must be installed between the terminal location in city 2 and city 1. In such cases, the performance, reliability, and possible cost advantages of using digital service may be completely dissipated.

3.4.3 Economics of use

Until late 1989, users considering digital transmission would primarily compare the potential use of DDS and Accunet T1.5 to single and multiple analog leased lines. In late 1989, AT&T and other communications carriers began to introduce fractional T1 facilities, resulting in users having to consider the economics associated with the use of this transmission facility with DDS and Accunet T1.5. In this section, we will examine the rate schedules associated with each of the three digital facilities that will form a basis for understanding the rationale for selecting an appropriate digital transmission facility. In addition, we will compare and contrast the rate structure of DDS to that of an analog line to understand why the use of DDS, in many instances, may not represent the least economical method for satisfying one's transmission requirements.

3.4.4 DDS

Similar to the cost of an analog leased line, the cost of a DDS line is primarily based upon the distance in miles between AT&T central

Table 3.12 AT&T dataphone digital service rate schedule monthly cost.

Mileage band	2.4 kbps		4.8 kbps		9.6 kbps		19.2 kbps		56 kbps	
	Fixed	Per mile	Fixed	Per mile	Fixed	Per mile	Fixed	Per mile	Fixed	Per mile
1–50	32.98	2.84	52.98	2.84	72.98	2.84	83.19	3.23	275.50	9.19
51–100	109.48	1.31	129.48	1.31	149.48	1.31	170.19	1.49	516.50	4.37
101–500	189.48	0.51	209.48	0.51	229.48	0.51	261.62	0.57	677.50	2.76
501+	284.48	0.32	304.48	0.32	324.48	0.32	366.26	0.36	1287.50	1.54

offices. Table 3.12 indicates the AT&T Dataphone Digital Service rate schedule in effect in early 1990.

In addition to the mileage cost indicated in Table 3.12, there are several other costs you must consider. These costs include the access lines to AT&T points of presence from each customer location, a flat rate AT&T bills customers for their central office DDS connection, and the cost of DSUs. To illustrate the cost of DDS service, let us assume you are considering the installation of a 450-mile 56-kbps digital circuit. Assume the local access lines and DDS central office connections have a one-time cost of $250 and a monthly recurring cost of $100. Table 3.13 indicates the computations required to determine the system life cost for the use of 56 kbps service. Note that the monthly DDS mileage cost is determined by adding the fixed cost of $677.50 to $2.76 per mile times 450 miles since the 450 miles of the DDS circuit is in the 101 to 500 mileage band and the per mile cost is based upon total circuit length falling in that band.

Table 3.13   56 kbps DDS system life cost computation.

	One-time cost ($)	Monthly recurring cost ($)
Access lines	250	100
AT&T central office	250	100
Mileage		1920
DSUs 2 @ $750	1500	____
	2000	2120
System life cost computation		
One time	2 000	
Recurring $2120 ∗ 36 months	76 320	
System life cost	78 320	
Monthly cost	$\dfrac{78\,320}{36} = 2176$	

Analog versus DDS

To provide readers with additional information concerning the economics associated with AT&T's DDS service as opposed to that vendor's private line analog service a simple Lotus 1-2-3 model was developed to project monthly line costs based upon distances of 1, 50, 100, 250, 500, 1000, and 2000 miles. The model developed is labeled DDS.WK1 on the convenience diskette sold as a supplement to this book. Table 3.14 contains the printout of the Lotus model that was developed to compare the monthly line cost of AT&T's analog and DDS facilities.

An examination of the cost entries contained in Table 3.14 indicates some interesting abnormalities concerning the price performance relationship of analog and DDS facilities. Since an analog leased line is capable of transmitting data at 19.2 kbps, its cost to performance ratio when performance is considered to be the obtainable data transmission rate on a line is slightly less than that obtainable from the use of a 19.2 kbps DDS facility. Here the better cost to performance ratio of an analog line is not totally unexpected since DDS is promoted as having a higher level of availability. However, what can we say about the cost relationship between the other four DDS facilities and an analog leased line?

The eighth column in Table 3.14 indicates the cost ratio between 56 kbps DDS and an analog line. If we assume that transmission on an analog leased line can occur at 19.2 kbps, in effect, the price ratio between 56 kbps DDS and an analog line should be approximately 2.9 if we simply considered the data transmission capacity of each facility. Note from column eight that the cost ratio between the two facilities ranges from a low of 3.75 to a high of 5.31. This indicates that the price structure of 56 kbps DDS is such that unless you absolutely require the data transportation capacity of that facility as an entity you may be better off considering the use of multiple analog leased lines. Even if you require a data transmission rate exceeding the 19.2 kbps data rate currently obtainable on analog leased lines it may be more economical to use a device known as an inverse multiplexer to share the transmission capacity of two or more analog lines as an entity rather than use a 56 kbps DDS facility. The reader is referred to the author's book *Data Communications Networking Devices 2nd Edition* for detailed information concerning the operation and utilization of inverse multiplexers.

To provide readers with a visual indication of the cost relationship between the five types of DDS facilities and an analog leased line, the cost columns contained in Table 3.14 were used to create a series of line graphs with the Lotus 1-2-3 PGRAPH program. The results obtained from the graphing of analog and DDS monthly circuit costs for distances from 1 to 2000 miles are illustrated in Figure 3.10. In that figure note the close cost relationship between analog and all DDS facilities except 56 kbps. This cost relationship indicates that users considering DDS should take advantage of its cost structure by obtaining a 19.2 kbps DDS

Table 3.14 Monthly line cost comparison.

Circuit Distance (miles)	Analog Line ($)	2.4kbps DDS ($)	4.8kbps DDS ($)	9.6kbps DDS ($)	19.2kbps DDS ($)	56 kbps DDS ($)	Ratio 56kbps DDS/Analog Monthly Cost ($)
1	75.82	35.82	55.82	75.82	86.42	284.69	3.75
50	138.48	174.98	194.98	214.98	244.69	735.00	5.31
100	280.28	240.48	260.48	280.48	319.19	953.50	3.40
250	356.78	316.98	336.98	356.98	404.12	1367.50	3.83
500	484.28	444.48	464.48	484.48	546.62	2057.50	4.25
1000	644.24	604.48	624.48	644.48	726.26	2827.50	4.39
2000	964.24	924.48	944.48	964.48	1086.26	4367.50	4.53

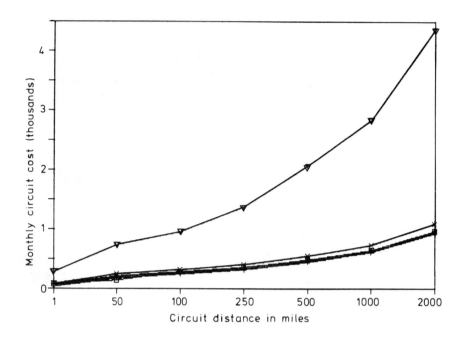

Figure 3.10 Analog plotted against DDS (analog + 2.4, 0 4.8, △ 9.6, × 19.2, ▽ 56)

facility if they project even a slight possibility of an increase in transmission requirements. Doing so will eliminate the installation costs associated with obtaining a 19.2 kbps DDS circuit at a later date.

Another interesting aspect of Figure 3.10 is the close cost relationship between analog and all DDS facilities other than 56 kbps DDS services. Thus, from an economic perspective, it may be less expensive to upgrade an existing analog leased line to operate at a higher data rate by obtaining higher speed modems than to replace that line by a higher speed DDS facility and have to pay a series of one-time charges for the local access and interexchange portions of a new DDS circuit.

3.4.5 Accunet T1.5

The 1.544 Mbps data transmission capability of Accunet T1.5 service provides a very cost effective method to integrate voice, data, and video transmission requirements between two locations. The use of Accunet T1.5, unlike DDS, will normally require the use of T1 multiplexers or channel banks to make effective use of the available bandwidth. In addition, since the functions of a DSU are built into T1 multiplexers, users of Accunet T1.5 will have a requirement for the use of a separate CSU on a T1 line.

To illustrate the economic tradeoffs between 56 kbps DDS and a 1.544 Mbps T1 line let us first examine AT&T's Accunet T1.5 service tariff that was in effect in early 1990. Table 3.15 lists the rate schedule for the circuit mileage between AT&T central offices.

Table 3.15   Accunet T1.5 service rate schedule monthly recurring charges.

Circuit miles	Fixed charge ($)	Per-mile charge ($)
1–51	1800	10.00
51-100	1825	9.50
100+	2025	7.50

DDS as opposed to Accunet T1.5

We can obtain an indication of the cost effectiveness of a T1 circuit by comparing the monthly cost of a 56 kbps DDS circuit to that of a T1 circuit. A T1 circuit can be used to support the transmission of twenty-four 56 or 64 kbps data sources, however, the monthly per mile charge between a 56 kbps DDS and a 1.544 Mbps T1.5 circuit is almost equivalent for circuits up to 50 miles in length, while at distances exceeding 500 miles the monthly circuit cost of an Accunet T1.5 facility is less than 5 times the cost of 56 kbps digital service although the T1.5 services provides 24 times the capacity of the DDS service.

As with other system cost computations, you must consider the installation and monthly cost of access lines to each AT&T point of presence as well as the cost of CSUs and multiplexers or channel banks when using Accunet T1.5 facilities. Once you do so, you will probably determine the breakeven point between separate 56 kbps DDS circuits and one Accunet T1.5 line to be between four and seven DDS circuits. The reason we say 'probably' is because of the number of variables that must be considered when developing the system cost of each facility, including operating company access line charges and DSU, CSU, and multiplexer costs.

3.4.6 Accunet spectrum of digital services

From a comparison of DDS and T1.5 monthly charges, it is obvious that end-users that required the use of a few 56 kbps circuits were previously forced to use a 1.544 Mbps facility even though the use of that facility resulted in a large amount of unused bandwidth. To alleviate this situation, as well as to promote the use of digital transmission based upon groupings of one or more 64 kbps time slots in a T1 carrier facility, AT&T and other vendors introduced fractional T1 service. AT&T's fractional T1 service is marketed under the name Accunet Spectrum of Digital Services (ASDS) and provides data transmission rates that are fractions of the 1.544 Mbps T1 transmission rate, ranging from a 56/64 kbps channel to a 768 kbps channel.

Comparison to other digital services

Table 3.16 contains AT&T's ASDS rate schedule which was in effect in early 1990. By comparing the mileage band rates between DDS, Accunet T1.5, and ASDS and their data transmission capability we can examine the relative cost/performance ratio of each facility. Although all tariffs are subject to change, we can obtain an indication of the cost performance relationship between each of the three AT&T digital transmission offerings by computing the monthly cost of different length circuits based upon each 1000 bits per second of transmission provided by each facility. Using the tariffs contained in Tables 3.12, 3.15, and 3.16 we can compute the cost per 1000 bps of transmission for five types of DDS line facilities, 1.544 Mbps Accunet T1.5, and the six Accunet Spectrum of Digital Services data rates for a 1000-mile circuit. Table 3.14 contains the monthly cost of 1000-mile DDS circuits. Dividing each cost by the data rate obtainable on the line in kbps results in the monthly cost per 1000 bps of transmission capacity. Thus, 2.4 kbps DDS would have a monthly cost of $251.87 per 1000 bps on a 1000-mile circuit. Similarly, a 1000-mile 56 kbps DDS circuit would have a monthly cost per 1000 bps of transmission capacity of $50.49.

Table 3.17 summarizes the monthly cost per 1000 bps of transmission for DDS, Accunet T1.5, and ASDS 1000-mile circuits. From Table 3.17 it is obvious that Accunet T1.5 service provides the best cost performance ratio of all three of AT&T's digital transmission services. Next, all fractional T1 (ASDS) service offerings provide a cost performance ratio more than four times better than each DDS offering. Due to the disparity between ASDS and DDS, it is a reasonable expectation for fractional T1 services to eventually replace a majority of AT&T and other carrier older digital transmission services.

Table 3.16 Accunet spectrum of digital services rate schedule.

Mileage band	56/64 kbps Fixed ($)	56/64 kbps Per mile ($)	128kbps Fixed ($)	128kbps Per mile ($)	256 kbps Fixed ($)	256 kbps Per mile ($)	384kbps Fixed ($)	384kbps Per mile ($)	512kbps Fixed ($)	512kbps Per mile ($)	768 kbps Fixed ($)	768 kbps Per mile ($)
1–50	72.00	2.84	138.00	5.40	277.00	10.79	415.00	16.19	525.00	20.45	788.00	30.67
51–100	149.00	1.31	284.00	2.49	567.00	4.98	851.00	7.47	1076.00	9.43	1614.00	14.15
101+	248.00	0.32	472.00	0.61	943.00	1.22	1416.00	1.82	1789.00	2.30	2683.00	3.46

Per channel charge ($)

Central office connection	Monthly	Installation
Per 56/64 kbps channel	16.40	196.00
Per 128 kbps channel	30.00	500.00
Per 256 kbps channel	35.00	500.00
Per 384 kbps channel	40.00	500.00
Per 512 kbps channel	45.00	500.00
Per 768 kbps channel	50.00	500.00

Table 3.17 Monthly cost per 1000 bps transmission capacity (1000 mile interchange circuit).

Digital service	Monthly cost per 1000 bps ($)
DDS	
2.4 kbps	251.87
4.8 kbps	130.10
9.6 kbps	67.13
19.2 kbps	37.83
56.0 kbps	50.49
Accunet T1.5	6.17
ASDS	
56/64 kbps	10.14/8.88
128 kbps	8.45
256 kbps	8.45
384 kbps	8.43
512 kbps	7.99
768 kbps	8.00

From an examination of the costs associated with fractional T1 services it is obvious that the spectrum of data transmission rates under ASDS can provide substantial savings for many users. These savings are most pronounced when a cost comparison to DDS occurs. In addition, significant cost savings are obtained when the rate for a full T1 circuit is compared to the cost of most 64 kbps groupings under ASDS.

To obtain a detailed appreciation for some of the abnormalities in digital transmission service tariffs we will compare and contrast the cost of 56 kbps DDS to 56/64 kbps ASDS and 768 kbps ASDS to 1.544 Mbps Accunet T1.5 service. Table 3.18 contains the monthly cost comparison for 56 kbps DDS and 56/64 kbps ASDS circuits from 1 to 2000 miles in length. This table was developed using Lotus 1-2-3 and the model representing the cost comparison is contained on the file DDSASDS.WK1 on the convenience diskette you can obtain from the publisher of this book.

To assist readers that may prefer to use or modify the Lotus model and do not have the convenience disk, Table 3.19 contains the cell contents of the model displayed in Table 3.18.

Note that the fourth column in Table 3.18 indicates that the monthly cost ratio between 56 kbps DDS and 56/64 kbps ASDS is at least 3.41 and rises to 5.04 for a circuit distance of 500 miles. Figure 3.11 plots the circuits' costs contained in Table 3.18,

Table 3.18 Monthly line cost comparison 56 kbps versus 56/64 kbps ASDS.

Circuit distance (miles)	56 kbps DDS	56/64 kpbs ASDS	Ratio DDS/ASDS monthly cost
1	284.69	74.84	3.80
50	735.00	214.00	3.43
100	953.50	280.00	3.41
250	1367.50	328.00	4.17
500	2057.50	408.00	5.04
1000	2827.50	568.00	4.98
2000	4367.50	888.00	4.92

illustrating the widening cost gap between the two services that provide an equivalent data transmission capacity. Due to this, it is reasonable to expect a growth in the availability of ASDS to be countered by a migration of users off DDS unless tariffs for the latter are significantly reduced.

A second comparison of two digital service offerings which for many readers produces unexpected results involves 768 kbps ASDS and Accunet T1.5. Table 3.20 compares the monthly cost of 768 kbps ASDS to 1.544 Mbps Accunet T1.5 for circuit distances of 1, 50, 100, 250, 500, 1000, and 2000 miles. In a similar way to several previous monthly line cost comparisons, Table 3.20 was created using Lotus 1-2-3. The file ACCUNET.WK1 on the convenience diskette contains the model which displays the line cost computations used to develop the data entries in Table 3.20.

For readers who do not have the convenience diskette, the cell contents of the file ACCUNET.WK1 are listed in Table 3.21. Readers so inclined can enter those cell entries into their own Lotus 1-2-3 model to compare 768 kbps ASDS to Accunet T1.5 tariffs and manipulate the entries based upon tariff changes or different distances.

In examining the entries in Table 3.20 the reader will note that for certain circuit distances the cost of a 768 kbps circuit actually exceeds the cost of a full T1 circuit operating at 1.544 Mbps. To obtain the exact breakeven points you can use the previously presented tariffs by setting the cost of Accunet T1.5 service equal to 768 kbps ASDS. An example of this is shown below for the 101+ mileage band where X represents the unknown mileage where the circuit costs are equal.

$$2025 + 7.50X = 2683 + 3.46X$$

Table 3.19 Cell contents of Lotus model shown in Table 3.18.

```
B1:   (T)  '      MONTHLY LINE COST COMPARISON
B3:   (T)  '      56KBPS versus 56/64KBPS ASDS
B5:   (T)  'Circuit
C5:   (T)  '  56KBPS
D5:   (T)  '56/64KBPS
E5:   (T)  '  RATIO
B6:   (T)  'Distance
C6:   (T)  '   DDS
D6:   (T)  '   ASDS
E6:   (T)  'DDS/ASDS
B7:   (T)  '  (miles)
E7:   (T)  'Monthly Cost
B9:   (T)  1
C9:   (T)  284.69
D9:   (T)  72+2.84
E9:   (T)  +C9/D9
B10:  (T)  50
C10:  (T)  275.5+9.19*50
D10:  (T)  72+2.84*50
E10:  (T)  +C10/D10
B11:  (T)  100
C11:  (T)  516.5+4.37*100
D11:  (T)  149+1.31*100
E11:  (T)  +C11/D11
B12:  (T)  250
C12:  (T)  677.5+2.76*250
D12:  (T)  247+0.32*250
E12:  (T)  +C12/D12
B13:  (T)  500
C13:  (T)  677.5+2.76*500
D13:  (T)  +C13/D13
B14:  (T)  1287.5+1.54*1000
D14:  (T)  248+1000*0.32
E14:  (T)  +C14/D14
```

Solving for X, we obtain

$$4.04X = 658 \text{ or } X = 163 \text{ miles}$$

To obtain the breakeven point for the 1 to 50 mileage band we would solve the following equation

$$1800 + 10.00X = 788 + 30.67X$$

Solving for X, we obtain

$$20.67X = 1012 \text{ or } X = 49 \text{ miles}$$

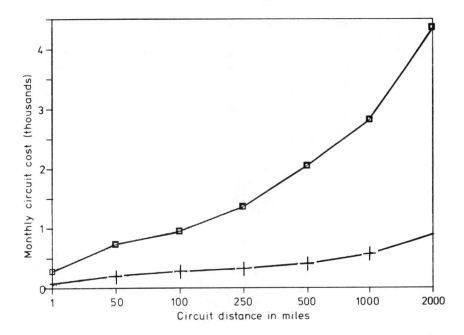

Figure 3.11 DDS plotted against ASDS (□ 56K bps DDS, + 66/64K kbps ASDS)

Table 3.20 Monthly line cost comparison 768 kbps ASDS versus Accunet T1.5.

Circuit distance (miles)	768 kbps ASDS	1.544 mbp T1.5	Ratio T1.5/ASDS monthly cost
1	818.67	1810.00	2.21
50	2321.50	2300.00	0.99
100	3029.00	2775.00	0.92
250	3548.00	3900.00	1.10
500	4413.00	5775.00	1.31
1000	6143.00	9525.00	1.55
2000	9603.00	17025.00	1.77

Based upon the preceding computations, the cost of Accunet T1.5 and 768 kbps ASDS digital transmission are equivalent at 49 and 163 miles. To obtain a visual indication of the monthly cost of 768 kbps ASDS and 1.544 Mbps T1 service the costs contained in Table 3.20 were plotted as line graphs. Figure 3.12 illustrates the plotted cost comparisons and indicates that for circuits up to 250 miles in length, organizations should consider obtaining a full T1 circuit instead of a 768 kbps ASDS circuit. Only for distances in excess of 250 miles does the cost difference between the two facilities begin to substantially increase.

Table 3.21 Cell contents of ACCUNET.WK1 file.

```
B1:   (T)  '      MONTHLY LINE COST COMPARISON
B3:   (T)  '      768KBPS ASDS VERSUS ACCUNET T1.5
B5:   (T)  'Circuit6
C5:   (T)  ' 768 KBPS
D5:   (T)  ' 1.54MBPS
E5:   (T)  ' RATIO
B6:   (T)  'Distance
C6:   (T)  '  ASDS
D6:   (T)  '   T1.5
E6:   (T)  'T1.5/ASDS
B7:   (T)  ' (miles)
E7:   (T)  'Monthly Cost
B9:   (T)  1
C9:   (T)  788+30.67
D9:   (T)  1810
E9:   (T)  +D9/C9
B10:  (T)  50
C10:  (T)  788+30.67*50
D10:  (T)  1800+50*10
E10:  (T)  +D10/C10
B11:  (T)  100
C11:  (T)  1614+14.15*100
D11:  (T)  1825+9.5*100
E11:  (T)  +D11/C11
B12:  (T)  250
C12:  (T)  2683+3.46*250
D12:  (T)  2025+7.5*250
E12:  (T)  +D12/C12
B13:  (T)  500
C13:  (T)  2683+3.46*500
D13:  (T)  2025+7.5*500
E13:  (T)  +D13/C13
B14:  (T)  1000
C14:  (T)  2683+3.46*1000
D14:  (T)  2025+7.5*1000
E14:  (T)  +D14/C14
```

Although we have identified one pricing abnormality between the cost of 768 kbps, FT1, and the cost of a full T1 circuit, in general, FT1 pricing has the potential to cause most companies to restructure their communications networks. Until now, many companies and government agencies were reluctant to obtain digital transmission facilities due to the differences between cost/performance ratios associated with 56 kbps DDS and an analog leased line that supports 19.2 kbps operations. With

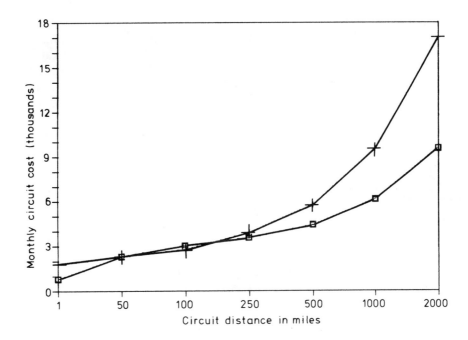

Figure 3.12 768 kbps plotted against 1.544 Mbps. (□ 768 kbps ASDS, + 1.544 Mbps)

56/64 kbps ASDS offering a price structure similar to that of analog leased lines we can expect most, if not all, new transmission requirements associated with the use of continuous line availability to be satisfied by the use of ASDS or similar facilities offered by other communications carriers. Perhaps the only counteracting force to the growth in the use of FT1 facilities is its availability. Currently, not all carriers offer fractional T1 capabilities in the same cities and access to FT1 may be further limited due to the unavailability of a T1 local loop from the local operating company to the point of presence (POP) of the interchange carrier which is required to access FT1 facilities. In spite of these problems, the availability of FT1 can be expected to significantly increase as the installation of tens of thousands of miles of fiber optic cable has resulted in a tremendous increase in transmission bandwidth that carriers are reselling in large increments to end-users.

By performing analyses similar to those presented in this chapter, readers can, if necessary, update the economic comparisons presented in this chapter to determine cost performance ratios between different facilities and breakeven points that will enable management to select the most appropriate facility to satisfy end-user requirements.

MULTIPLEXING AND LINE SHARING EQUIPMENT

In this chapter we will focus our attention upon the use of several types of multiplexers and line sharing devices that enable multiple data sources to be transmitted over a common line facility. The acquisition of each of the devices examined in this chapter is primarily justified by the economic savings their utilization promotes.

In the first section of this chapter, we will investigate the operation and utilization of several types of multiplexers. This will be followed by focusing attention upon a second category of line sharing equipment known by such terms as modem, line and port sharing units. Although we will focus our attention upon the operation and utilization of multiplexing and line sharing equipment, we will defer until Chapter 5 detailed information concerning the methods that can be employed to determine the location or locations to install such equipment. In that chapter we will examine the application of graph theory to several equipment location problems.

4.1 MULTIPLEXERS AND DATA CONCENTRATORS

With the establishment of distributed computing, the cost of providing the required communications facilities became a major focus of concern to users. Numerous network structures were examined to determine the possibilities of using specialized equipment to reduce these costs. For many networks where geographically distributed users accessed a common computational facility, a central location could be found which would serve as a hub to link those users to the computer. Even when terminal traffic was low and the cost of leased lines could not be justified on an individual basis, quite often the cumulative cost of providing communications to a group of users could be reduced if a mechanism was available to enable many terminals to share common communications facilities. This mechanism was provided by the utilization of multiplexers whose primary function is to provide the user with a reduction of communications costs. This device enables one high-speed line to be used to carry the formerly separate transmissions of a group of lower speed lines. The use of multiplexers should be considered when a number of data terminals communicate from within a similar geographical area or when a number of leased lines run in parallel for any distance.

4.1.1 Evolution

From the historical perspective, multiplexing technology can trace its origination to the early development of telephone networks. Then, as today, multiplexing was the employment of appropriate technology to permit a communications circuit to carry more than one signal at a time.

In 1902, twenty-six years after the world's first successful telephone conversation, an attempt to overcome the existing ratio of one channel to one circuit occurred. Using specifically developed electrical network terminations, three channels were derived from two circuits by telephone companies.

The third channel was denoted as the phantom channel, hence the name 'phantom' was applied to this early version of multiplexing. Although this technology permitted two pairs of wires to effectively carry the load of three, the requirement to keep the electric network finely balanced to prevent crosstalk limited its practicality.

4.1.2 Comparison with other devices

In the past, differences between multiplexers and concentrators were pronounced, with multiplexers being prewired, fixed logic devices; they produced a composite output transmission by sharing frequency bands (frequency division multiplexing) or time slots (time division multiplexing) on a predetermined basis, with the result that the total transmitted output was equal to the sum of the individual data inputs. Multiplexers were also originally transparent to the communicator, so that data sent from a terminal through a multiplexer to a computer was received in the same format and code by the computer as its original form.

In comparison, concentrators were developed from mini-computers by the addition of specialized programming and origin-ally performed numerous tasks that could not be accomplished through the use of a multiplexer. First, the intelligence provided by the software in concentrators permits a dynamic sharing technique to be employed instead of the static sharing technique used in traditional multiplexers. If a terminal connected to a concentrator is not active, then the composite high-speed output of the concen-trator will not automatically reserve a space for that terminal as will a traditional multiplexer.

This scheme, commonly known as dynamic bandwidth allo-cation, permits a larger number of terminals to share the use of a high-speed line through the use of a concentrator than when such terminals are connected to a multiplexer, since the traditional multiplexer allocates a time slot or frequency band for each terminal, regardless of whether the terminal is active. For this reason, statistics and queuing theory play an important role in the planning and utilization of concentrators. Next, owing to the stored program capacity of concentrators, these devices can be programmed to perform a number of additional functions. Such functions as the preprocessing of sign-on information and code conversion can be used to reduce the burden of effort required by the host computer system.

The advent of statistical and intelligent multiplexers, which are discussed later in this section, has closed the gap between concentrators and multiplexers. Through the use of built-in microprocessors, these multiplexers can now be programmed to perform numerous functions previously available only through the use of concentrators. In fact, many vendors now market products labeled as data concentrators that are based upon the use of built-in microprocessors. Perhaps even more interesting is that several manuals now describe those concentrators as devices that perform statistical multiplexing.

4.1.3 Device support

In general, any device that transmits or receives a serial data stream can be considered a candidate for multiplexing. Data streams produced by the devices listed in Table 4.1 are among those that can be multiplexed. The intermix of devices as well as

Table 4.1   Candidates for data stream multiplexing.

Analog network private line modems
Analog switched network modems
Digital network data service units
Digital network channel service units
Data terminals
Data terminal controllers
Minicomputers
Concentrators
Computer ports
Computer-computer links
Other multiplexers

---

the number of any one device whose data stream is considered for multiplexing is a function of the multiplexer's capacity and capabilities, the economics of the application, and cost of other devices which could be employed in that role, as well as the types and costs of high-speed lines being considered.

4.1.4 Multiplexing techniques

Two basic techniques are used for multiplexing: frequency division multiplexing (FDM) and time division multiplexing (TDM). Within the time division technique, two versions are available—fixed time slots which are employed by traditional TDMs and variable use of time slots which are used by statistical and intelligent TDMs.

FDM

In the FDM technique, the available bandwidth of the line is split into smaller segments called data bands or derived channels. Each data band in turn is separated from another data band by a guard band which is used to prevent signal interference between channels, as shown in Figure 4.1. Typically, frequency drift is the main cause of signal interference and the size of the guard bands is structured to prevent data in one channel drifting into another channel.

Physically, an FDM contains a channel set for each data channel as well as common logic, as shown in Figure 4.2. Each channel set contains a transmitter and receiver tuned to a specific frequency, with bits being indicated by the presence or absence of signals at

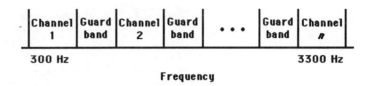

| Channel 1 | Guard band | Channel 2 | Guard band | ... | Guard band | Channel n |

300 Hz   3300 Hz

Frequency

Figure 4.1 FDM channel separations. In frequency division multiplexing the 3 kHz bandwidth of a voice-grade line is split into channels or data bands separated from each other by guard bands

each of the channel's assigned frequencies. In FDM, the width of each frequency band determines the transmission rate capacity of the channel, and the total bandwidth of the line is a limiting factor in determining the total number or mix of channels that can be serviced. Although a multipoint operation is illustrated in Figure 4.2, FDM equipment can also be utilized for the multiplexing of data between two locations on a point-to-point circuit. Data rates up to 1200 bps can be multiplexed by FDM. Typical FDM channel spacings required at different data rates are listed in Table 4.2.

As indicated in Table 4.2, the channel spacing on an FDM system is proportional to its data rate. In the 1960s and early 1970s when terminal transmission rates were relatively low, FDM could provide for the multiplexing of a fairly reasonable number of data sources over the 3000 Hz bandwidth of an analog leased line. As terminal transmission speeds increased the number of channels that could be supported by FDM significantly decreased,

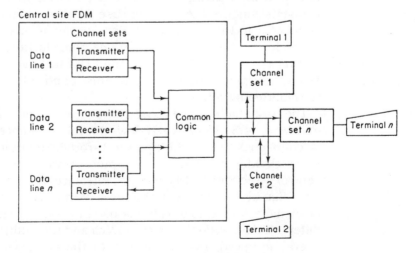

Figure 4.2 Frequency division multiplexing. Since the channel sets modulate the line at specified frequencies, no modems are required at remote locations

Table 4.2 FDM channel spacings.

Speed (bps)	Spacing (Hz)
75	120
110	170
150	240
300	480
450	720
600	960
1200	1800

making this multiplexing technique essentially obsolete for data transmission in the 1990s. Thus, the remainder of this section will focus its attention upon several types of time division multiplexing.

Time division multiplexing

In the FDM technique, the bandwidth of the communications line serves as the frame of reference. The total bandwidth is divided into subchannels consisting of smaller segments of the available bandwidth, each of which is used to form an independent data channel. In the TDM technique, the aggregate capacity of the line is the frame of reference, since the multiplexer provides a method of transmitting data from many terminals over a common circuit by interleaving them in time. The TDM divides the aggregate transmission on the line for use by the slower-speed devices connected to the multiplexer. Each device is given a time slot for its exclusive use so that at any one point in time the signal from one terminal is on the line. In the FDM technique, in which each signal occupies a different frequency band, all signals are being transmitted simultaneously.

The fundamental operating characteristics of a TDM are shown in Figure 4.3. Here, each low- to medium-speed data source is connected to the multiplexer through an input/output (I/O) channel adapter. The I/O adapter provides the buffering and control functions necessary to interface the transmission and reception of data to the multiplexer. Within each adapter, a buffer or memory area exists which is used to compensate for the speed differential between the data sources and the multiplexer's internal operating speed. Data is shifted to the I/O adapter at different rates (typically 110 to 9600 bps), depending upon the speed of the connected devices; but when data is shifted from the I/O adapter

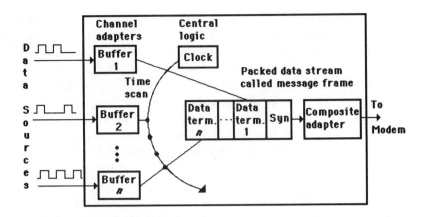

Figure 4.3 Time division multiplexing. In time division multiplexing, data is first entered into each channel adapter buffer area at a transfer rate equal to the device to which the adapter is connected. Next, data from the various buffers are transferred to the multiplexer's central logic at the higher rate of the device for packing into a message frame for transmission

to the central logic of the multiplexer, or from central logic to the composite adapter, it is at the much higher fixed rate of the TDM. On output from the multiplexer to each connected device the reverse is true, since data is first transferred at a fixed rate from central logic to each adapter and then from the adapter to the connected device at the data rate acceptable to the device. Depending upon the type of TDM system, the buffer area in each adapter will accommodate either bits or characters.

The central logic of the TDM contains controlling, monitoring, and timing circuitry which facilitates the passage of individual data sources to and from the high-speed transmission medium. The central logic will generate a synchronizing pattern which is used by a scanner circuit to interrogate each of the channel adapter buffer areas in a predetermined sequence, blocking the bits of characters from each buffer into a continuous, synchronous data stream which is then passed to a composite adapter. The composite adapter contains a buffer and functions similar to the I/O channel adapters. However, it now compensates for the difference in speed between the high-speed transmission medium and the internal speed of the multiplexer.

4.1.5 The multiplexing interval

When operating, the multiplexer transmits and receives a continuous data stream known as a message train, regardless of the activity of the data sources connected to the device. The message train is formed from a continuous series of message frames which represents the packing of a series of input data streams. Each message frame contains one or more synchronization characters followed by a number of basic multiplexing intervals whose number is dependent upon the model and manufacturer of the device. The basic multiplexing interval can be viewed as the first level of time subdivision which is established by determining the number of equal sections per second required by a particular application. Then, the multiplexing interval is the time duration of one section of the message frame.

When TDMs were first introduced, the section rate was established at 30 sections per second, which then produced a basic multiplexing interval of 0.033 second or 33 ms. Setting the interval to 33 ms made the multiplexer directly compatible to a 300-baud asynchronous channel which transmits data at up to 30 characters per second (cps). With this interval, the multiplexer was also compatible with 150-baud (15-cps) and 110-baud (10-cps) data channels, since the basic multiplexing interval was a multiple of those asynchronous data rates. Later TDMs had a section rate of 120 sections per second, which then made the multiplexer capable of servicing a range of asynchronous data streams up to 1200 bps.

4.1.6 TDM techniques

The two TDM techniques available are bit interleaving and character interleaving. Bit interleaving is generally used in systems which service synchronous terminals, whereas character interleaving is generally used to service asynchronous terminals. When interleaving is accomplished on a bit-by-bit basis, the multiplexer takes 1 bit from each channel adapter and then combines them as a word or frame for transmission. As shown in Figure 4.4A, this technique produces a frame containing one data element from each channel adapter. When interleaving is accomplished on a character-by-character basis, the multiplexer assembles a full character from each data source into one frame and then transmits the frame, as shown in Figure 4.4B.

For the character-by-character method, the buffer area required is considerably larger; and although memory costs have declined, TDM character interleaving is still slightly more expensive than TDM bit interleaving systems. Since the character-by-character interleaved method preserves all bits of a character in sequence, the TDM equipment can be used to strip the character of any

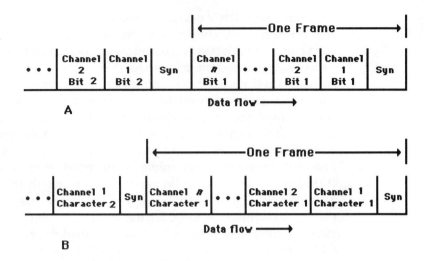

Figure 4.4 Time division interleaving bit-by-bit and character-by-character. When interleaving is accomplished bit-by-bit (top), the first bit from each channel is packed into a frame for transmission. (B) Time division multiplexing character-by-character. When interleaving is conducted on a character-by-character basis, one or more complete characters are grouped with a synchronization character into a frame for transmission

recognition information that may be sent as part of that character. Examples of this would be the servicing of such terminals as a Teletype Model 33 or an IBM Personal Computer transmitting asynchronous data, where a transmitted character contains 10 or 11 bits which include a start bit, 7 data bits, a parity bit, and 1 or 2 stop bits. When the bit-interleaved method is used, all 10 or 11 bits would be transmitted to preserve character integrity, whereas in a character-interleaved system, the start and stop bits can be stripped from the character, with only the 7 data bits and on some systems the parity bit warranting transmission.

To service terminals with character codes containing different numbers of bits per character, two techniques are commonly employed in character interleaving. In the first technique, the time slot for each character is of constant size, designed to accommodate the maximum bit width or highest level code. Making all slots large enough to carry American Standard Code for Information Interchange (ASCII) characters makes the multiplexer an inefficient carrier of a lower level code such as five-level Baudot. However, the electronics required in the device and its costs are reduced. The second technique used is to proportion the slot size to the width of each character according to its bit size. This technique maximizes the efficiency of the multiplexer, although the complexity of the logic and the cost of the multiplexer increases. Owing to the reduction in the cost of semiconductors, most character-interleaved multiplexers marketed are designed to operate on the proportional assignment method.

While bit interleaving equipment is less expensive, it is also less efficient when used to service asynchronous terminals. On the positive side, bit-interleaved multiplexers offer the advantage of faster resynchronization and shorter transmission delay, since character-interleaved multiplexers must wait to assemble the bits into characters; whereas, a bit-interleaved multiplexer can transmit each bit as soon as it is received from the terminal. Multiplexers, which interleave by character, use a number of different techniques to build the character, with the techniques varying between manufacturers and by models produced by manufacturers.

A commonly utilized technique is the placement of a buffer area for each channel adapter which permits the character to be assembled within the channel adapter and then scanned and packed into a data stream. Another technique which can be used is the placement of programmed read only memory within the multiplexer so that it can be used to assemble characters for all the input channels. The second technique makes a multiplexer resemble a concentrator since the inclusion of programmed read only memory permits many additional functions to be performed in addition to the assembly and disassembly of characters. Such multiplexers with programmed memory are referred to as intelligent multiplexers and are discussed later in this chapter.

4.1.7 TDM constraints

Prior to investigating some of the more common network applications for which TDMs are used, we should examine the major constraints that limit the number of channels supported by a TDM and the data transmission rates obtainable on those channels. To do so we will examine a typical TDM configuration from both a hardware and a network schematic configuration perspective. The top of Figure 4.5 illustrates an eight-channel TDM connected to a modem operating at 9600 bps as viewed from a network perspective. In the lower portion of that illustration, the eight-channel TDM is illustrated from a hardware perspective, assuming that the equipment is mounted in an industry standard 19-inch rack.

In examining the network schematic, let us focus our attention

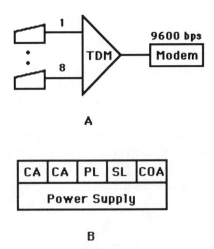

Figure 4.5 (A) Network and (B) hardware TDM schematics (CA channel adapter card, PL primary logic card, SL secondary logic card, COA composite adapter card)

upon the data rates the TDM can support. Although eight inputs are illustrated, no data rates were actually assigned to individual channels since prior to doing so you must consider several device constraints.

The first constraint you must consider is the data rate supported by each channel adapter card. Most multiplexers have channel adapters that support 2, 4, or 8 line terminations that are referenced as multiplexer ports or channels. Since the operational characteristics of the channel adapter govern the operational characteristics of each of the line terminations mounted in the adapter, in effect, all ports on the adapter have the same data rate and protocol support characteristics. Thus, if one port supports 300, 1200, 2400, and 4800 bps asynchronous transmission, all other ports on the adapter can be expected to have a similar support capability.

The actual data rate each port can be set to depends upon several factors in addition to the data rates supported by the channel adapter housing the port. These factors include the aggregate data input supported by the TDM, the data rate assigned to other ports, the data rate assigned to the composite adapter, and the overhead and efficiency of the TDM. Concerning the next to last factor, overhead is primarily a result of the multiplexer sampling the state of the RS-232 interface once every predefined number of data sample cycles and the gaps in transmission resulting from the necessity of sending synchronization characters from one multiplexer to another.

When a multiplexer performs the sampling of the RS-232 interface, it typically examines multiples of two leads on each port and encodes the state of the leads as a binary value, zero if the lead is low and one if the lead is high. In this manner, the multiplexer can pass the state of many control leads to a distant location. This enables, as an example, a ring indicator signal passed by an auto-answer modem connected to a multiplexer or a data terminal ready signal caused by a directly connected terminal being powered on to be passed to a distant computer system as illustrated in Figure 4.6.

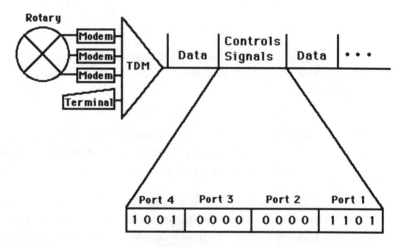

Figure 4.6 Multiplexer overhead. Once every *X* data sample cycles a TDM will sample the state of a number of RS-232 control leads on each port, encoding them as a binary 0 if not active and binary 1 if active. The passing of control signals is the major contribution to the overhead of TDMs

To illustrate the effect of control signal passing upon the overhead of a TDM, let us assume every 25th cycle the device samples control signals. If the composite adapter is connected to a 9600 bps modem, then 1/25 or 384 bps is used for the transmission of control signals, precluding the transmission of data. Due to this, the maximum data rate that all input ports could accommodate without the TDM losing data would be 9600–384 or 9216 bps, assuming there were no other overhead factors or constraints to consider. Since the transmission rates supported by each port are usually a multiple of 300 bps, the aggregate data input of all ports would probably be limited to 9000 bps.

The protocol overhead associated with multiplexers can be expected to lower the actual data transmission of TDMs by another 10 to 15%. Continuing with our previous example, this could lower the effective data transmission servicing capacity of the TDM from 9000 bps to 8000 bps or less.

Although many vendors provide detailed information concerning data rate constraints and protocol overhead associated with their TDMs, some vendors only include this information in manuals that are received after you purchase the equipment. Thus, it is imperative that you check the previously mentioned constraints prior to purchasing a TDM to ensure its overhead will not adversely affect your network application.

Counteracting the overhead of TDMs are several operational efficiencies that, upon occasion, negate the overhead of the device. Two of the more common operational efficiencies are the use of a proportional width time slot and the stripping of non-essential bits from asynchronous characters, such as start, stop, and parity bits. If vendor literature does not provide detailed information concerning the aggregate data rate their equipment can support based upon a specific composite adapter operating rate, you can estimate that rate with a fair degree of accuracy if you know the overhead and efficiency factors of the TDM. As an example of this, again assume the TDM uses 1 cycle every 25 cycles for the passing of control information and its composite adapter operates at 9600 bps. Then, the overhead is 384 bps. If we assume that the TDM is to service eight 1200 bps terminals, without considering any possible efficiencies provided by the multiplexer, our first impression would be that the device would be limited to supporting seven terminals. This is because 8 * 1200 is 9600 bps, however, as previously computed, less than 9000 bps of data can be effectively transmitted as 384 bps is reserved for control signaling and 900 bps or more for the protocol overhead. Now let us investigate the effect of the TDM stripping start and stop bits prior to transmission while the distant multiplexer reconstructs each character by the addition of those bits prior to transmitting them to their destination.

A 1200 bps data source using 10 bits per character presents 120 characters per second to a multiplexer port. If the multiplexer strips each start and stop bit, only 8 bits per character are actually transmitted over the multiplexed line. Thus, the effective data rate per port is 120 cps * 8 bits per character or 960 bits per second. If all eight multiplexer ports transmit similar ASCII characters whose start and stop bits can be stripped, the effective data input rate becomes 7680 bps, a rate low enough to be serviced by the composite adapter's effective operating rate which was computed by considering the passing of control characters and the overhead associated with the protocol used by the multiplexers.

The hardware schematic illustrated in the lower portion of Figure 4.5 will be used to discuss some of the physical constraints associated with TDMs as well as similar equipment. In that illustration, note that there are five cards inserted into the upper bay or rack-mount nest. Most rack-mount equipment have housings that include a bus built into the backplane of the nest, as well as slots for the insertion of adapter cards. Similar to a personal computer, the insertion of adapter cards adds to the functionality and capability of the TDM.

If each channel adapter is capable of supporting four ports, the hardware schematic illustrated in Figure 4.5 indicates that this particular TDM can support a maximum of eight data sources. To expand the capability of the TDM you can consider several options, depending upon the method by which the device is manufactured. First, you might be able to remove the secondary logic card and manually use it to replace a failed primary logic card, if the need arises. Then, you could install a third channel adapter card to increase the number of data sources supported to 12. Another option would be to install a third bay, adding five more slots into which different adapter cards can be inserted. When selecting this option, you must consider the power requirements of the additional adapter cards which could require an additional power supply to operate. Thus, you must consider the number of data sources each adapter card supports, the number of adapter cards that can be installed in a bay, as well as the number of bays and the power requirements to support adapter cards installed in each bay.

4.1.8 TDM applications

The most commonly used TDM configuration is the point-to-point system, which is shown in Figure 4.7. This type of system, which is also called a two-point multiplex system, links a mixture of terminals to a centrally located multiplexer. As shown, the terminals can be connected to the multiplexer in a variety of ways. Terminals can be connected by a leased line running from the terminal's location to the multiplexer, by a direct connection if the user's terminals are within the same building as the multiplexer and a cable can be laid to connect the two, or terminals can use the switched network to call the multiplexer over the dial network. For the latter method, since the connection is not permanent, several terminals can share access to one or more multiplexer channels on a contention basis.

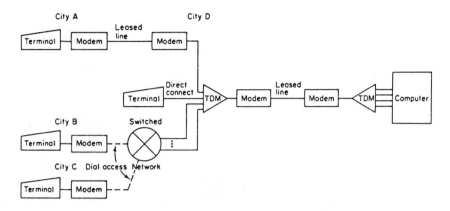

Figure 4.7 Time division multiplexing point-to-point. A point-to-point or two-point multiplexing system links a variety of data users at one or more remoted locations to a central computer facility

As shown in Figure 4.7, the terminals in cities B and C use the dial network to contend for one multiplexer channel which is interfaced to an automatic answer unit on the dial network. Whichever terminal accesses that channel maintains use of it and thus excludes other terminals from access to that particular connection to the system. As an example, one might have a network which contains 50 terminals within a geographical area wherein between 10 to 12 are active at any time; and one method to deal with this environment would be through the installation of a 12-number rotary interfaced to a 12-channel multiplexer. If all of the terminals were located within one city, the only telephone charges that the user would incur in addition to those of the leased line between multiplexers would be local call charges each time a terminal user dialed the local multiplexer number.

Series multipoint multiplexing

A number of multiplexing systems can be developed by linking the output of one multiplexer into a second multiplexer. Commonly called series multipoint multiplexing, this technique is most effective when terminals are distributed at two or more locations and the user desires to alleviate the necessity of obtaining two long-distance leased lines from the closer location to the computer. As shown in Figure 4.8, four low-speed terminals are multiplexed at city A onto one high-speed channel which is transmitted to city B where this line is in turn multiplexed along with the data from a number of other terminals at city B. Although the user requires a

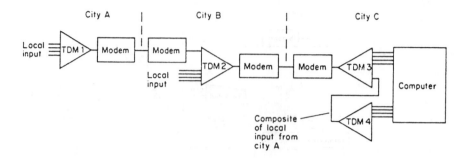

Figure 4.8 Series multipoint multiplexing. Series multipoint multiplexing is accomplished by connecting the output of one multiplexer as input to a second device

leased line between city A and city B, only one line is now required to be installed for the remainder of the distance from city B to the computer at city C. If city A is located 50 miles from city B, and city B is 2000 miles from city C, 2000 miles of duplicate leased lines are avoided by using this multiplexing technique.

Multipoint multiplexing requires an additional pair of channel cards to be installed at multiplexers 2 and 3 and higher-speed modems to be interfaced to those multiplexers to handle the higher aggregate throughput when the traffic of multiplexer 1 is routed through multiplexer 2; but, in most cases the cost savings associated with reducing duplicated leased lines will more than offset the cost of the extra equipment. Since this is a series arrangement a failure of either TDM2 or TDM3 or a failure of the line between these two multiplexers will terminate service to all terminals connected to the system.

Hub-bypass multiplexing

A variation of series multipoint multiplexing is hub-bypass multiplexing. To be effectively used, hub-bypass multiplexing can occur when a number of remote locations have the requirement to transmit to two or more locations. To satisfy this requirement, the remote terminal traffic is multiplexed to a central location which is the hub, and the terminals which must communicate with the second location are cabled into another multiplexer which transmits this traffic, bypassing the hub. Figure 4.9 illustrates one application where hub-bypassing might be utilized. In this example, eight terminals at city 3 require a communications link with one of two computers; six terminals always communicate

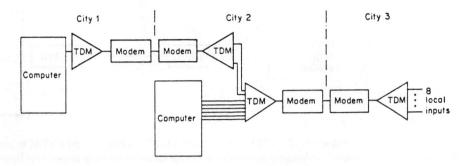

Figure 4.9 Hub-bypass multiplexing. When a number of terminals have the requirement to communicate with more than one location, hub-bypass multiplexing should be considered

with the computer at city 2, while two terminals use the facilities of the computer at city 1. The data from all eight terminals are multiplexed over a common line to city 2 where the two channels that correspond to the terminals which must access the computer at city 1 are cabled to a new multiplexer, which then remultiplexes the data from those terminals to city 1. When many terminal locations have dual location destinations, hub-bypassing can become very economical. However, since the data flows in series, an equipment failure will terminate access to one or more computational facilities, depending upon the location of the break in service.

Although hub-bypass multiplexing can be effectively used to connect collocated terminals to different destinations, if more than two destinations exist a more efficient switching arrangement can be obtained by the employment of a port selector or a multiplexer that has a port selection capability.

A port selector or multiplexer with port selection capability functions as a dynamic data switch, establishing a temporary connection between a port on the input side of the device or, in the case of a multiplexer, a channel on the multiplexing frame and its output destination. The reader is referred to the portion of this chapter covering statistical and intelligent multiplexers which describes the operation and utilization of switching and port contention features of those devices.

Front-end substitution

Although not commonly utilized, a TDM may be installed as an inexpensive front end for a computer, as shown in Figure 4.10.

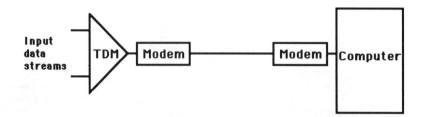

Figure 4.10 TDM system used as a front end. When a TDM is used as a front-end processor, the computer must be programmed to perform demultiplexing

When used as a front end, only one computer port is then required to service the terminals which are connected to the computer through the TDM. The TDM can be connected at the computer center, or it can be located at a remote site and connected over a leased line and a pair of modems. Since demultiplexing is conducted by the computer's software, only one multiplexer is necessary.

However, owing to the wide variations in multiplexing techniques of each manufacturer, no standard software has been written for demultiplexing; and, unless multiple locations can use this technique, the software development costs may exceed the hardware savings associated with this technique. In addition, the software overhead associated with the computer performing the demultiplexing may degrade its performance to an appreciable degree and must be considered.

Inverse multiplexing

A multiplexing system which is coming into widespread usage is the inverse multiplexing system. As shown in Figure 4.11, inverse multiplexing permits a high-speed data stream to be split into two

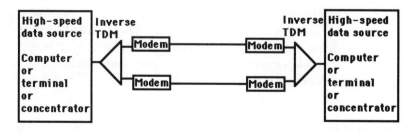

Figure 4.11 Inverse multiplexing. An inverse multiplexer splits a serial data stream into two or more individual data streams for transmission at lower data rates

or more slower data streams for transmission over lower-cost lines and modems.

Because of the tariff structure associated with wideband facilities, the utilization of inverse multiplexers can result in significant savings in certain situations. As an example, their use could permit 38 400 bps transmission over two voice-grade lines at a fraction of the cost which would be incurred when using wideband facilities.

As an example of the economics associated with the potential use of inverse multiplexers, the reader is referred to the monthly line cost comparison between an analog and a 56 kbps DDS leased line presented in Chapter 3. From Table 3.14, you will note that a 2000 mile analog line has a cost of approximately $964 per month, while a 56 kbps DDS circuit has a cost of $4368 per month. Thus, the use of two analog lines could provide an aggregate transmission capacity of 38.4 kbps if each line operates at 19.2 kbps for a total line cost of $1928 per month. Then, if the cost of a pair of inverse multiplexers and four modems is less than the cost of two digital service units used on DDS plus the difference between the cost of one digital line and two analog circuits, inverse multiplexing will be more economical. In addition, two analog lines can serve as a backup to one another enabling transmission at 19.2 kbps to occur if one circuit should become inoperative. In comparison, the failure of the DDS circuit would cause the transmission system to become inoperative.

4.1.9 Multiplexing economics

The primary motive for the use of multiplexers in a network is to reduce the cost of communications. In analyzing the potential of multiplexers, one should first survey terminal users to determine the projected monthly connect time of each terminal. Then, the most economical method of data transmission from each individual terminal to the computer facility can be computed. To do this, direct dial costs should be compared with the cost of a leased line from each terminal to the computer site.

Once the most economical method of transmission for each individual terminal to the computer is determined, this cost should be considered the 'cost to reduce'. The telephone mileage costs from each terminal city location to each other terminal city location should be determined in order to compute and compare the cost of utilizing various techniques, such as line dropping and the multiplexing of data by combining several low- to medium-speed terminals' data streams into one high-speed line for transmission to the central site.

In evaluating multiplexing costs, the cost of telephone lines from each terminal location to the 'multiplexer center' must be computed and added to the cost of the multiplexer equipment. Then, the cost of the high-speed line from the multiplexer center to the computer site must be added to produce the total multiplexing cost. If this cost exceeds the cumulative most economical method of transmission for individual terminals to the central site, then multiplexing is not cost-justified. This process should be reiterated by considering each city as a possible multiplexer center to optimize all possible network configurations. In repeating this process, terminals located in certain cities will not justify any calculations to prove or disprove their economic feasibility as multiplexer centers, because of their isolation from other cities in a network.

An example of the economics involved in multiplexing is illustrated in Figure 4.12. In this example, assume the volume of terminal traffic from the devices located in cities A and B would result in a dial-up charge of $3000 per month if access to the computer in city G was over the switched network. The installation of leased lines from those cities to the computer at city G would cost $2000 and $2200 per month, respectively. Furthermore, let us assume that the terminals at cities C, D, and E only periodically communicate with the computer, and their dial-up costs of $400, $600, and $500 per month, respectively, are much less than the cost of leased lines between those cities and the computer. Then, without multiplexing, the network's most economical communications cost would be:

Location	Cost per month
city A	$2000
city B	2200
city C	400

Location	Cost per month
city D	600
city E	500
Total cost	$5700

Let us further assume that city C is centrally located with respect to the other cities so we could use it as a homing point or multiplexer center. In this manner, a multiplexer could be installed in city C, and the terminal traffic from the other cities could be routed to that city, as shown in of Figure 4.12B. Employing

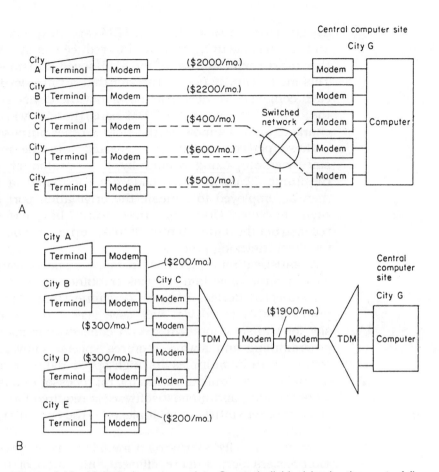

Figure 4.12 Multiplexing economics. On an individual basis, the cost of five terminals accessing a computer system (A) can be much more expensive than when a time division multiplexer is installed (B)

multiplexers would reduce the network communications cost to $2900 per month which produces a potential savings of $2800 per month, which should now be reduced by the multiplexer costs to determine net savings. If each multiplexer costs $500 per month, then the network using multiplexers will save the user $1800 each month. Exactly how much can be saved, if any, through the use of multiplexers depends not only on the types, quantities, and distributions of terminals to be serviced but also on the leased line tariff structure and the type of multiplexer employed.

4.1.10 Statistical and intelligent multiplexers

In a traditional TDM, data streams are combined from a number of devices into a single path so that each device has a time slot assigned for its use. While such TDMs are inexpensive and reliable, and can be effectively employed to reduce communications costs, they make inefficient use of the high-speed transmission medium. This inefficiency is due to the fact that a time slot is reserved for each connected device, whether or not the device is active. When the device is inactive, the TDM pads the slot with nulls or pad characters and cannot use the slot for other purposes.

These pad characters are inserted into the message frame since demultiplexing occurs by the position of characters in the frame. Thus, if these pads are eliminated, a scheme must then be employed to indicate the origination port or channel of each character. Otherwise, there would be no way to correctly reconstruct the data and route it to its correct computer port during the demultiplexing process.

A statistical multiplexer is, in many respects, very similar to a concentrator since both devices combine signals from a number of connected devices in such a manner that there is a certain probability that a device will have access to the use of a time slot for transmission. Whereas a concentrator may require user programming and always requires special software in the host computer to demultiplex its high-speed data stream, statistical multiplexers are built around a microprocessor that is programmed by the vendor, and no host software is required for demultiplexing since another statistical multiplexer at the computer site performs that function.

By dynamically allocating time slots as required, statistical multiplexers permit more efficient utilization of the high-speed transmission medium. This permits the multiplexer to service more terminals without an increase in the high-speed link as would a traditional multiplexer. The technique of allocating time slots on a demand basis is known as statistical multiplexing and means that data is transmitted by the multiplexer only from the terminals that are actually active.

Depending upon the type of TDM, either synchronization characters or control frames are inserted into the stream of message frames. Synchronization characters are employed by conventional TDMs, while control frames are used by TDMs which employ a high-level data link control (HDLC) protocol or version of that protocol between multiplexers to control the transmission of message frames.

The construction technique used to build the message frame also defines the type of TDM. Conventional TDMs employ a fixed frame approach as illustrated in Figure 4.13. Here, each frame consists of one character or bit for each input port or channel scanned at

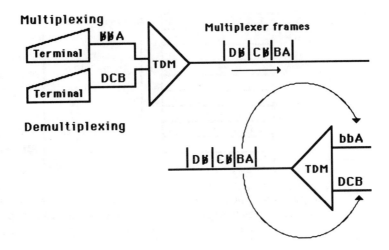

Figure 4.13 Multiplexing and demultiplexing by TDMs. b = absence of line activity during multiplexer scan, ∅ = null character inserted into message frame

a particular period of time. As illustrated, even when a particular terminal is inactive, the slot assigned to that device is included in the message frame transmitted since the presence of a pad or null character in the time slot is required to correctly demultiplex the data. In the lower portion of Figure 4.13, the demultiplexing process which is accomplished by time slot position is illustrated. Since a typical data source may be idle 90% of the time, this technique contains obvious inefficiencies.

Statistical frame construction

A statistical multiplexer employs a variable frame building technique which takes advantage of terminal idle times to enable more terminals to share access to a common circuit. The use of variable frame technology permits previously wasted time slots to be eliminated, since control information is transmitted with each frame to indicate which terminals are active and have data contained in the message frame.

One of many techniques that can be used to denote the presence or absence of data traffic is the activity map which is illustrated in Figure 4.14. When an activity map is employed, the map itself is transmitted before the actual data. Each bit position in the map is used to indicate the presence or absence of data from a particular multiplexer time slot scan. The two activity maps and data characters illustrated in Figure 4.14 represent a total

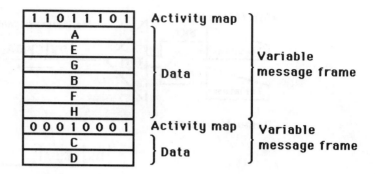

Figure 4.14 Activity mapping to produce variable frames. Using an activity map where each bit position indicates the presence or absence of data for a particular data source permits variable message frames to be generated

of 10 characters which would be transmitted in place of the 16 characters if no activity mapping occurred.

Another statistical multiplexing technique involves buffering data from each data source and then transmitting the data with an address and byte count. The address is used by the demultiplexer to route the data to the correct port, while the byte count indicates the quantity of data to be routed to that port.

Figure 4.15 illustrates the message frame of a four-channel statistical multiplexer employing the address and byte count frame composition method during a certain time interval. Note that since channels 3 and 4 had no data traffic during the two particular time intervals, there was no address and byte count nor data from those channels transmitted on the common circuit. Also note that the data from each channel is of variable length. Typically, statistical multiplexers employing an address and byte count frame

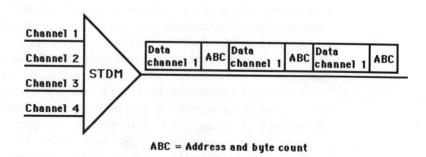

Figure 4.15 Address and byte count frame composition. ABC Address and byte count

composition method wait until either 32 characters or a carriage return is encountered prior to forming the address and byte count and forwarding the buffered data. The reason 32 characters was selected as the decision criterion is that it represents the average line length of an interactive transmission session.

A few potential technical drawbacks of statistical multiplexers exist which users should note. These problems include the delays associated with data blocking and queuing when a large number of connected terminals become active or when a few terminals transmit large bursts of data. For either situation, the aggregate throughput of the multiplexer's input active data exceeds the capacity of the common high-speed line, causing data to be placed into buffer storage.

Another reason for delays is when a circuit error causes one or more retransmissions of message frame data to occur. Since the connected terminals may continue to send data during the multiplexer-to-multiplexer retransmission cycle, this can also fill up the multiplexer's buffer areas and cause time delays.

If the buffer area should overflow, data would be lost which would create an unacceptable situation. To prevent buffer overflow, all statistical multiplexers employ some type of technique to transmit a traffic control signal, formally referred to as flow control, to attached terminals and/or computers when their buffers are filled to a certain level. Such control signals inhibit additional transmission through the multiplexer until the buffer has been emptied to another predefined level. Once this level has been reached, a second control signal is issued which permits transmission to the multiplexers to resume.

Buffer control

The three major buffer control techniques employed by statistical multiplexers include inband signaling, outband signaling, and clock reduction. Inband signaling involves transmitting XOFF and XON characters to inhibit and enable the transmission of data from terminals and computer ports that recognize these flow control characters. Since many terminals and computer ports do not recognize these control characters, a second common flow control method involves raising and lowering the Clear to Send (CTS) control signal on the RS-232 or CCITT V.24 interface. Since this method of buffer control is outside the data path where data is transmitted on pin 2, it is known as outband signaling.

Both inband and outband signaling are used to control the data flow of asynchronous devices. Since synchronous devices transmit data formed into blocks or frames, one would most likely break a block or frame by using either inband or outband signaling. This would cause a portion of a block or frame to be received, which would result in a negative acknowledgement when the receiver performs its cyclic redundancy computation. Similarly, when the remainder of the block or frame is allowed to resume its flow to the receiver, a second negative acknowledgement would result.

To alleviate these potential causes of decrease of throughput, multiplexer vendors typically reduce the clocking speed furnished to synchronous devices. Thus, a synchronous terminal operating at 4800 bps might first be reduced to 2400 bps by the multiplexer halving the clock. Then, if the buffer in the multiplexer continues to fill, the clock might be further reduced to 1200 bps.

Service ratio

The measurement used to denote the capability of a statistical multiplexer is called its service ratio, which compares its overall level of performance in comparison to a conventional TDM. Since synchronous transmission by definition denotes blocks of data with characters placed in sequence in each block, there are no gaps in this mode of transmission. In comparison, a terminal operator transmitting data asynchronously may pause between characters to think prior to pressing each key on the terminal. Thus, the service ratio of STDMs for asynchronous data is higher than the service ratio for synchronous data. Typically, STDM asynchronous service ratios range between 2:1 and 3.5:1, while synchronous service ratios range between 1.25:1 and 2:1, with the service ratio dependent upon the efficiency of the STDM as well as its built-in features, including the stripping of start and stop bits from asynchronous data sources. In Figure 4.16, the operational efficiency of both a statistical and conventional TDM are compared. Here we have assumed that the STDM has an efficiency of twice that of the TDM.

Assuming four 1200 bps and ten 300 bps data sources are to be multiplexed, the conventional TDM illustrated in the top part of Figure 4.16 would be required to operate at a data rate of at least 7800 bps, thus requiring a 9600 bps modem if transmission was over an analog facility. For the STDM shown in the lower portion of this illustration, assuming a two-fold increase in efficiency over the conventional TDM, the composite data rate required will be 3900 bps. This permits the employment of a lower operating rate

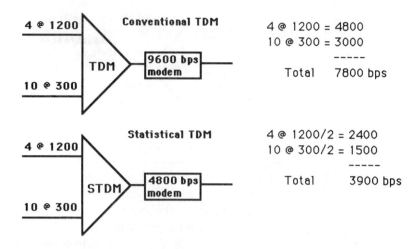

Figure 4.16 Comparing statistical and conventional TDMs. An STDM typically has an efficiency of two to four times a conventional TDM. Using an efficiency level twice the conventional TDM results in a composite operating data rate requirement of 3900 bps which is serviced by the use of a 4800 bps modem

modem which is also a lower-cost modem. In addition, the STDM can accept a combined input data rate increase of 1800 bps from additional sources prior to requiring the 4800 bps modem to be upgraded. If an input data rate increase of over 1800 bps were directed to the conventional TDM, a significantly more expensive wideband line would probably be required to replace the voice-grade facility whose data rate, in many locations, is limited to 9600 bps.

Data source support

Some statistical multiplexers only support asynchronous and synchronous data sources. When a statistical multiplexer supports synchronous data sources, it is extremely important to determine the method used by the STDM vendor to implement this support.

Some statistical multiplexer vendors employ a bandpass channel to support synchronous data sources. When this occurs, not only is the synchronous data not multiplexed statistically, but the data rate of the synchronous input limits the overall capability of the device to support asynchronous transmission. Figure 4.17 illustrates the effect of multiplexing synchronous data via the use of a bandpass channel. When a bandpass channel is employed, a

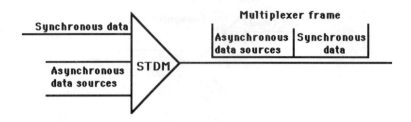

Figure 4.17 The use of a bandpass channel to multiple synchronous data

fixed portion of each message frame is reserved for the exclusive multiplexing of synchronous data, with the portion of the frame reserved proportional to the data rate of the synchronous input to the STDM. This means that only the remainder of the message frame is then available for the multiplexing of all other data sources.

As an example of the limitations of bandpass multiplexing, consider an STDM that is connected to a 9600 bps modem and supports a synchronous terminal operating at 7200 bps. If bandpass multiplexing is employed, only 2400 bps is then available in the multiplexer for the multiplexing of other data sources. In comparison, assume another STDM statistically multiplexes synchronous data. If this STDM has a service ratio of 1.5 : 1, then a 7200 bps synchronous input to the STDM would, on the average, take up 4800 bps of the 9600 bps operating line. Since the synchronous data is statistically multiplexed, when that data source is not active other data sources serviced by the STDM will flow through the system more efficiently. In comparison, the bandpass channel always requires a predefined portion of the high-speed line to be reserved for synchronous data, regardless of the activity of the data source.

Switching and port contention

Two features normally available with more sophisticated statistical multiplexers are switching and port contention. Switching capability is also referred to as alternate routing and requires the multiplexer to support multiple high-speed lines whose connection to the multiplexer is known as a node. Thus, switching capability normally refers to the ability of the multiplexer to support multiple nodes. Figure 4.18 illustrates how alternate routing can be used to compensate for a circuit outage. In the example shown, if the line connecting locations 1 and 3 should become inoperative, an

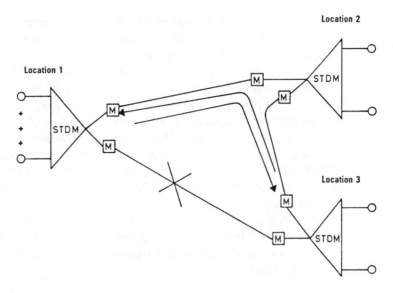

Figure 4.18 Switching permits load balancing and alternate routing if a high-speed line should become inoperative. M Modem

alternate route through location 2 could be established if the STDMs support data switching.

Port contention is normally incorporated into large capacity multinodal statistical multiplexers that are designed for installation at a central computer facility. This type of STDM may demultiplex data from hundreds of data channels, however, since many data channels are usually inactive at a given point in time, it is a waste of resources to provide a port at the central site for each data channel on the remote multiplexers. Thus, port contention results in the STDM at the central site containing a lesser number of ports than the number of channels of the distant multiplexers connected to that device. Then, the STDM at the central site contends the data sources entered through remote multiplexer channels to the available ports on a demand basis. If no ports are available, the STDM may issue a 'NO PORTS AVAILABLE' message and disconnect the user or put the user into a queue until a port becomes available.

ITDMs

One advancement in statistical multiplexer technology resulted in the introduction of data compression into a few STDMs. Such devices intelligently examine data for certain characteristics and are known as intelligent time division multiplexers (ITDM). These devices take advantage of the fact that different characters occur with different frequencies and use this quality to reduce the average number of bits per character by assigning short codes to frequently occurring characters and long codes to seldom-encountered characters.

The primary advantage of the intelligent multiplexer lies in its ability to make the most efficient use of a high-speed data circuit in comparison to the other classes of TDMs. Through compression, synchronous data traffic which normally contains minimal idle times during active transmission periods can be boosted in efficiency. Intelligent multiplexers typically permit an efficiency four times that of conventional TDMs for asynchronous data traffic and twice that of conventional TDMs for synchronous terminals. Thus, in analyzing the traffic handling capacity of ITDMs you can usually work with higher service ratios than that available with STDMs.

STDM/ITDM statistics

Although the use of statistical and intelligent multiplexers can be considered on a purely economic basis to determine if the cost of such devices is offset by the reduction in line and modem costs, the statistics that are computed and made available to the user of such devices should also be considered. Although many times intangible, these statistics may warrant consideration even though an economic benefit may at first be hard to visualize. Some of the statistics normally available on statistical and intelligent multiplexers are listed in Table 4.3. Through a careful monitoring of these statistics, network expansion can be preplanned to cause a minimum amount of potential busy conditions to users. In addition, frequent error conditions can be noted prior to user complaints and remedial action taken earlier than normal when conventional devices are used.

Using system reports

One of the most common problems associated with the use of a statistical or intelligent multiplexer service ratio is that vendors providing this figure tend to exaggerate, using a best case scenario to compute the ratio. As an example, vendors might consider all asynchronous users to be performing interactive data entry functions and ignore the possibility that some users are performing

Table 4.3   Intelligent multiplexer statistics.

Multiplexer loading: % of time device not idle

Buffer utilization: % of buffer storage in use

Number of frames transmitted

Number of bits of idle code transmitted

Number of negative acknowledgements received

$$\text{Traffic density} = \frac{\text{non-idle bits}}{\text{total bits}}$$

$$\text{Error density} = \frac{\text{NAKs received}}{\text{frames transmitted}}$$

$$\text{Compression efficiency} = \frac{\text{total bits received}}{\text{total bits compressed}}$$

$$\text{Statistical loading} = \frac{\text{number of actual characters received}}{\text{maximum number which could be received}}$$

$$\text{Character error rate} = \frac{\text{characters with bad parity}}{\text{total characters received}}$$

---

full screen emulated access to a mainframe via a protocol converter. Similarly, vendors will probably ignore file transfer activities since they would also increase data transmission and lower the computation of the multiplexer's service ratio.

One obvious question to ask is 'what is the effect of connecting too many data sources to a statistical or intelligent TDM based upon an inflated service ratio?' To understand the effect resulting from this situation, let us examine the cause and effect of buffer control on a terminal operator's display.

Figure 4.19 illustrates a statistical multiplexer for which a service ratio of 4:1 for asynchronous transmission is assumed. In this illustration, assume all 24 multiplexer ports are connected to mainframe computer ports. As more and more terminal users become actively connected to computer ports through the STDM system, begin to pull files, scroll through screens, or perform other data transmission intensive operations, the data flow into the multiplexer rapidly increases and could conceivably approach 38.4 kbps. Since the multiplexer transfers data onto the line at 9.6 kbps, the difference between the input and output data flow

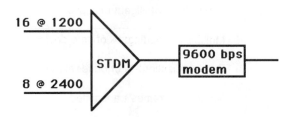

Figure 4.19 Overconfigured STDM. As all ports become fully active transmitting data into the STDM the data flow into the device approaches 38.4 kbps; however, the data flow from the STDM to the line is 9.6 kbps. This causes the STDM's buffer to fill rapidly

will rapidly fill the STDM's buffer. To prevent buffer overflow, the multiplexer will implement buffer or flow control when the buffer fills to a predetermined level.

When the multiplexer implements flow control, it signals the computer ports to disable or stop data transmission, providing the multiplexer with the ability to dump data out of its buffers. At another predefined buffer level, the STDM will issue another set of buffer or flow control signals to enable transmission to resume.

If a large number of file transfer operations are in progress, the multiplexer will rapidly enable and disable transmission again and again. To the typical terminal operator connected to the computer through the STDM system, the multiplexer's actions will result in random pauses in the display of data on their screen. In addition to obviously affecting response time, the random nature of the pauses will adversely affect the productivity of terminals operators and result in numerous complaints. These complaints are usually directed at the host computer's capacity as the symptoms closely resemble the effect of a saturated computer system. Only after hardware capacity planners review the utilization of the mainframe do most organizations begin to examine the possibility that their multiplexers are overloaded.

One of the best mechanisms available to determine potential multiplexer overloading conditions and initiate corrective action is through the use of system reports generated by most multiplexers.

System reports generated by statistical and intelligent multiplexers can include the parameters listed in Table 4.3 as well as other data elements. In this section, we will examine the use of several system report parameters to understand how this information can be used to more accurately size data sources to the capacity of statistical and intelligent multiplexers.

Figure 4.20 illustrates a Line Status Report generated by some

```
HH:MM:SS LINE 9600 BPS

Outbound 10 MIN AVG 1082

Inbound  10 MIN AVG  327
```

Figure 4.20 Typical line status report. The typical multiplexer line status report indicates the average inbound and outbound data traffic with respect to the line operating rate between two multiplexers in the system

multiplexers. This report is generated at predefined intervals and indicates the inbound and outbound character rates per second averaged over the prior interval of time. In addition, some multiplexers also provide the peak character input rate over a smaller period of time.

As indicated in Figure 4.20, the high-speed line is operating at 9600 bps, which is equivalent to 1200 cps. Thus, over the prior 10 minute period, data being transmitted through the local multiplexer to the remote multiplexer (outbound) represents a line utilization of 1082/1200 times 100 or 90.2%. Similarly, data being transmitted from the remote site through the remote multiplexer (inbound) represents a line occupancy rate of 27.3%.

As a general rule of thumb, any line occupancy in excess of 80 to 85% sustained over a period of time will result in an excessive amount of flow control. This is because the line occupancy calculations based upon inbound and outbound data compared to the line capacity rate does not include the effect of the overhead associated with the protocol used to transfer data between multiplexers. Typically, the protocol overhead may utilize 10 to 15% or more of the line's total traffic handling capacity. Thus, without examining other report parameters a line occupancy report can be used to determine whether or not your multiplexer system has or is approaching an overload condition.

If line occupancy is excessive, you can consider one of several options to improve multiplexer performance. First, you can replace existing modems with higher speed devices to increase the transmission rate on the line, in effect, reducing the line occupancy. If it is not feasible to increase the transmission rate between multiplexers you can consider removing one or more data sources that may be excessively using the capacity of the multiplexer. In some cases, the identification of more active data sources can be facilitated by the reports some multiplexers provide which indicate inbound and outbound traffic on an individual port basis as well as on a composite basis.

Another report element available from some multiplexers includes the number of flow controls issued by each channel during the predefined interval of time. If this report element is available you can directly determine which ports are being adversely affected and use this information to take corrective action.

A third report element provided by some multiplexers indicates the occupancy of its transmit buffers over a predefined period of time. Figure 4.21 indicates an example of this report element that can be a separate multiplexer report or incorporated into a multiplexer's system report.

```
HH:MM:SS LINE 9600 BPS

    LOCAL TRANSMIT BUFFER   10 MIN AVG 1842 CHAR

    REMOTE TRANSMIT BUFFER 10 MIN AVG   436 CHAR
```

Figure 4.21 Typical multiplexer buffer report. The buffer report can be used to determine throughput delays through multiplexers. This information can be used to determine what effect multiplexers have on composite response time delays seen from the terminal operator's perspective

In effect, the buffer report indicates the number of characters contained in the multiplexer awaiting transmission onto the high-speed line. By comparing the average contents of the local and remote transmit buffers with the high-speed line transmission rate, you can determine inbound and outbound delays through the multiplexer system. This information is extremely useful in attempting to determine the contributing factors that may be resulting in an unacceptable response time for interactive terminal users.

To illustrate the use of multiplexer buffer occupancy information, consider the local transmit buffer 10-minute average of 1842 characters shown in Figure 4.21. This is equivalent to 14 736 bits, which, when transmitted at 9600 bps, requires approximately 1.5 seconds until the first character entering the transmit buffer is placed onto the line. This means that outbound data traffic through the multiplexer is adding 1.5 seconds to the total response time end-users see between pressing an Enter key on their terminal and having the first character of the computer's response displayed. Concerning the remote transmit buffer, note that its occupancy results in less than four-tenths of a second delay. Normally, if the local multiplexer is considered to be located at the computer site while the remote multiplexer is located where terminal users are located, you will find a similar disproportion between local and remote buffer occupancy. this disproportion is due to terminal queries being relatively short in comparison to computer responses generated by those queries. Thus, in most cases, you will probably concentrate your efforts towards determining methods that can reduce the occupancy of the buffer of the local multiplexer.

Features to consider

In Table 4.4, the reader will find a list of the primary selection features one should consider when evaluating statistical multiplexers. Although many of these features were previously discussed, a few features were purposely omitted from consideration until now. These features include auto baud detect, flyback display, and echoplex, and primarily govern the type of terminal devices that can be efficiently supported by the statistical multiplexer.

Table 4.4 Statistical multiplexer selection features.

Feature	Parameters to consider
Auto baud detect	Data rates detected
Flyback delay	Settings available
Echoplex	Selectable by channel or device
Protocols supported	2780/3780, 3270, HDLC/SDLC, other
Data type supported	Asynchronous, synchronous
Service ratios	Asynchronous, synchronous
Flow control	XON-XOFF, CTS, clocking
Multinodal capability	Number of nodes
Switching	Automatic or manual
Port contention	Disconnect or queued when all ports in use
Data compression	Stripping bits or employs compression algorithm

Auto baud detect is the ability of a multiplexer to measure the pulse width of a data source. Since the data rate is proportional to the pulse width, this feature enables the multiplexer to recognize and adjust to different speed terminals accessing the device over the switched telephone network.

On electromechanical printers, a delay time is required between sending a carriage return to the terminal and then sending the first character of the next line to be printed. This delay time enables the print head of the terminal to be repositioned prior to the first character of the next line being printed. Many statistical multiplexers can be set to generate a series of fill characters after detecting a carriage return, enabling the print head of an electromechanical terminal to return to its proper position prior to receiving a character to be printed. This feature is called flyback delay and can be enabled or disabled by channel on many multiplexers.

Since some networks contain full-duplex computer systems that echo each character back to the originating terminal, the delay from twice traversing through statistical multiplexers may result in the terminal operator obtaining the feeling that his or her terminal is non-responsive. When echoplexing is supported by an STDM, the multiplexer connected to the terminal immediately echoes each character to the terminal, while the multiplexer connected to the computer discards characters echoed by the computer. This enables data flow through the multiplexer system to be more responsive to the terminal operator. Since error detection and correction is built into all statistical multiplexers, a character echo from the computer is not necessary to provide visual transmission validation and is safely eliminated by echoplexing.

The other options listed in Table 4.4 should be self-explanatory, and the user should check vendor literature for specific options available for use on different devices.

4.2 MODEM- AND LINE-SHARING UNITS

Cost-conscious company executives are always happy to hear of ways to save money on the job. One of the things a data communications manager can best do to make his or her presence felt is to produce a realistic plan for reducing expenses. It may be evident that a single communication link is less costly than two or more. What is sometimes less obvious is the most economical and effective way to make use of even a single link.

Multiplexing is usually the first technique that comes to mind, but there are many situations where far less expensive, albeit somewhat slower, equipment is quite adequate. Here, terminals are polled one by one through a 'sharing device' that acts under the instructions of the host computer. Typically, the applications where this method would be most useful and practical would be those where messages are short and where most traffic between host computer and terminal moves in one direction during any one period of time. The technique which can be called 'line-sharing' (as distinct from multiplexing) may work in some interactive situations, but only if the overall response time can be kept within tolerable limits. The technique is not as a rule useful for remote batching or RJE, unless messages can be carefully scheduled so as not to get in each other's way because of the long run-time for any one job. Although line-sharing is inexpensive, it has some limits to its usefulness, particularly in situations where a multiplexer can be used to produce additional economic leverage.

4.2.1 Operation

A TDM operates continuously to sample in turn each channel feeding it, either bit by bit or character by character; and this produces an aggregate transmission at a speed equal to the sum of the speeds of all its terminals.

A conventional TDM operation is illustrated in Figure 4.22A. For example, a multiplexer operating character by character assembles its first frame by taking the letter A from the first terminal, the letter E from the second, and the letter I from the third terminal. During the next cycle, the multiplexer takes the second character of each message (B, F, and J, respectively) to make up its second

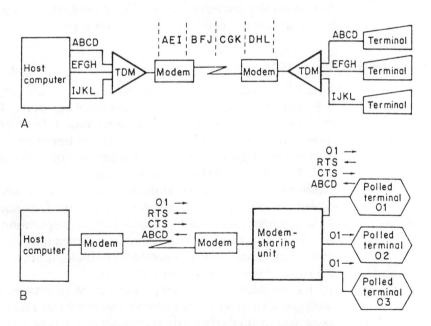

Figure 4.22 Multiplexing versus line-sharing. Top: Time division multiplex network. Bottom: Modem-sharing network. Multiplexer needs: A time division multiplex system (A) requires one computer port for each terminal and a multiplexer at each end. A sharing system (B) needs only one computer port. Because it requires terminals to be polled, a sharing system can be cost-effective for interactive operation, but may not be so for long messages such as are likely to move in remote job entry or remote batch types of applications

frame. The sampling continues in this way until traffic on the line is reversed to allow transmission from the computer to the terminals. The demultiplexing side of the TDM (operating on the receiving side of the network) assembles incoming messages and distributes them to their proper terminals or computer ports.

A line-sharing network is connected to the host computer by a local link, through which the host polls the terminals one by one. The central site transmits the address of the terminal to be polled throughout the network by way of the sharing unit. This is illustrated in Figure 4.22B. The terminal assigned this address (01 in the diagram) responds by transmitting a Request to Send (RTS) signal to the computer, which returns a Clear to Send (CTS), to prompt the terminal to begin transmitting its message (ABCD in diagram). When the message is completed, the terminal drops its RTS signal, and the computer polls the next terminal.

Throughout this sequence, the sharing device continuously routes the signals to and from the polled terminal and handles supporting tasks, such as making sure the carrier signal is on the line when the terminal is polled and inhibiting transmission from all terminals not connected to the computer.

4.2.2 Device differences

There are two types of devices that can be used to share a polled line: modem-sharing units and line-sharing units. They function in much the same way to perform much the same task—the only significant difference being that the line-sharing unit has an internal timing source, while a modem-sharing unit gets its timing signals from the modem it is servicing.

A line-sharing unit is mainly used at the central site to connect a cluster of terminals to a single computer port, as shown in Figure 4.23. It does, however, play a part in remote operation, when a data stream from a remote terminal cluster forms one of the inputs to a line-sharing unit at the central site to make it possible to run with a less expensive single-port computer.

In a modem-sharing unit, one set of inputs is connected to multiple terminals or processors, as shown in Figure 4.23. These lines are routed through the modem-sharing unit to a single modem. Besides needing only one remote modem, a modem-sharing network needs only a single two-wire (for half-duplex) or four-wire (for full-duplex) communications link. A single link between terminals and host computer allows all of them to connect with a single port on the host, a situation that results in still greater savings.

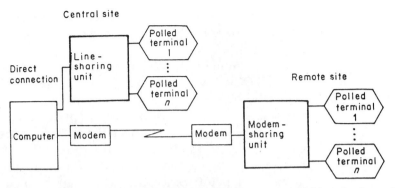

Figure 4.23 Line-sharing and modem-sharing use compared. Line-sharing units tie central site terminals to the computer, but modem-sharing units handle all the remote terminals. A line-sharing unit requires internal timing, whereas a modem-sharing unit gets its timing from the modem to which it is connected. In either case, access to the host is made through a single communications link—either a 2-wire or 4-wire—and a single port at the central site computer

If multiplexing were used in this type of application the outlay would likely be greater, because of the cost of the hardware and the need for a dedicated host computer port for each remote device. A single modem-sharing unit, at the remote site, is all that is needed for a sharing system, but multiplexers come in pairs, one for each end of the link.

The polling process makes sharing units less efficient than multiplexers. Throughput is cut back because of the time needed to poll each terminal and the line turnaround time on half-duplex links. Another problem is that terminals must wait their turn. If one terminal sends a long message others may have to wait an excessive amount of time, which may tie up operators if unbuffered terminals are used; but terminals with buffers to hold messages waiting for transmission will ease this situation.

4.2.3 Sharing unit constraints

Sharing units are generally transparent within a communications network. There are, however, four factors that should be taken into account when making use of these devices: the distance separating the data terminals and the sharing unit (generally set at no more than 50 ft under RS-232-C interface specifications); the number of terminals that can be connected to the unit; the various types of modem with which the unit can be interfaced; and whether the terminals can accept external timing from a modem through a sharing unit. Then, too, the normal constraints of the polling process, such as delays arising from turnaround and response and the size of the transmitted blocks, must be considered in designing the network.

The 50 ft limit on the distance between terminal and sharing unit (RS-232/CCITT V.24 standard) can cause problems if terminals cannot be clustered closely. A way to avoid this constraint is to obtain a sharing unit with a DCE option. This option permits a remote terminal to be connected to the sharing unit through a pair of modems, as illustrated in Figure 4.24. This in turn allows the users the economic advantage of a through connection out to the farthest point. Since the advantage of modem-sharing units over a multipoint line is the reduction in the total number of modems when terminals are clustered, only one or at most a few DCE options should be used with a modem-sharing unit, as it could defeat the economics of clustering the terminals to utilize a common modem.

It is advisable to check carefully into what types of modem can be supported by modem-sharing units, since some modems permit a great deal more flexibility of network design than others. For instance, if the sharing unit can work with a multiport modem, the extra modem ports can service remote batch terminals or dedicated terminals that frequently handle long messages. An example of this flexibility of design is shown in Figure 4.25. Some terminals that

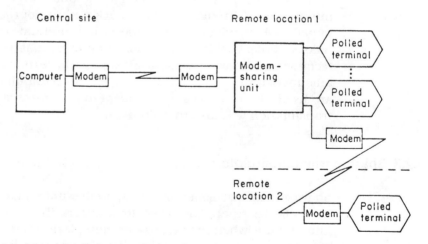

Figure 4.24 Extending the connection. Line- or modem-sharing units form a single link between a host computer and terminals. This system contains a modem-sharing unit with inputs from the terminals at its own site as well as from remote terminals. A line-sharing unit at the central site can handle either remote site devices or local devices more than 50 ft away from the host computer, which is the maximum cable length advisable under the RS-232-C/CCITT V.24 standards

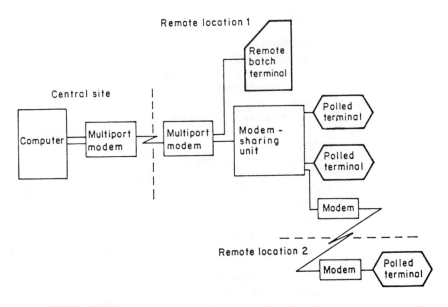

Figure 4.25 Multiple applications can share the line. Through the use of a modem-sharing unit with a data communications equipment interface, a terminal distant from the cluster (location 2) can share the same line segment (computer to location 1) that is used to transmit data to those terminals at location 1. With a second application that requires a remote batch terminal at location 1, additional line economies can be derived by installing multiport modems so both the polled terminals and the RBT can continue to share the use of one leased line from the computer to location 1

cannot accept external timing can be fitted with special circuitry through which the timing originates at the terminal itself instead of at the modem.

4.2.4 Economics of utilization

The prices of sharing units range from $500 to $3000, depending mainly upon the number of terminals that can be connected through the unit. At present this number varies, the most versatile units being able to handle up to 32 terminals.

As shown in Table 4.5, a typical multiplexing system containing a line leased at $1000 a month and designed to service four 1200 bps terminals (Part A of the table) might cost the user $2160 a month; a system with a modem-sharing unit designed to service four polled 4800 bps terminals (Part B of the table) would cost $1900 a month, or 12% less. The leased line contributes the largest part of the system's cost, thus the percentage saved with a less expensive line

Table 4.5 Comparison of monthly rental costs.

A.	Multiplexing	Monthly cost ($)
	Two TDMs at $90 each	180
	Two 4800 bps modems at $120 each	240
	Four computer ports at $35 each	140
	Leased line	1000
	Four terminals at $150 each	600
	Total monthly cost $2160	

B.	Using a modem-sharing unit	Monthly cost ($)
	Two 4800 bps modems at $120 each	240
	Computer port	35
	Modem-sharing unit	25
	Leased line	1000
	Four terminals at $150 each	600
	Total monthly cost $1900	

C. How percentage savings increase
as leased line cost decreases

	$1000 a month leased line	$1000 a month leased line
Multiplexing	$2160	$1660
Modem-sharing unit	$1900	$1400
Percentage savings	12%	16%

can be even greater. For instance (Part C of the table), a line leased
for $500 a month would increase the overall saving to 16%.

4.3 PORT-SHARING UNITS

An alternative to the utilization of modem- and line-sharing
units in a communications network can be obtained through the
employment of devices known as port-sharing units. In addition,
the proper employment of such devices can be used to complement
or supplement modem- and line-sharing units and in certain
situations may result in large economies being realized.

4.3.1 When to consider their use

Port-sharing units are devices that are installed between a host
computer and modem and that control access to and from the
host for up to six terminals with the number of terminals limited
by the capabilities of current hardware. In this way, port-sharing

units are able to cut down on the number of computer ports needed for these terminals. The port-sharing unit is versatile, inexpensive (about $500), and available from many modem and terminal manufacturers. Its utilization can save the cost of one or more relatively expensive computer channels that does essentially the same job but may have more capabilities than are needed. Port-sharing units can be used to service both local and remote terminals and so expand the job that can be done by a single port of the host computer.

To put the concept of port-sharing into perspective, the user should be aware of related devices designed to cut networking costs. Modem-sharing units and line-sharing units are available to minimize modem and line costs at remote locations, but they do not deal with the problem of overloading the host computer's ports. Modem- and line-sharing units are partial solutions to the high cost of data communications networking, but they are limited to the types of modems they can handle; and they can, by themselves, complicate the life of the network designer.

A problem that surfaces when either modem- or line-sharing units are used by themselves is the distribution of polled terminals within the network. For either kind of sharing unit to be effective, the terminals should be placed so that several are grouped close together. A typical modem-sharing unit employed to connect a number of terminals at a remote location for access to one computer port via a single pair of modems is illustrated in Figure 4.26. Some modem-sharing units can be obtained with a DCE interface option which is an RS-232-C interface by which remote terminals at two or more locations can be connected to the modem-sharing unit through the installation of a pair of modems between the terminal and the modem-sharing unit. Such a configuration

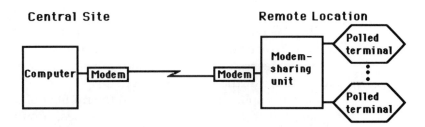

Figure 4.26 Modem-sharing unit usage. A modem-sharing unit permits a number of polled terminals to share the usage of a single line, one pair of modems, and a single computer port

is shown in Figure 4.27. Although the use of the interface shown in Figure 4.27 permits the network to have a more flexible configuration, with a number of terminals remote from the sharing unit, the number of such terminals that can be served by any one unit is usually limited to one or two.

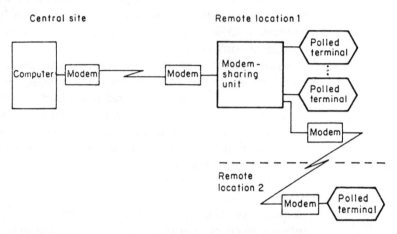

Figure 4.27 Network expansion using modem-sharing units with data communications equipment (DCE) interface. Remote terminals at two or more locations can share a common polled circuit when a DCE interface is present on the modem-sharing unit

Another disadvantage of this arrangement is that it is rather like putting all your eggs in one basket. If either modem on the high-speed link between the computer and the modem-sharing unit should fail, or if the circuit itself goes down, all the remote terminals become inoperative. Multiplexed terminals can use the dial-up network to restore data communications if the dedicated line fails. Polled terminals, however, do not have this advantage, since the host computer software is set up to seek and recognize the addresses of specific terminals in a certain order on the line. Therefore polled terminals must stay in their respective places, relative to each other, along the communications route. Any change in route necessitates changes in hardware at the terminals as well as software at the host computer.

As new applications develop and the number of remote terminals connected to the host computer increases, a situation can arise where the network designer runs out of ports to service the network. If no additional ports are available, a costly computer upgrade or the installation of a second computer system would represent a major economic burden. A method to obviate or postpone these types of equipment upgrades is through the utilization of port-sharing units.

4.3.2 Operation

Port sharing, then, is presented either as an alternative or as a supplement to modem and line sharing, in networks without multiplexers. A port-sharing unit is connected to a computer port and can transmit and receive data to and from two to six either synchronous or asynchronous modems, as shown in Figure 4.28.

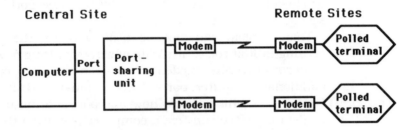

Central Site   **Remote Sites**

Figure 4.28 Using a port-sharing unit. The port-sharing unit lies between the host computer and the modems at the central site. One advantage is that if a failure occurs on the communications line or at the modem, only the terminal on that particular line goes down. On a polled, multidrop line, a line failure renders all terminals beyond it inaccessible

Data from the computer port is broadcast by the port-sharing unit, which passes the broadcast data from the port to the first modem that raises a receiver-carrier detect (RCD) signal. Data for any other destination will be blocked by the unit until the first modem stops receiving. The port-sharing unit thus provides transmission by broadcast and reception by contention for the port connected to it. Like a modem-sharing unit, a port-sharing unit is transparent with respect to data transmission. Data rates are limited only by the capabilities of the terminal. modem, and computer port.

In order to gain the same results without a port-sharing unit a multidrop configuration would, however, be required. Both the port-sharing unit and a multidrop network allow a large number of terminals to be served by one computer port; but in a multidrop network the failure of any part of the circuit will put all terminals beyond the failure out of action. In the configuration in Figure 4.28, however, failure of modem or outage on the line will only cut out a terminal on that segment. Failure of a computer port or of the port-sharing unit would, of course, bring down the entire network, but these devices are stable and such failures are fairly unusual.

4.3.3 Port-sharing as a supplement

Port-sharing units may also be used alongside modem-sharing units. If modem-sharing units alone are used, a situation can arise where there are not enough ports to serve the network, as in the top of Figure 4.29. If each modem-sharing unit serves its full complement of terminals and all the computer ports are in use, expansion of the network, even by just one port, may require a second mainframe computer.

This problem can also be dealt with by the use of a port-sharing unit at the central site which by cutting down the number of ports currently needed allows a network to expand without additional computer ports. This is illustrated at the bottom of Figure 4.29 which shows how one port-sharing unit with a two-modem interface can free a computer port from the configuration shown at the top of that illustration.

One versatile feature of port-sharing units is an option that allows the unit to accept a local interface instead of the normal RS-232-C interface, so that up to two local terminals may be operated without modems at the central site, as shown in Figure 4.30.

While both modem-sharing units and port-sharing units are similar in the way they are used, there is an important difference in the normal placing of their interfaces. In Table 4.6, a comparison of the characteristics of a port-sharing unit with those of modem- and line-sharing units will be found. For additional information on the latter two devices the reader is referred to Section 4.2.

4.3.4 Comparing cost with alternate components

In Figure 4.31, the reader is presented with two alternate means of connecting four 2400 bps remotely located terminals to a central computer facility. In the top portion of that illustration, a port-sharing unit and four individual lines and four pairs of modems are installed to enable the terminals to communicate on a poll and select basis with the computer. For this configuration, the failure of any modem or line will only render the terminal connected to the failing modem or line inoperative. In the lower portion of Figure 4.31, a pair of four-channel synchronous multiplexers has been

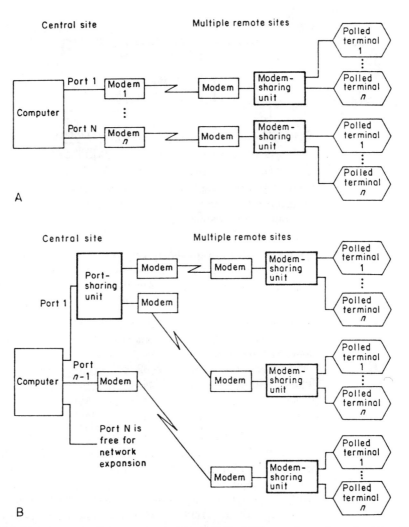

Figure 4.29 Two sharing techniques combined. When only modem-sharing units are used (A) a time may come when every port is in use and no further expansion on the network is possible. Rather than add another computer to serve a single new terminal, the user may prefer to invest in a port-sharing unit (B) that will solve the problem for about $500

installed to service the four terminals which are now restricted to being collocated unless other equipment is installed in addition to the devices shown in that illustration. Table 4.7 compares the monthly cost of a four-terminal network in multiplexed and port-sharing configurations. The breakeven point comes when the cost of each leased line reaches $103 a month. This figure can be arrived at by taking the total known costs (for multiplexers,

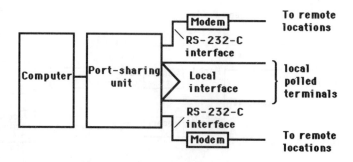

Figure 4.30 Connecting local peripherals. A local interface option to port-sharing lets local and remote sites to be served by the same port. Peripherals are polled as if they were at remote sites

Table 4.6 Features of sharing units.

Feature	Modem-sharing/ line-sharing unit	Port-sharing unit
Transmit mode	Broadcast	Broadcast
Receive mode	Contention	Contention
Number of modems interfaced	2–32	2–6
Terminals supported	Polled	Polled
Options	RS-232-C interface (MSU to modem)	Local interface (PSU to terminal)
Normal interface placement	Between modem and terminal	Between computer port and modem

computer ports, modems, and four terminals, at an average of $150 a month apiece), and adding an unknown cost—for the leased line—which remains constant whether the user employs port-sharing units or chooses a multiplexed network configuration. Balanced against this is the somewhat smaller total rental amount for a single port-sharing unit, one computer port, four lower-speed modems, and four terminals, all at the same rate of $150 a month.

4.3.5 More leased lines

The lower part of Table 4.7, however, shows an increase in the number of leased lines from one to four. The upper part of the table, therefore, gives a fixed cost of $1420 with a variable amount on a one-time basis for a single leased line, while the lower part

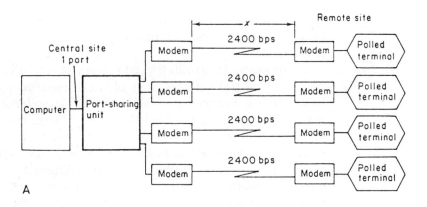

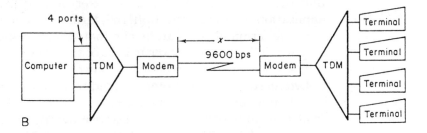

Figure 4.31 Comparing port-sharing units with multiplexers. (A) Port-sharing unit servicing four polled terminals. (B) Using multiplexers to service the terminals. When a leased line is equidistant from all terminals to the computer, a cost comparison becomes simple

Table 4.7 Comparison of monthly costs.

Multiplexed configuration costs	
Two 4-channel TDMs at $120	$240
Four computer ports at $35	140
Two 9600 bps modems at $220	440
Four terminals at $150	600
One leased line	x
	$1420 + x$
Port-sharing unit configuration costs	
One port-sharing unit at $25	$ 25
One computer port at $35	35
Eight 2400 bps modems at $55	440
Four terminals at $150	600
Four leased lines	$4x$
	$1110 + 4x$

equating: $1420 + x = 1110 + 4x$, $x = 103$

x = monthly cost of a leased line

shows a significantly lower equipment cost but gives a variable cost for leased lines four times that for a single-line multiplexed configuration.

In this example, $1420 less $1110 equals $310, or $3x$ (with x still representing the variable cost of the leased line). Dividing $310 by 3 gives a breakeven point of $103. Therefore, until monthly leased line charges total $103 for each line, the use of a port-sharing unit is more economical. Although the preceding cost comparison assumed that the cost of the terminals used on the port-sharing and multiplexer networks illustrated in Figure 4.23 were equivalent, this may not necessarily be true. Since terminals used on a port-sharing network generally require a buffer area, these terminals may be more expensive than non-buffered ones that could be used on the multiplexer network. If, owing to the application requirement, buffered terminals become necessary, then the terminal cost can be eliminated from consideration since they would be necessary regardless of the network employed.

In addition, without increasing network costs users can add up to two more local or remotely located terminals to a configuration based on a port-sharing unit, since the table is based on the costs related to four terminals and the average port-sharing unit can support up to six. The only additional cost would be for the rental of the terminal units; none would be incurred for additional modems or leased lines when local terminals are connected.

In order to support two additional terminals in a multiplexed configuration, however, the user would have to pay substantially more. Not only is an additional $35 per computer port required, but since the multiplexer is operating at the transmission limit of a leased voice-grade circuit, substantially more expensive wideband facilities would have to be installed to service the upgraded multiplexers. In addition, as explained earlier, the cost of adding two computer ports can be further aggravated if all ports are already in use on the computer, so that any extra load requires another entire processing unit.

The port-sharing unit, therefore, is most evidently a cost-saving tool when the user is already straining his computer system to its limits. Saving money is a constant preoccupation for all cost-conscious data communications managers and port-sharing should be considered in any polled-terminal situation where instantaneous response is not the most important network condition; yet there are times, such as when the computer runs out of capacity, when the cost of any further network expansion takes a leap from a few hundred dollars to perhaps tens of thousands for another computer.

5

LOCATING DATA CONCENTRATION EQUIPMENT

One of the most commonly encountered problems facing network designers is the selection of locations to install data concentration equipment. Although network designers must consider many factors, including the availability of space for equipment and personnel to provide maintenance vendors with access to such equipment, the major factor used to consider a location for data concentration equipment is economics. In general, when you have a number of locations transmitting and receiving data within a geographical area you will attempt to select a location for the installation of data concentration equipment that represents a minimum cost of transmission from all locations within the geographical area to the selected location. Since graph theory can be used to provide a firm methodology for selecting a data concentration location that represents a minimum cost location with respect to all other locations, we will first examine this subject area. Using the relationship between graph theory and network topology will provide us with the information required to use graph theory to manually perform or automate the equipment location process which is the major emphasis of the second section of this chapter.

5.1 GRAPH THEORY AND NETWORK DESIGN

One of the more interesting aspects of data communications networks is their topological relationship to graphs. You can view a communications network as a series of transmission paths that is used to interconnect different devices to include terminals, multiplexers, concentrators, port selectors, and similar equipment.

5.1.1 Links and nodes

If you consider transmission paths as branches while equipment clustered at a common location is used to represent a node, you can redesign a communications network in the form of a graph consisting of branches which are formally referred to as links and nodes which are connected to one another by one or more links. To illustrate this concept consider the network illustrated at the top portion of Figure 5.1 and its graphical model illustrated at the bottom of that illustration.

In converting the network schematic at the top of Figure 5.1 to its graphical format note that the host computer and the two modems at the central site location are considered as an entity and denoted as node 1, while the terminal and modem at remote sites A and B are also considered as an entity for nodes 2 and 3. Finally, the modem, control unit, and set of terminals at remote location C are considered to represent node 4 when the communications network is redrawn as a graph.

Now that we have briefly examined the relationship of graph theory to communications networks, let us focus our attention upon the properties of graphs which will enable us to consider the use of a connection matrix that can be developed to describe the paths between nodes and the relationship between the links connecting each node. Once this is accomplished we will focus our attention upon the typical network design problem concerning where to locate data concentration equipment and the use of graph theory to solve this problem. Thus, the intent of this chapter is to provide the reader with practical information in the form of graph theory knowledge that can be applied to solve a common network design problem. Later in this book we will use the knowledge of graph theory presented in this chapter to solve another common network design problem—obtaining an optimum route for a multidrop line.

5.1.2 Graph properties

In examining the network represented in graph format in the lower portion of Figure 5.1, it should be recognized that prior

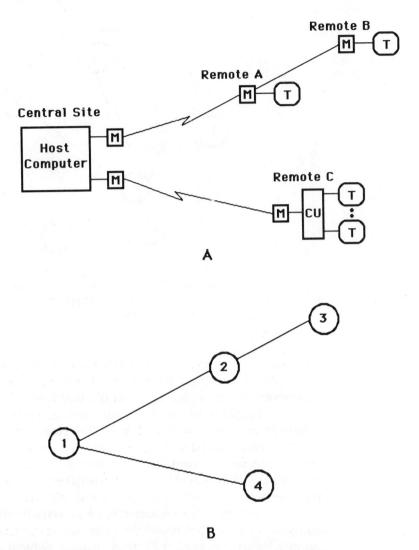

Figure 5.1 Network and graph relationship. A communications network can be represented as a graph by considering each location as a node, while circuits between nodes are represented as links. (A) simple communications network (M modem, CU control unit, T terminal. (B) Network in graph format

organizational requirements and constraints resulted in the original network design the graph represents. Rather than consider requirements and constraints at this time, let us start anew without prior conditions by examining the representation of a potential network in which four remote locations are to be connected to a host computer. Figure 5.2 illustrates a graph that contains

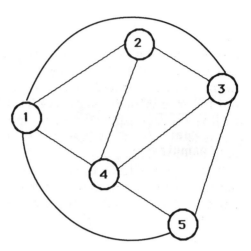

Figure 5.2 Five-node graph. This five-node graph can represent a central computer site and four remote locations or it can represent five remote locations clustered within one geographical area

five nodes and which will be used to both discuss the properties of graphs as well as develop and examine the properties of a connection matrix resulting from the topology of the graph.

The versatility associated with using graphs to represent networks can be envisioned by considering a few of the possible network configurations Figure 5.2 could represent. This diagram could represent a central computer site and four remote sites that must communicate directly with the central site or it could represent the possible routes allowed for the construction of a single multidrop line connecting each remote site to a central computer. As another possibility, the diagram could represent five remote locations clustered within a geographical area that must communicate with a distant computer system, such as five cities in a state east of Mississippi that must communicate with a computer located in Denver.

The five-node graph illustrated in Figure 5.2 contains nine links, where each link represents a line or branch connecting two nodes. As such, each link can be defined by a set of node pairs, such as (1,2), (1,3), (1,4), (1,5), and so on. If we assume that the flow of communications represented by a graph is bidirectional we do not have to distinguish between link (i,j) and link (j,i), where i and j represent node numbers. Thus, we can define link (i,j)=link (j,i) and will do so. Furthermore, we can define the graph representing a set of N nodes and L links as $G(N,L)$.

Network subdivisions

If we subdivide a network, we can represent the subdivision as a subgraph of $G(N,L)$. As an example of network subdivision assume the network illustrated at the top of Figure 5.1 was subdivided into the sets of node pairs (1,4) and (1,2), (2,3) and (3,5). Then, if $G_1(N_1,L_1)$ represents the subgraph of the network whose node pair is (1,4) while $G_2(N_2,L_2)$ represents the subgraph whose set of node pairs is (1,2), (2,3), (3,5) and whose links connect node 1 to 2, 2 to 3 and 3 to 5, then the union of G_1 and G_2 (represented mathematically as $G_1 \cup G_2$) represents the undivided or original network. Thus, $G_1 \cup G_2$ is the graph whose set of nodes is $N_1 \cup N_2$ and whose set of links is $L_1 \cup L_2$.

Routes

If i and j are distinct nodes in the graph $G(N,L)$, we can define the term route as an ordered list of links (i,i_1), (i_1,i_2), ... (i_n,j) such that i appears only at the end of the first link while j appears only at the end of the last link. With the exception of nodes i and j, all other nodes in the route will appear exactly twice, as they represent an entrance into a node from one link as well as an exit of the node by a link homing on another node. Based upon the preceding route properties it will not contain a loop nor will it represent the retracing of a link.

Cycles and trees

Two additional properties of graphs that warrant attention are cycles and trees. A cycle is a route that has the same starting and ending nodes. Thus, the route (1,2), (2,4), (4,5) in Figure 5.2 could be converted into the cycle (1,2), (2,4), (4,5), (5,1) by using link (5,1) to return to node 1. The reader should note that link (5,1) could be replaced by links (5,3), (3,1) to obtain a different cycle that also returns to node 1. A tree is a collection of links that connect all nodes in a graph and whose links contain no cycles.

Although a comparison between a route and a tree may appear trivial, in actuality the difference between the two is both distinct and has a key applicability to one specific area of network design. Unlike a route that may or may not connect all nodes in a graph, a tree will connect all nodes. This means that an analysis of the length of different trees that can be constructed from a common graph can be used, as an example, to determine the optimum route for a multidrop line that is used to interconnect network locations represented as nodes on a graph.

5.1.3 The Basic connection matrix

We can describe a graph $G(N.L)$ that contains N nodes and L links by an N-by-N matrix. In this matrix we can assign the value of each element based upon whether or not a link connects nodes i to j. Thus, if X is the connection matrix, we can describe the value of each element X_{ij} as follows

$X_{ij} = 0$ if no link connects i to j
$X_{ij} = 1$ if there is a link between i and j

In the preceding definition we will use the variable i to represent the ith row of the connection matrix, while the variable j will be used to represent the jth column of the connection matrix. Figure 5.3 represents the connection matrix for the graph illustrated in Figure 5.2.

$$\mathbf{X} = \begin{bmatrix} 0 & 1 & 1 & 1 & 1 \\ 1 & 0 & 1 & 1 & 0 \\ 1 & 1 & 0 & 1 & 1 \\ 1 & 1 & 1 & 0 & 1 \\ 1 & 0 & 1 & 1 & 0 \end{bmatrix}$$

Figure 5.3 Basic connection matrix. In a basic connection matrix, $X_{ij}=1$ when a link connects nodes i to j; otherwise $X_{ij}=0$

Considering graph weights

Although a basic connection matrix illustrates the relationship between links and nodes, that relationship is expressed as a binary relationship. In reality, we normally wish to consider the assignment of values to links where such values can represent the length of a link, its cost, transmission capacity, or some similar value as long as the values for all links are expressed in the same term. The assignment of values to links results in a real number known as a weight being placed on, above, or below each link on a graph.

If we denote the weight of a link between nodes i and j as W_{ij}, then we can assume that $W_{ij}=W_{ji}$ since we will not distinguish between link (i,j) and link (j,i). Similarly, if there is no link between nodes i and j, W_{ij} will be assigned the value 0.

To illustrate the use of graph weights, let us consider a five-node graph in which each node is connected by a link to another node. Let us assume that the link distances between nodes are as indicated in Table 5.1.

Table 5.1 Link distances.

Link	Distance (Miles)
(1,2)	9
(1,3)	11
(1,4)	8
(1,5)	13
(2,3)	7
(2,4)	14
(2,5)	12
(3,4)	8
(3,5)	6
(4,5)	6

The distances listed in Table 5.1 can be used to construct a weighted connection matrix. This matrix is illustrated in Figure 5.4 and could represent a geographical area consisting of a city and suburbs in which five offices are located. In this instance, a typical network design problem you may encounter is to determine the optimum location for the installation of a control unit among the five offices. In this type of problem, you would consider each location as a potential site to install the control unit. Since a terminal in each of the other offices would be connected to the control unit by the use of a leased line, you would want to select the control unit installation location to minimize the distance to all other offices.

$$
\mathbf{X} =
\begin{bmatrix}
0 & 9 & 11 & 8 & 13 \\
9 & 0 & 7 & 14 & 12 \\
11 & 7 & 0 & 8 & 6 \\
8 & 14 & 8 & 0 & 6 \\
13 & 12 & 6 & 6 & 0
\end{bmatrix}
$$

Figure 5.4 Weighted connection matrix. In a weighted connection matrix, each element is assigned a common value that can represent line cost, distance, or traffic handling capacity

As previously discussed, a weighted connection matrix can be used to represent all possible connections between a number of offices within a geographical area. If we assume that one terminal device is to be located at each office and we wish to connect those terminals to a common control unit, the question arises to find the location to place the control unit. In effect, this problem is a minimum route distance problem that can be solved by the manipulation of the elements of the previously developed weighted connection matrix.

In the next section of this chapter we will use the information concerning graph theory presented in this section to solve several typical data concentration equipment location problems. First we will examine the placement of one terminal per location. Next, we will vary the number of terminals we will develop, and modify a Basic language program you can use to automate the equipment location process.

5.2 EQUIPMENT LOCATION TECHNIQUES

One of the most common problems associated with the use of data concentration equipment is determining an optimum location to install such equipment. When the terminal population that will be serviced by data concentration equipment is clustered within a building or small geographical area, including a city and its suburbs, the problem of equipment location is typically reduced to selecting a convenient site that has available space, electrical power, and personnel available to provide access to installers and repair personnel if, at a later date, servicing or the upgrading of equipment becomes necessary. In this type of situation, little thought is given nor usually required to consider the cost of communications between each terminal device and potential data concentration locations to determine an optimum location based upon the cost of communications.

5.2.1 Examining distributed terminals

In place of the situation where terminal devices are clustered, let us consider the effect upon the distribution of terminals over a wider geographical area. For illustrative purposes, let us assume there are five locations at which one terminal will be installed. Let us further assume that the distances between terminal locations are as indicated in Table 5.2.

Table 5.2 Distances between terminal locations.

Terminal locations	Distance (Miles)
1–2	90
1–3	110
1–4	80
1–5	130
2–3	70
2–4	140
2–5	120
3–4	80
3–5	60
4–5	60

In examining the distances between terminal locations, it is not apparent which location would be optimum with respect to their distance to all other locations for the installation of a multiplexer or concentrator. If we consider each terminal location as a node, we can consider the distances between nodes as a weighted link for the development of a weighted graph. Then we can apply our prior discussion of graph theory to solve this problem.

Using the data contained in Table 5.2, we can develop a weighted graph as illustrated in Figure 5.5. Note that this graph uses nodes to represent terminal locations while the distances between locations are expressed as link weights.

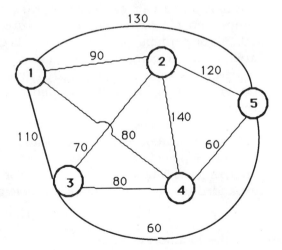

Figure 5.5 Graphical representation of distributed terminal locations. This graph represents the geographical distribution of terminals in miles from one another

We can use the distances between terminal locations contained in Table 5.2 or the graphical representation of the distributed terminal locations illustrated in Figure 5.5 to create a weighted connection matrix. This matrix is illustrated in Figure 5.6 and allows us to easily consider each location as a potential site for the installation of data concentration equipment.

$$
X = \begin{bmatrix}
0 & 90 & 110 & 80 & 130 \\
90 & 0 & 70 & 140 & 120 \\
110 & 70 & 0 & 80 & 60 \\
80 & 140 & 80 & 0 & 60 \\
130 & 120 & 60 & 60 & 0
\end{bmatrix}
$$

Figure 5.6 Weighted connection matrix. This weighted connection matrix uses the assignment of mileage to each element

5.2.2 Using a weighted connection matrix

A weighted connection matrix can be used to represent all possible connections between terminal locations within a geographical area. When we desire to find an optimum location to place data concentration equipment, in effect, we are attempting to solve a minimum route distance problem. This problem is easily solved by the manipulation of the elements contained in the previously developed weighted connection matrix.

Although we can easily analyze the elements in the weighted connection matrix contained in Figure 5.6, suppose there were 20, 30, or perhaps 50 or even 100 offices within the geographical area we had to consider. In such situations it would be preferable to develop a computer program to analyze the connection matrix to determine an optimum location to install data concentration equipment.

Due to the use of computer programs facilitating the solution of data concentration equipment location problems, let us examine the development and utilization of a computer program for analyzing the 5-by-5 element connection matrix and which can be expanded to solve more complex problems.

5.2.3 Automating the location process

Figure 5.7 contains a Basic language program listing which, when executed, computes the route distance from each node in the

```
REM PROGRAM TO COMPUTE NODE LOCATION
CLS
DIM X(5, 5), DISTANCE(5)
FOR I = 1 TO 5
FOR J = 1 TO 5
READ X(I, J)
NEXT J
NEXT I
DATA 0,90,110,80,130
DATA 110,70,0,80,60
DATA 80,140,80,0,60
DATA 130,120,60,60,0
REM FIND MINIMUM ROUTE DISTANCE
FOR I = 1 TO 5
DISTANCE(I) = 0
FOR J = 1 TO 5
DISTANCE(I) = DISTANCE(I) + X(I, J)
NEXT J
NEXT I
REM PRINT RESULTS
FOR J = 1 TO 5
LOW = DISTANCE(1)
K = 1
FOR I = 1 TO 5
IF LOW < DISTANCE(I) GOTO 1
LOW = DISTANCE(I)
K = I
1 NEXT I
PRINT "NODE "; K; " ROUTE DISTANCE ="; LOW
DISTANCE(K) = 9999
NEXT J
```

Figure 5.7 Node location program listing

graph illustrated in Figure 5.5. In effect, this program can be used to obtain the information necessary to select an optimum node location from a five-node graph and can be easily modified to operate upon graphs containing additional nodes. This program is contained in the file NODE.BAS on the convenience diskette available from the publisher of this book.

The DIM (dimension) statement allocates space for a two-dimensional 5-by-5 (25) element array labeled X which will represent the connection matrix and a one-dimensional five-element array labeled DISTANCE. The first pair of FOR–NEXT loop statements initialize the element values of the connection matrix as each time a loop occurs the READ statement assigns a value in a DATA statement to X_{ij} based upon the values of I and J in the FOR–NEXT loop. Note that the values in the DATA statements correspond to the row values of the connection matrix previously listed in Figure 5.4.

The second pair of FOR–NEXT statement loops in the program

listing first initialize each element of the one-dimensional DISTANCE array to zero. Next, the route distance from node i to all other nodes is computed as J varies from 1 to 5. In effect, the preceding operations sum the row values of the connection matrix.

The last portion of the program listed in Figure 5.7 prints the results based upon the values of the elements of the DISTANCE array. First, the variable LOW, which represents the lowest number or route distance is set to the value of the first element in the DISTANCE array. Next, as the variable I varies from 1 to 5 which correspond to all elements in the DISTANCE array, the value of LOW is compared to the value of each element of the DISTANCE array. If the value of LOW is not less than the value of the appropriate DISTANCE element, the value of the DISTANCE element is assigned to LOW and the variable I which indicates the node associated with the DISTANCE element is assigned to the variable K. If the value of LOW is less than the value of the appropriate DISTANCE element, a branch to the statement labeled with 1 occurs, in effect, bypassing the assignment of the DISTANCE element to LOW and the value of K to I. Once the I loop is completed, K represents the node number that has the lowest or shortest route distance while the variable LOW contains the value of the route distance. After the PRINT line is executed, the Kth element of the DISTANCE array is assigned the value 9999. In effect, this operation precludes the selection of this node a second time when J is incremented by one and the J loop is again executed. Thus, the nested FOR–NEXT J and I loops result in the printing of the route distance by node in ascending distance. Figure 5.8 illustrates the execution of the program based upon the use of the connection matrix illustrated in Figure 5.4.

```
NODE 3    ROUTE DISTANCE = 320
NODE 4    ROUTE DISTANCE = 360
NOTE 5    ROUTE DISTANCE = 370
NODE 1    ROUTE DISTANCE = 410
NODE 2    ROUTE DISTANCE = 420
```

Figure 5.8 Execution of node location program

As illustrated in Figure 5.8, node 3 represents the optimum location to place a data concentration device based upon the previously described problem. In this example, the placement of data concentration equipment at node 3 results in a reduction of 40 miles in comparison to the selection of node 4, 50 miles with respect to the selection of node 5, 90 miles over the selection of node 1, and 100 miles in comparison to selecting node 2.

5.2.4 Extending the node location problem

In solving the previous node location problem, it was assumed that only one terminal would be installed at each location and that all terminals would communicate over leased lines. These two assumptions enabled the use of a symmetrical connection matrix since the cost of a leased line from A to B is the same as a line from B to A and limiting one terminal per location insures that the weight of link X_{ij} equals the weight of link X_{ji}.

Suppose there are some locations that will have more than one terminal installed. What effect does this situation have on the node location problem and the symmetry of the connection matrix? To illustrate the effect of increasing the terminal population, let us first consider dial or switched network access from each terminal to a data concentration device located at a node. Next, we will examine the use of leased lines to support a non-uniform distribution of terminals. Then, we can use the previously developed networking information to examine the effect of using a mixture of switched network and leased line facilities to service a terminal population within a geographical area by a common data concentration equipment.

5.2.5 Switched network utilization

In place of a uniform distribution of one terminal per node, let us assume a variable distribution of terminals. In addition, let us further assume that the switched telephone network will be used as the data transportation medium to the location where a multiplexer or another type of data concentration equipment will be located.

To determine the cost associated with the use of the switched network from one location to another would require the development of a complex table in which the cost of a call from each location to every other location would be listed for the first minute and each additional call minute. Fortunately, the tariff structure for switched network telephone calls is based upon mileage bands, with calls between cities that fall into the same mileage band distance billed at the same rate. Due to this, in many instances, it becomes possible to simplify the construction and application of a cost table. If we assume the terminal locations in the geographical area we are examining are located within the same switched network mileage band, we can use the same cost elements in computing the cost per call from one location to all other locations, that is, we will assume the cost of the first minute and each succeeding minute is the same, say, from location 1 dialing location 3 as it is for location 1 dialing location 5 and location 2 dialing location1, and so on. Otherwise, we would have to determine the mileage band for calls from each node to all other nodes.

Assuming the mileage bands for all locations calling all other locations are equivalent, our cost table can be easily constructed. Table 5.3 illustrates the construction of a Switched Network Cost Table. In constructing this table, you would normally include some additional information that was omitted for simplicity, such as the average call duration in minutes and the cost per minute. These two missing columns of data were replaced by the Avg Cost/Call column.

Table 5.3 Switched network cost table.

Location	Number of terminals	Calls/day per terminal	Average cost per call	Total cost per day ($)	Monthly cost ($)
1	1	2	1.00	2.00	44.00
2	2	1	2.00	4.00	88.00
3	2	3	1.50	9.00	198.00
4	1	4	2.00	8.00	176.00
5	3	2	2.00	12.00	264.00

The row entries in the Total Cost/Day column in Table 5.3 were computed by multiplying the entries in column 2 by the entries in column 3 by the Cost/Call entry in column 4. Next, it was assumed that the organization was actively transmitting data an average of 22 days per month. Thus, the Monthly Cost column was completed by multiplying the Total Cost/Day column entries by 22.

The entries in column 6 of Table 5.3 can be used to develop a non-symmetrical connection matrix where X_{ij} may or may not be equal to X_{ji}. This is because a non-uniform distribution of terminals, a non-uniform number of calls per day per terminal, and a non-uniform cost per call either by themselves or collectively contribute to the weight of X_{ij} being less than, equal to or greater than the weight of link X_{ji}, where the link weight from i to j is the monthly cost of communications from location i to location j.

Based upon the use of column 6 in Table 5.3, we can create the connection matrix illustrated in Figure 5.9. In creating the connection matrix, the monthly cost of communications from location 1 ($44) is assumed to be the cost from that location to all other locations. Similarly, the cost of communications from location 2 to all other locations was assumed to be $88. Note that the differences in the number of terminals, calls per day, and cost per call between locations 1 and 2 ensured $X_{12} \neq X_{21}$.

In attempting to use the connection matrix illustrated in Figure 5.9 as a basis for use in the previously described Basic NODE analysis program, your first inclination might be to simply substitute the entries in the connection matrix into the DATA statement values in the program. If you did so, your DATA statements would appear as indicated in Figure 5.10.

Using the previously discussed modifications, the execution of the program would result in the computation of route distances, which now represent the monthly cost of communications, as indicated in Figure 5.11. However, the question arises—are these distances or costs correct?

To verify the correctness of the program execution, let us examine a route distance. From Figure 5.9, the route distance for node 1 is 176, which represents the distance or cost from location 1 to all

$$
\mathbf{X} = \begin{bmatrix}
0 & 44 & 44 & 44 & 44 \\
88 & 0 & 88 & 88 & 88 \\
198 & 198 & 0 & 198 & 198 \\
176 & 176 & 176 & 0 & 176 \\
264 & 264 & 264 & 264 & 0
\end{bmatrix}
$$

Figure 5.9 Switched network utilization connection matrix. When the number of terminals or call duration per terminal vary a weighted connection matrix will not be symmetrical

```
DATA 0,44,44,44,44
DATA 88,0,88,88,88
DATA 198,198,0,198,198
DATA 176,176,176,0,176
DATA 264,264,264,264,0
```

Figure 5.10 Modified DATA statements

```
NODE 1 ROUTE DISTANCE = 176
NODE 2 ROUTE DISTANCE = 352
NODE 4 ROUTE DISTANCE = 704
NODE 3 ROUTE DISTANCE = 792
NODE 5 ROUTE DISTANCE = 1056
```

Figure 5.11 Executing of node location program using revised data

other locations. Since the connection matrix is not symmetrical as it does not represent an even bidirectional weight, what the program computed represents the reverse direction of the problem, that is, the placement of data concentration equipment at each location requires the computation of the total route distance or cost from all other node locations to that location. Thus, the program must be modified to sum the connection element values by column instead of by row. Figure 5.12 illustrates the program segment change in which the *I* and *J* FOR--NEXT loops were reversed to enable the summation of element values by column. Figure 5.13 illustrates the execution of the program based upon the previously described program modifications.

```
REM FIND MINIMUM ROUTE DISTANCE
FOR J = 1 TO 5
DISTANCE(J) = 0
FOR I = 1 TO 5
DISTANCE(J) = DISTANCE(J) + X(I, J)
NEXT I
NEXT J
```

Figure 5.12 Changing the program to sum by column

```
NODE 5 ROUTE DISTANCE = 506
NODE 3 ROUTE DISTANCE = 572
NODE 4 ROUTE DISTANCE = 594
NODE 2 ROUTE DISTANCE = 682
NODE 1 ROUTE DISTANCE = 726
```

Figure 5.13 Execution of revised node location program

5.2.6 Other program modifications

To simplify the computation of the cost of leased lines based upon their distance between rate centers, the Bell System developed a vertical and horizontal (*VH*) Coordinate Grid System that overlays all of the continental United States and a large portion of Canada at an approximate 30 to 45 degree shift from a true North to South orientation. The *VH* Coordinate Grid System varies both *V* and *H* from 0 to 10 000, with *H* varying from 0 to 10 000 going from right to left on the *VH* map, while *V* varies from 0 to 10 000 going from top to bottom on the map. This results in some upper Maine locations having *VH* coordinates of 3000, 0 while upper Washington state locations have *VH* coordinates of approximately 8000, 10 000. At the lowest *V* level, the Florida Keys and some locations in southern

Texas have a *V* coordinate of approximately 10 000 while the *H* coordinate value varies from approximately 0 at the eastern edge of the Florida Keys to approximately 4000 near the tip of southern Texas. Figure 5.14 illustrates the AT&T *VH* Coordinate Grid System overlaid on the eastern and mid-western portions of the United States.

The *VH* Coordinate Grid System is used by most communications carriers, as well as a number of independent firms, as the

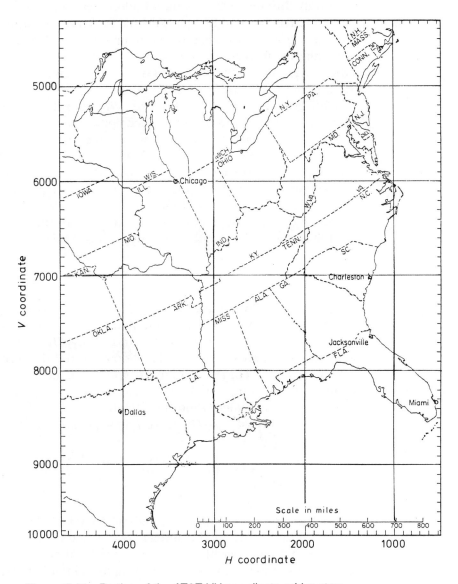

Figure 5.14 Portion of the AT&T VH coordinate grid system

foundation for developing programs that compute the location to place a data concentration node within a geographical area, the path that represents a minimum route multidrop circuit, and other network design functions. Since each rate center corresponds to an area code and three-digit telephone prefix, a number of firms sell software that allows users to enter those six digits that represent office locations to obtain their *VH* coordinate location. Other firms sell tables listing *VH* coordinates of thousands of cities in the US and Canada, while some vendors market a database of *VH* coordinates that can be incorporated into user-developed software. Assuming you have access to one or more methods to obtain *VH* coordinates for your organizational locations, let us examine how the previously described Basic language program could be modified to automatically compute link distances.

The grid formed to define the *VH* boundaries between two locations represents a two-dimensional plane. Due to this, a slightly modified version of the Pythagorean theorem can be used to calculate the distance between pairs of *VH* coordinates representing two locations. In the Pythagorean theorem the hypotenuse of a right triangle is shown to be equal to the square root of the sum of the squares of the other two sides of the triangle. Thus, if *C* is the hypotenuse and *A* and *B* are the other two sides of the triangle, the length of the hypotenuse becomes

$$C = \left(A^2 + B^2\right)^{1/2}$$

In the *VH* Coordinate Grid System, you can envision *A* and *B* to be the difference between pairs of *VH* coordinates. Thus, you can replace *A* by $V_1 - V_2$ and *B* by $H_1 - H_2$, where the subscripts 1 and 2 represent locations 1 and 2. Finally, to convert *VH* coordinate points to mileage you must divide the resulting sum of the squares by 10 prior to taking the square root, thus, the formula for calculating the distance (*D*) in miles between two locations expressed as *VH* coordinates becomes

$$D = \mathrm{INT}\left[\left(\frac{(V_1 - V_2)^2 + (H_1 - H_2)2}{10}\right)^{1/2} + 0.5\right]$$

In the preceding equation, 0.5 is added to the result of the computation prior to the integer being taken since a communications carrier is permitted by tariff to round the computed mileage to the next higher mile in performing its cost calculations.

As an example of the utilization of the *VH* coordinate system, let us compute the mileage between Denver and the geographical center of Georgia located in the famous town of Macon. The *VH* coordinates of Denver are 7501, 5899 while Macon's *VH* coordinates are 7364, 1865. Thus, the distance between those two locations is

$$D = \text{INT} \left[\left(\frac{(7501 - 7364)^2 + (5899 - 1865)^2}{10} \right)^{1/2} + 0.5 \right] = 1277 \text{ miles}$$

Based upon the preceding description of the *VH* Coordinate Grid System, you can easily modify the Basic program listed in Figure 5.5 to compute distances between nodes rather than work with predefined link distances. Here you would either input *VH* coordinates for each location or the area code and three-digit prefix of the telephone exchange for each location. For the latter, you could integrate a commercially available database into your program that would allow you to retrieve the *VH* coordinates for a location based upon knowing the area code and telephone prefix of the location. Once the *VH* coordinates for each node are determined, you could use the previously noted equation to determine the link distances between nodes. Thereafter, the program would operate as previously described to compute the total route distance from each node to all of the other nodes in the network. Finally, for networks that have a large number of nodes you could modify the program to sort and list the route distances in ascending order by node. This would allow users to easily consider alternate data concentration locations if a better location is not suitable for installing the required equipment for some reason. Now that we have examined the properties of graphs and the use of a connection matrix to determine the optimum location to place data concentration equipment, we will continue our examination of the use of graph theory to solve another common network design problem—where to route a multidrop line to minimize its distance. Thus, in Chapter 6 we will conclude our application of graph theory to network design by examining its utilization to determine an optimum multidrop line route.

6

MULTIDROP LINE
ROUTING TECHNIQUES

One of the most frequent problems encountered by organizations is to determine an economical route for the path of a multidrop circuit. This type of circuit is used to interconnect two or more locations that must be serviced by a common mainframe computer port. Although there are several commercial services that the reader can subscribe to as well as a free service offered by AT&T to obtain a routing analysis, in many situations, this analysis can be conducted internally within the organization. Doing so not only saves time but may also eliminate some potential problems that can occur if one relies upon programs that do not consider whether the resulting number of drops on a circuit can support the data traffic while providing a desired level of performance.

In this chapter, we will examine the use of several algorithms that can be employed to minimize the routing distance and resulting cost of a multidrop circuit. Since there is a finite limit to the number of drops a multidrop circuit can support, we will also investigate a method that will enable users to estimate the worst case and average terminal response times as the number of drops increase. Then if the response time exceeds the design goal of the organization, the network manager can consider removing one or more drops and placing them on a different multidrop circuit. Due to the applicability of graph theory for solving multidrop routing problems, we will use information previously presented in this book concerning that area of mathematics as a foundation for solving additional communications related problems. Thus, the reader is referred to Chapter 5 for a review of graph theory techniques previously presented in this book.

6.1 MULTIDROP ROUTING ALGORITHMS

In this section, we will examine the operation and utilization of a popular algorithm that can be employed to develop a multidrop network structure. This algorithm, which is known as the Prim algorithm in recognition of its developer, was publicised in 1957 in the *Bell System Technical Journal*. Because this algorithm results in the development of a minimum spanning tree (MST) in which the link distances between nodes are minimized, the resulting tree structure obtained by the use of this algorithm is known as a minimum spanning tree while the algorithm is commonly referred to as a MST algorithm. Although this algorithm results in the development of an optimum network structure, it does not consider such constraints as traffic flow or response time. Thus, later in this chapter we will examine methods by which such constraints can be considered.

6.1.1 The minimum-spanning-tree technique

When the total number of drops to be serviced does not exceed the capacity of software operating on a computer connected to a multidrop line, the MST technique can be used. This technique results in the most efficient routing of a multidrop line by the use of a tree architecture which is used to connect all nodes with as few branches as possible. When applied to a data communications network, the MST technique results in the selection of a multidrop line whose drops are interconnected by branches or line segments which minimize the total distance of the line connecting all drops. Since the distance of a circuit is normally proportional to its cost, this technique results in a multidrop line which is also cost optimized. To better understand the procedure used in applying the MST technique, let us first examine an example of its use.

The upper portion of Figure 6.1A illustrates the location of a mainframe computer with respect to four remote locations that require a data communications connection to the computer. Assuming that remote terminal usage requires a dedicated connection to the computer, such as busy travel agency offices might require to their corporate computer, an initial network configuration might require the direct connection of each location to the computer by separate leased lines. The lower portion of Figure 6.1B illustrates this network approach.

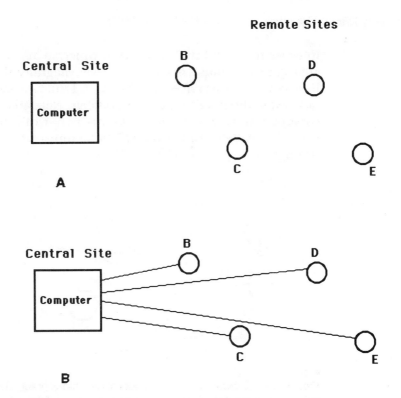

Figure 6.1 Terminal locations to be serviced. (A.) Terminal locations with respect to central site computer. (B.) Individual site connection to computer

When separate leased lines are used to connect each terminal location to the mainframe, a portion of many line segments can be seen to run in parallel. Thus, from a visual perspective, it is apparent that the overall distance of one circuit linking all locations to the computer will be less than the total distance of individual circuits. Other factors that can reduce the cost of a composite multidrop circuit in comparison to separate leased lines includes differences in the number of computer ports and modems required between the use of multidrop line and individual leased lines.

A multidrop line requires the use of one computer port with a common modem servicing each of the drops connected to the port. A total of $n + 1$ modems are thus required to service n drops on a multidrop circuit. In comparison, separate point-to-point leased lines would require one computer port per line as well as $n * 2$ modems, where n equals the number of required point-to-point lines.

Applying Prim's algorithm

In order to apply Prim's algorithm which is also known as a MST algorithm, we must first convert the diagram showing terminal locations to be serviced in Figure 6.1 into a graph. Figure 6.2 illustrates the result of this conversion. Note that the central site computer has been replaced as node 1, while the remote sites previously labeled B, C, D, and E were replaced by nodes labeled 2 through 5.

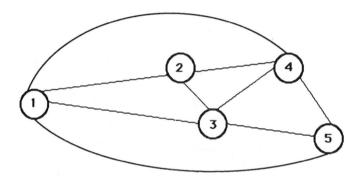

Figure 6.2 Conversion of network locations into a graph. This figure illustrates the conversion of the network locations contained in Figure 6.1 into a graph. Note that the central site computer was assumed to be node 1

Now that we have established a graph representing the network, the next step to be performed prior to applying Prim's algorithm is to assign link weights to the graph. Here, the assignment of link weights will be based upon the distance between nodes since the cost of a leased line is normally proportional to its length. Due to the complexity of tariffs, this may not always be correct, and the reader may wish to assign values to link weights based upon the actual cost of leased lines between each node.

For illustrative purposes, let us assume the distances between the nodes previously illustrated in Figure 6.2 correspond to the entries in Table 6.1. We can then use those distances between nodes as the link weight assignments and revise Figure 6.2. Figure 6.3 illustrates this revision in which each link has been assigned a link weight.

Prim's algorithm lets us start the construction of a MST by selecting any node in a graph. Once a node is selected, you then construct a two-node subgraph by connecting the first node to the nearest node, in effect, selecting the minimum link distance

Table 6.1   Node distance relationship.

Link	Node Distance
1,2	30
1,3	60
1,4	60
1,5	90
2,3	50
2,4	40
3,4	20
3,5	50
4,5	30

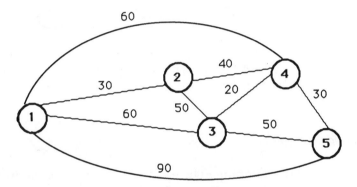

Figure 6.3   Assignment of link weights. This figure illustrates the assignment of node distances to the network graph contained in Figure 6.2

between the first node and all other nodes in the graph. Next, you will expand the two-node subgraph into a three-node subgraph by connecting one of the nodes in the two-node subgraph to the nearest node not contained in the subgraph. This process is repeated until all of the nodes are connected to one another.

To illustrate the use of Prim's algorithm, let us apply it to the graph containing link weights representing the mileage between nodes previously illustrated in Figure 6.3. Table 6.2 lists the steps involved in developing a MST based upon the creation and expansion of a subgraph and the resulting link addition each time the subgraph is expanded. In this example, the construction of the MST commenced by selecting node 1 as the starting node, however, you could obtain the same tree structure by selecting any other node in the graph as the starting node. Figure 6.4 illustrates the resulting MST based upon Prim's algorithm. Note that this tree has a link weight of 120.

Table 6.2 Constructing the minimum spanning tree.

Step	Nodes in subgraph	Link addition
1	1	(1,2)
2	1,2	(2,4)
3	1,2,4	(4,3)
4	1,2,3,4	(4,5)
5	1,2,3,4,5	—

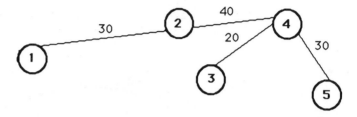

Figure 6.4 Resulting minimum spanning tree. This minimum-spanning-tree has a link weight of 120

Considering fan-out

In examining Figure 6.4, one item of special interest that warrants attention is the dual links that home on node 4. In a multidrop network configuration, a modem installed at node 4 would have to contain a 'fan-out' feature to support multiple links. Otherwise, the use of conventional multidrop modems would preclude the use of the MST configuration previously illustrated in Figure 6.4. In such situations where you cannot or prefer not to use modems with a fan-out feature, you may want to use a modified MST technique that results in a minimum tree length with only one link routed from a node to any other node.

6.1.2 Modified minimum-spanning-tree technique

In the modified MST technique, you should select the farthest location from the node connected to the computer first. In our example, this would be node 5. Next, form subgraphs similar to the manner previously described, however, add the following constraints:

(1) If two links currently connect a node in a subgraph, exclude

the use of that node for a link when you expand the subgraph by selecting a link to the nearest nonconnected node.
(2) Home on the destination link last.

Based upon the preceding constraints, Table 6.3 lists the steps followed in developing a modified MST. Figure 6.5 illustrates the resulting tree. Note that the link weight of the tree has increased to 130, however, it does not require the use of modems with a fan-out feature.

Table 6.3 Constructing a modified minimum spanning tree.

Step	Nodes in subgraph	Link addition
1	5	(5,4)
2	5,4	(4,3)
3	5,4,3	(3,2)
4	5,4,3,2	(2,1)
5	5,4,3,2,1	—

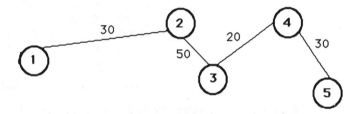

Figure 6.5 Revised tree. The revised tree contains a maximum of two links connecting a node, eliminating the necessity of using modems with a fanout feature when constructing the network configured by the graph

In examining Table 6.3, let us review each of the steps to illustrate the procedure required to avoid a fan-out situation. In step 1, the most distant node, node 5 in this example, is selected. From node 5 the nearest node is node 4, hence, link (5,4) is added for the formation of our multidrop line. Since the distances from node 4 to other nonconnected nodes is less than the distance from node 5 to other nonconnected nodes we will resume our work at node 4. From that node we would then select node 3 as the nearest node and add the link (4,3) to the formation of our multidrop line. Next, in examining the distance from nodes 3, 4, and 5 to the remaining unconnected nodes we would select node 4 to work with if we were developing a conventional MST structure. However, if we work with node 4 it would violate our previously stated constraint designed to prevent a fan-out situation as node 4 already has two links connected to it. Thus, to prevent a fan-out situation from occurring, we should select node 3 to work with.

By selecting node 3 instead of node 4 to use as a base for forming a link to node 2, we eliminate a fan-out from occurring. However, we also replace a link (4,2) whose weight is 40 by a link (3,2) whose weight is 50, resulting in an increased link weight during the formation of the modified MST. Lastly, we use node 2 as a base and connect it to node 1 to complete our modified MST whose structure does not include a fan-out.

6.1.3 Using a connection matrix

To illustrate the use of a connection matrix, let us focus our attention upon the initial graph previously illustrated in Figure 6.3. The connection matrix for that graph is illustrated in Figure 6.6.

$$
\mathbf{X} = \begin{bmatrix}
0 & 30 & 60 & 60 & 90 \\
30 & 0 & 50 & 40 & 0 \\
60 & 50 & 0 & 20 & 50 \\
60 & 40 & 20 & 0 & 30 \\
90 & 0 & 50 & 30 & 0
\end{bmatrix}
$$

Figure 6.6 Connection matrix for graph in Figure 6.9

We can computerize the development of a MST by first initializing a two-dimensional matrix using the connection matrix values shown in Figure 6.6 for each element array value. Once this is accomplished, we can initialize a one-dimensional array whose element values contain the nodes in the graph that must be connected to form a tree. Thus, this array would contain five elements whose values would be 1, 2, 3, 4, and 5.

The computer program developed to determine the MST would first scan column 1 of the two-dimensional matrix, searching for the minimum distance from node 1 to another node. In our example, element X_{21} would be selected, since its value is the lowest of all values in column 1. Since nodes 1 and 2 are then connected, the elements X_1 and X_2 in the one-dimensional node array whose values were 1 and 2 would be assigned the value zero to denote they are included in a subgraph used to form a tree. Similarly, since $X_{ij} = X_{ji}, X_{12}$ in the two-dimensional matrix would be assigned the value zero prior to searching column 2 in the two-dimensional array for the element with the smallest value. Figure 6.7 illustrates the composition of the node matrix and the connection matrix after the first column in the connection matrix was processed.

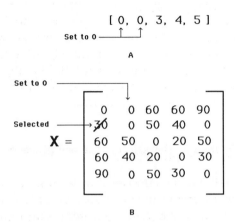

Figure 6.7 Node and connection matrix values. This figure illustrates the composition of the node and connection matrices after the first column in the connection matrix is produced

The selection of element X_{21} in the connection matrix can also be used as an identifier of the next column in the connection matrix to search. This is because the selection of element X_{21} indicates not only the selection of a link (1,2), but, in addition, that the remaining element values in column 1 are greater than element values in column 2. Hence the development of the MST should commence with node 2. Thus, column 2 in the two-dimensional connection matrix is examined next for the minimum element value.

The search of column 2 in the connection matrix previously illustrated in Figure 6.7 results in the selection of element X_{42} whose value is 40. The selection of that element indicates that link (2,4) is added to the developing MST as well as the next column to search, in this instance column 4. Figure 6.8 illustrates the values for the node matrix and the connection matrix at this time. Note that since $X_{ij} = X_{ji}, X_{34}$ was assigned the value zero after X_{43} was selected. Also note that X_3 and X_4 in the node matrix were set to zero since the selection of link (4,3) indicates the connection of node 4 to node 3.

In examining the revised node matrix illustrated in Figure 6.8, note that only element X_5 whose value is 5 is non-zero. This means that the MST can be completed by connecting node 5 to a previously connected node. Searching column 5 in the connection matrix indicates that element X_{45} has the lowest non-zero value, indicating

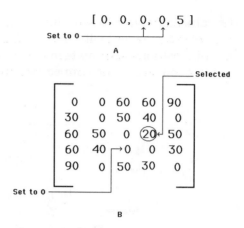

Figure 6.8   Revised (A) node and (B) connection matrix values

that the selection of link (4,5) is all that remains to complete the development of the MST.

From the preceding description of the manipulation of the values of the elements in the node and connection matrices, the reader will understand how MST computer programs can be developed. Essentially, the key to such programs is a searching routine which minimizes computer processing time when a large number of nodes results in a large n-by-n matrix whose columns must be searched n times to find the lowest value in each column.

6.2 AUTOMATING THE MINIMUM-SPANNING-TREE PROCESS

Now that we have discussed the manipulation of the elements in node and connection matrices to develop a MST, let us focus our attention upon a Basic language program that can be used to perform the required computation to solve this type of problem.

6.2.1 Basic language program

Figure 6.9 contains a Microsoft Quick Basic language program listing that can be executed to solve a modified MST problem that limits each node to one entry and one exit link, in effect, precluding the use of modems with a fan-out capability. The entries in this program which will soon be described are designed to automate the selection of a MST for the graph illustrated in Figure 6.10. In this illustration you will note every location is connected to every other

```
REM CONNECTION MATRIX FOR MODIFIED MINIMUM SPANNING TREE - NO FANOUT
CLS
PRINT "LINK SELECTION SUMMARY"
DIM n(5), x(5, 5)
REM initialize node matrix element values
FOR i = 1 TO 5
        n(i) = i
        NEXT i
REM initialize connection matrix element values
FOR j = 1 TO 5
FOR i = 1 TO 5
        READ x(i, j)
        IF x(i, j) = 0 THEN x(i, j) = 9999 'make missing links into large #
        NEXT i, j
        DATA 0,1,3,2,4,1,0,6,2,8,3,6,0,3,5,2,2,3,0,2,4,8,5,2,0
WEIGHT = 0'link weight counter
REM start in column 1
j = 1    'j is the column pointer into connection matrix
1 IF n(j) > 0 GOTO 2'node selected not connected
        FOR k = 1 TO 5
        IF n(k) > 0 THEN j = n(k)'pick first unconnected node
        NEXT k
2       i = 1'pick a legal value in row
4        x = x(i, j)
        IF n(i) > GOTO 3
        i = i + 1
        GOTO 4
3               FOR i = 1 TO 5 'search column j for smallest value
                    IF n(i) = 0 THEN x(i, j) = 9999
                    IF x(i, j) <= x AND n(j) > 0 THEN
                    x = x(i, j)
                    indexi = i    'i index of smallest value in column
                    indexj = j    'j index of smallest value in column
                END IF
                NEXT i
                IF x = 9999 GOTO 20'when smallest value=9999 we end
                WEIGHT = WEIGHT + x
REM segment selected is link connecting nodes j to i
PRINT "LINK CONNECTS NODES"; indexj; " TO "; indexi; " LINK WEIGHT="; x
        n(indexj) = 0'set node element to 0 to represent connection
     REM test if all nodes connected
        FOR i = 1 TO 5
        IF n(i) > 0 THEN 10 'if a node element >0 all nodes not connected
        NEXT i
        END
10      REM since Xij=Xji, set Xji to high value to preclude its use
        x(indexj, inhdexi) = 9999
REM search column denoted by indexi which represents node just connected
        j = indexi
        GOTO 1
20 PRINT "TOTAL LINK WEIGHT =", WEIGHT
```

Figure 6.9 Modified minimum-spanning-tree program

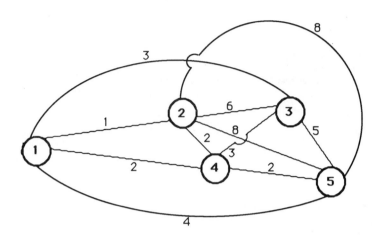

Figure 6.10 Graph to be automated. The data statements in the Basic language program listing contained in Figure 6.9 describe the link-mode relationship of this graph

location. If this is not feasible due to such real world problems as physical access constraints, you can eliminate one or more nodes by assigning a very large value to all links connected to a particular node. Readers that have obtained a convenience diskette will find this program's source code listing in the file MATRIX.BAS.

The DIM statement in Figure 6.9 allocates five elements for the node array labeled n and 25 elements for the connection array labeled x since the program was written to solve a five-node graph problem. The first FOR–NEXT loop initializes the element values of the n array to their node numbers. That is, n_1 is assigned the value 1, n_2 is assigned the value 2, and so on.

The program listing contained in Figure 6.9 next contains a dual pair of FOR–NEXT loops using the variable i as the inner loop index and j as the outer loop index. When this pair of FOR–NEXT loops is executed, the READ $x(i,j)$ statement within the loops assigns values in the DATA statement to the two-dimensional connection array based upon rows within a column. This is because i varies from 1 to 5 each time j changes its values. Figure 6.11 illustrates the connection matrix formed by the dual FOR–NEXT loops in the program listing.

The IF statement that follows the READ statement tests the value of each element assigned to the connection matrix. If the value is zero, which denotes a missing link, it is changed to 9999. This change will preclude its use when the program searches each column to locate the lowest value in that column. The variable WEIGHT after the DATA statement is initialized to zero as it will serve

$$\mathbf{n} = \begin{bmatrix} 0 & 1 & 3 & 2 & 4 \\ 1 & 0 & 6 & 2 & 8 \\ 3 & 6 & 0 & 3 & 5 \\ 2 & 2 & 3 & 0 & 2 \\ 4 & 8 & 5 & 2 & 0 \end{bmatrix}$$

Figure 6.11 Connection matrix formed by Basic program. The program listing in Figure 6.9 uses the i index for rows and j index for columns

as the counter that will hold the cumulative link weights as each link is selected.

Although we can start in any column, for ease of reference the program starts in column 1 by assigning the value of 1 to the variable j. Next, the statement labeled with the number 1 for branching purposes uses the column pointer to check the value of the node matrix element associated with that column. If the value is not zero, this indicates that the node was not connected and a branch to the statement labeled 2 occurs. If the node was previously selected, the FOR–NEXT loop using k as the loop variable picks the first nonconnected node by searching for an element value in the n matrix that is greater than zero and assigning j to that value.

The statement labeled with the number 2 initializes the variable i to 1, in effect, commencing the search of the connection matrix at row 1. Next, the variable x is assigned the element value of the x matrix for column j and row i. When an element in the node matrix is greater than zero a branch to the statement labeled with the number 3 occurs. Otherwise, the value of the variable i is incremented by 1 and a branch back to the statement labeled with the number 4 occurs.

The FOR–NEXT loop labeled with the number 3 searches the connection matrix for the smallest value. The statement IF n(i)=0 THEN x(i,j)=9999 assigns the relatively high value of 9999 to the element in the connection matrix when the node matrix element that matches the connection matrix row is zero. When this occurs, it indicates that the node is already connected, thus assigning the value 9999 precludes the selection of the element. Next, the statement IF x(i,j)<=x AND n(j)>0 tests the value of the element against the first value in the column and the value of the node element associated with the column. When $x(i,y) <= x$, the selected connection matrix element is less than the prior selected element. When $n(j) > 0$, the node is not yet connected. Thus, when both conditions are true, the next three statements are executed.

The first statement following the previously discussed IF statement assigns x to the value contained in the $x(i,j)$ element as that is now the lowest legal value in the column. The next two statements assign the index of the smallest value in the column based upon the row and column of the element to the variables index$i$ and index$j$, respectively. After the FOR–NEXT loop is completed the value of the smallest value element is compared to 9999. If the smallest value element equals 9999, all elements in the connection matrix have been operated upon and the program terminates. Otherwise, the WEIGHT variable is incremented by the value assigned to x, the latter representing the lowest link value in the column just searched.

After displaying the selected link by indicating the nodes it connects and their link weight, the program sets the node element associated with the column just processed to zero. This is done to preclude the column from being searched again since it indicates that the node represented by the column is connected by a link. The last FOR–NEXT loop which uses i as an index tests the node matrix for an element whose value is greater than zero since this condition indicates that one or more nodes remain to be connected. When this occurs, a branch to the statement labeled with the number 2 also occurs. Then, since $X_{ij} = X_{ji}, X_{ji}$ is set to a value of 9999 to preclude its use, using the value of the variables index$j$ and index$i$ to represent the row and column, respectively. Once the column has been searched and the lowest value element selected, the row position will be used as a pointer for the next column to be searched. This is accomplished by the statement j=index$i$, after which a branch back to the statement with the label number 1 occurs.

The execution of the modified MST program results in the selection of links between nodes based upon their link weight. Figure 6.12 illustrates the execution of the program listed in Figure 6.9. Note that the MST selected has a total link weight of 10 which is the lowest weight associated with a tree that connects all nodes and whose structure precludes a fan-out situation.

```
LINK SELECTION SUMMARY
LINK CONNECTS NODES 1  TO  2  LINK WEIGHT= 1
LINK CONNECTS NODES 2  TO  4  LINK WEIGHT= 2
LINK CONNECTS NODES 4  TO  5  LINK WEIGHT= 2
LINK CONNECTS NODES 5  TO  3  LINK WEIGHT= 5
TOTAL LINK WEIGHT =              10
```

Figure 6.12 Minimum-spanning-tree program output

6.3 CONSIDERING NETWORK CONSTRAINTS

The MST algorithm, while economically accurate, does not consider two key network constraints which could make its implementation impractical—the terminal response time of the locations interconnected and the capacity of a front-end processor to service the total number of locations connected on one multidrop line.

6.3.1 Terminal response time factors

Normally, full-screen display terminals are used on a multidrop circuit. The terminal response time is defined as the time from the operator pressing the enter key to the first character appearing on the terminal's screen in response to the data sent to the computer. This response time depends upon a large set of factors, of which the major ones are listed in Table 6.4.

Table 6.4 Terminal response time factors.

Line speed
Type of transmission line
Modem turnaround time
Number of characters serviced per polling used
Computer processing time
Polling service time

The line speed refers to the transmission data rate which determines how fast data can be transported between the terminal and the computer once the terminal is polled or selected. The type of transmission line, full- or half-duplex, determines whether or not an extra delay will be incurred to turn the line around after each poll. If a half-duplex transmission protocol is used, then the modem turnaround time will affect the terminal response time.

The number of characters serviced per poll refers to how the communications software services a terminal capable of storing 1920 characters on a full screen of 25 lines by 80 characters per line. To prevent one terminal from hogging the line, most communications software divide the screen into segments and services a portion of the screen during each poll sequence.

The type of polling can occur 'round robin' where each terminal receives servicing in a defined order or it can occur based upon a predefined priority. Although the computer processing time can greatly affect the terminal response time, it is normally beyond the control of the communications staff. The polling service time is the time it takes to poll a terminal so the communications software can service another segment of the screen when the data to be read or written to the terminal exceeds one segment. Finally, the probability of a transmission error occurring will affect the probability of transmitting the same data again, since detected errors are corrected by the retransmission of data.

6.3.2 Estimating response time

To estimate the average terminal response time requires an estimate of the average number of users that are using the terminals on a multidrop circuit. Next, the average number of characters to be transmitted in response to each depression of the enter key must be estimated. This data can then be used to estimate the average terminal response time.

Suppose there are 10 terminals on the multidrop circuit and at any one time 4 are active, with approximately 10 lines of 30 characters on the display when the enter key is pressed. If the communications software services segments of 240 characters, two polls will be required to service each terminal. Assuming a transmission rate of 4.8 kbps, which is equivalent to approximately 600 characters per second, it requires a minimum of 240/600 or 0.4 s to service the first segment on each terminal, excluding communications protocol overhead. Using a 25% overhead factor which is normally reasonable for most protocols, the time to service the first segment becomes 0.5 s, resulting in the last terminal having its first segment serviced at a time of 2.0 s if all four active users requested servicing at the same time. Since 60 characters remain on each screen, the second poll requires 60/600 or 0.1 s per terminal plus 25% for overhead, or a total of 0.5 s until the fourth terminal is again serviced. Adding the time required to service each segment results in a total time of 2.5 s transpiring in the completion of the data transfer from the fourth terminal to the computer.

Now let us assume that the average response is 300 characters. Then, the transmission of two screen segments is also required in the opposite direction. The first segment would then require 2.0 s for displaying on each terminal while the second segment requires 0.3 s plus 25% overhead or 0.375 s until the first character starts to appear on the fourth terminal, for a total response time (inbound and outbound) of 2.5 plus 2.375 or 4.875 s.

If a 'round robin' polling sequence is used, the computer has an equal probability of polling any of the four terminals when the enter key is pressed. Thus, the computed 4.875 s response time is the worst case response time. The best case response time would be the response time required to service the first terminal sending data, which in the previous example would be 2.1 s inbound and 2.0 soutbound until the first character is received, or a total of 4.1 s. Thus, the average terminal response time would be (4.1 + 4.875)/2 or approximately 4.5 s.

6.3.3 Front-end processing limitations

A second limitation concerning the use of multidrop circuits is the capability of the front-end processor. In a large network that contains numerous terminal locations, the polling addressing capability of the front-end processor will limit the number of drops that can be serviced. Even if the processor could handle an infinite number of drops, polling delay times as well as the effect of a line segment impairment breaking access to many drops usually precludes most circuits to a maximum of 16 or 32 drops.

6.3.4 Summary

When the number of drops in a network requires the use of multiple multidrop circuits, the network designer will normally consider the use of a more complex algorithm by the addition of a variety of constraints to the previously covered algorithms. While such algorithms are best applied to network design problems by the use of computer programs, the reader can consider a practical alternative to these complex algorithms. This alternative is the subdivision of the network's terminal locations into servicing areas, based upon defining a servicing area to include a number of terminals that will permit an average response time that is acceptable to the end-user. Then each segment can be analyzed using the MST algorithm to develop a minimum cost multidrop line to service all terminals within the servicing area.

SIZING COMMUNICATIONS EQUIPMENT AND LINE FACILITIES

Of many problems associated with the acquisition of data communications networking devices, including port selectors, multiplexers, and concentrators, one item often requiring resolution is the configuration or sizing of the device. The process of ensuring that the configuration of the selected device will provide a desired level of service is the foundation upon which the availability level of a network is built and, in many instances, is directly related to the number of dial-in lines connected to the device.

The failure to provide a level of access acceptable to network users can result in a multitude of problems. First, a user encountering a busy signal might become discouraged, take a break, or do something other than redial a telephone number of a network access port. Such action obviously will result in a loss of user productivity. If network usage is in response to customer inquiries, a failure to certify a customer purchase, return, reservation, or other action in a timely manner could result in the loss of customers to a competitor. This is similar to the situation where a long queue in front of a bank teller can result in the loss of customer accounts if the unacceptable level of service persists.

In this chapter, we will focus our attention upon the application of telephone traffic formulas to the sizing of data communications equipment and line facilities. Although most telephone traffic formulas were developed during the 1920s, many are applicable to such common problems as determining the number of dial-in business and WATS lines required to service terminal users as well as the number of ports or channels that should be installed in communications equipment connected to the dial-in lines. To obtain an appreciation of the sizing process, we will first examine several methods that can be used to size equipment and line facilities. This will be followed by a detailed examination of the application of telephone traffic sizing formulas to data communications. More formally referred to as traffic dimensioning formulas, in this chapter we will examine the application of the erlang B, erlang C, and Poisson formulas to data communications equipment and facility sizing problems.

7.1 SIZING METHODS

There are many devices and line facilities that can be employed in a data communications network whose configuration or sizing problems are similar. Examples of line facilities include the number of dial-in local business and WATS lines required to be connected to telephone company rotaries, while examples of communications equipment sizing includes determining the number of channels on multiplexers, data concentrators, and port selectors.

7.1.1 Experimental modeling

Basically, two methods can be used to configure the size of communications network devices. The first method, commonly known as experimental modeling, involves the selection of the device configuration based upon a mixture of previous experience and intuition. Normally, the configuration selected is less than the base capacity plus expansion capacity of the device. This enables the size of the device to be adjusted or upgraded without a major equipment modification if the initial sizing proved inaccurate. An example of experimental modeling is shown in Figure 7.1.

A rack-mounted time division multiplexer is shown Figure 7.1A. Initially, the multiplexer was obtained with five dual-channel adapters to support ten channels of simultaneous operation. Assuming the base unit can support eight dual-channel adapters, if the network manager's previous experience or gut intuition proves wrong, the multiplexer can be upgraded easily. This is shown in Figure 7.1B, where the addition of three dual-channel adapters permits the multiplexer to support 16 channels in its adjusted configuration.

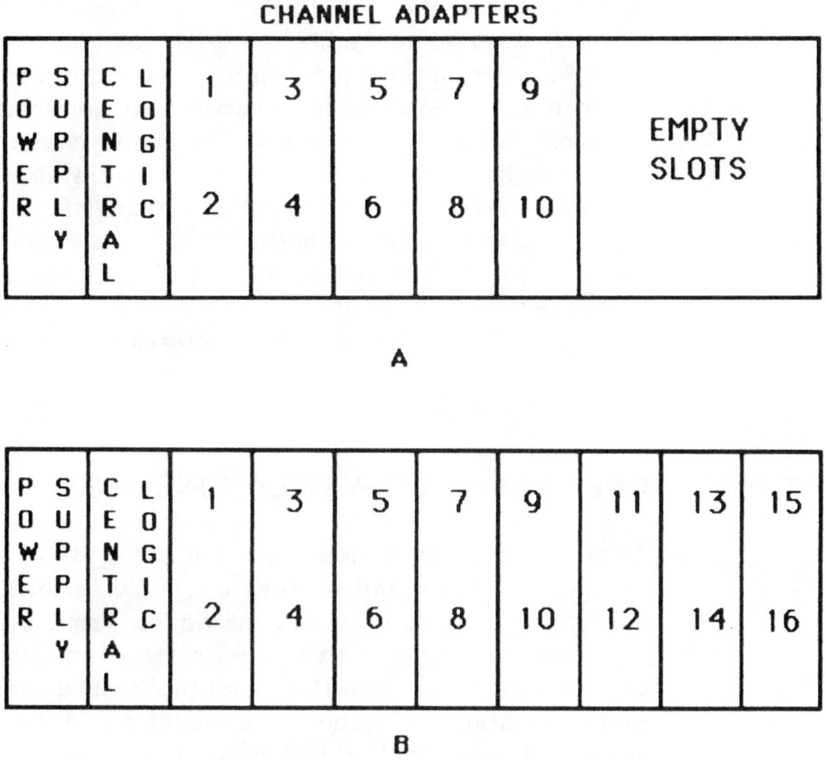

CHANNEL ADAPTERS

P S O U W P E P R L 　Y	C L E O N G T I R C A L	1 2	3 4	5 6	7 8	9 10	EMPTY SLOTS

A

P S O U W P E P R L 　Y	C L E O N G T I R C A L	1 2	3 4	5 6	7 8	9 10	11 12	13 14	15 16

B

Figure 7.1 Experimental modeling. Experimental modeling results in the adjustment of a network configuration based upon previous experience and gut intuition. (A) Initial configuration. (B) Adjusted configuration

7.1.2 The scientific approach

The second method that can be employed to size network components ignores experience and intuition. This method is based upon a knowledge of data traffic and the scientific application of mathematical formulas to traffic data. Hence it is known as the scientific approach or method of equipment sizing. While some of the mathematics involved in determining equipment sizing can become quite complex, a series of tables generated by the development of appropriate computer programs can be employed to reduce many sizing problems to one of a simple table lookup process.

Although there are advantages and disadvantages to each method, the application of a scientific methodology to equipment sizing is a rigorously defined approach. Thus, there should be a much higher degree of confidence and accuracy of the configuration selected when this method is used. On the negative side, the use of a scientific method requires a firm knowledge or accurate estimate of the data traffic. Unfortunately, for some organizations, this may be difficult to obtain. In many cases, a combination of two techniques will provide an optimum situation. For such situations, sizing can be conducted using the scientific method with the understanding that the configuration selected may require adjustment under the experimental modeling concept. In the remainder of this chapter, we will focus our attention upon the application of the scientific methodology to equipment sizing problems.

7.2 TELEPHONE TERMINOLOGY RELATIONSHIPS

Most of the mathematics used for sizing data communications equipment evolved out of work originally performed to solve the sizing problems of telephone networks. From a discussion of a few basic telephone network terms and concepts, we will see the similarities between the sizing problems associated with data communications equipment and facilities and the structure of the telephone network. Building upon this foundation, we will learn how to apply the mathematical formulas developed for telephone network sizing to data communications network configurations.

To study the relationship between telephone network and communications component sizing problems, let us examine a portion of the telephone network and study the structure and calling problems of a small segment formed by two cities, each assumed to contain 1000 telephone subscribers.

7.2.1 Telephone network structure

The standard method of providing an interconnection between subscribers in a local area is to connect each subscriber's telephone to what is known as the local telephone company exchange. Other synonymous terms for the local telephone company exchange include the 'local exchange' and 'telephone company central office'. When one subscriber dials another connected to the same exchange, the subscriber's call is switched to the called party number through the switching facilities of the local exchange. If we assume each city has only one local exchange, then all calls originating in that city and to a destination located within that city will be routed through one common exchange.

Since our network segment selected for analysis consists of two cities, we will have two telephone company exchanges, one located in each city. To provide a path between cities for intercity calling, a number of lines must be installed to link the exchanges in each city. The exchange in each city can act then as a switch, routing the local subscribers in each city to parties in the other city.

Trunks and dimensioning

As shown in the top part of Figure 7.2, a majority of telephone traffic in the network segment consisting of the two cities will be among the subscribers of each city. Although there will be telephone traffic between the subscribers in each city, it normally will be considerably less than the amount of local traffic in each city. The path between the two cities connecting their telephone central offices is known as a trunk.

One of the problems in designing the telephone network is determining how many trunks should be installed between

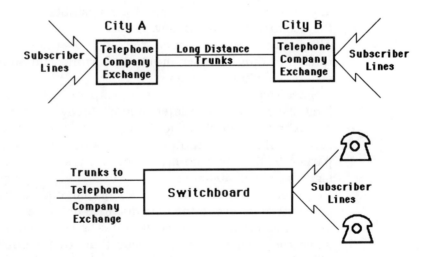

Figure 7.2 Telephone traffic sizing problems. Although most subscriber calls are routed locally through the local telephone company exchange or local switchboard to parties in the immediate area, some calls require access to trunks. The determination of the number of trunks required to provide an acceptable grade of service is known as line dimensioning and is critical for the effective operation of the facility

telephone company exchanges. A similar sizing problem occurs many times in each city at locations where private organizations desire to install switchboards. An example of the sizing problem with this type of equipment is illustrated in the lower portion of Figure 7.2. In effect, the switchboard functions as a small telephone exchange, routing calls carried over a number of trunks installed between the switchboard and the telephone company exchange to a larger number of subscriber lines connected to the switchboard. The determination of the number of trunks required to be installed between the telephone exchange and the switchboard is called dimensioning and is critical for the efficient operation of the facility. If insufficient trunks are available, company personnel will encounter an unacceptable number of busy signals when trying to place an outside telephone call. Once again, this will obviously affect productivity.

Returning to the intercity calling problem, consider some of the problems that can occur in dimensioning the number of trunks between central offices located in the two cities. Assume that based upon a previously conducted study it was determined that no more than 50 people would want to have simultaneous telephone conversations where the calling party was in one city and the called party in the other city. If 50 trunks were installed between cities and the number of intercity callers never exceeded 50, at any moment the probability of a subscriber completing a call to the distant city would always be unity, guaranteeing success. Although the service cost of providing 50 trunks is obviously more than providing a lesser number of trunks, no subscriber would encounter a busy signal.

Since some subscribers might postpone or choose not to place a long distance call at a later time if a busy signal is encountered, a maximum level of service will produce a minimum level of lost revenue. If more than 50 subscribers tried to simultaneously call parties in the opposite city, some callers would encounter busy signals once all 50 trunks were in use. Under such circumstances, the level of service would be such that not all subscribers are guaranteed access to the long distance trunks and the probability of making a long distance call would be less than unity. Likewise, since the level of service is less than that required to provide all callers with access to the long distance trunks, the service cost is less than the service cost associated with providing users with a probability of unity in accessing trunks. Similarly, as the probability of successfully accessing the long distance trunks decreases, the amount of lost revenue or customer waiting costs will increase. Based upon the preceding, a decision model factoring

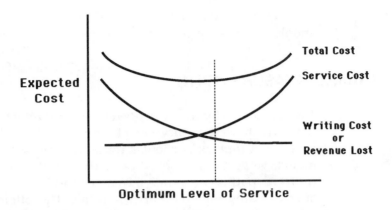

Figure 7.3 Using a decision model to determine the optimum level of service. The location where the total cost is minimal represents the optimum level of service one should provide

into consideration the level of service versus expected cost can be constructed as shown in Figure 7.3.

The decision model

For the decision model illustrated in Figure 7.3, suppose the optimum number of trunks required to link the two cities is 40. The subscriber line-to-trunk ratio for this case would be 1000 lines to 40 trunks, for a 25 : 1 ratio.

To correctly dimension the optimum number of trunks linking the two cities requires an understanding both of economics as well as subscriber traffic. In dimensioning the number of trunks, a certain trade-off will result that relates the number of trunks or level of service to the cost of providing that service and the revenue lost by not having enough trunks to satisfy the condition when a maximum number of subscribers in one city dial subscribers in another. To determine the appropriate level of service, a decision model as illustrated in Figure 7.3 is required. Here, the probability of a subscriber successfully accessing a trunk corresponds to the level of service provided. As more trunks are added, the probability of access increases as well as the cost of providing such access. Correspondingly, the waiting cost of the subscriber or the revenue loss to the telephone company decreases as the level of service increases, where the total cost represents the combination of service cost and waiting cost. The point where the cost is minimal represents the optimal number of trunks or level of service that should be provided to link the two cities.

7.3 TRAFFIC MEASUREMENTS

Telephone activity can be defined by the calling rate and the holding time which is the duration of the call. The calling rate is the number of times a particular route or path is used per unit time period, while the holding time is the duration of the call on the route or path. Two other terms that warrant attention are the offered traffic and the carried traffic. The offered traffic is the volume of traffic routed to a particular telephone exchange during a predetermined time period, while the carried traffic is the volume of traffic actually transmitted through the exchange to its destination during a predetermined period of time.

7.3.1 The busy hour

The key factor required to dimension a traffic path is knowledge of the traffic intensity during the time period known as the busy hour (BH). Although traffic varies by day and time of day, and is generally random, it follows a certain consistency one can identify. In general, traffic peaks prior to lunch time and then rebuilds to a second daily peak in the afternoon. The busiest one-hour period of the day is known as the busy hour. It is the busy hour traffic level that is employed in dimensioning telephone exchanges and transmission routes since one wants to size the exchange or route with respect to its busiest period.

Telephone traffic can be defined as the product of the calling rate per hour and the average holding time per call. This measurement can be expressed mathematically as

$$T = C * D$$

where
C = calling rate per hour
D = average duration per call

Using the above formula, traffic can be expressed in call-minutes (CM) or call-hours (CH), where a call-hour is the quantity reprsented by one or more calls having an aggregate duration of one hour.

If the calling rate during the busy hour of a particular day is

500 and the average duration of each call is 10 minutes, the traffic flow or intensity would be 500 * 10 or 5000 CM, which would be equivalent to 5000/60 or approximately 83.3 CH.

7.3.2 Erlangs and call-seconds

The preferred unit of measurement in telephone traffic analysis is the erlang, named after A. K. Erlang, a Danish mathematician. The erlang is a dimensionless unit in comparison to the previously discussed call-minutes and call-hours. It represents the occupancy of a circuit where one erlang of traffic intensity on one traffic circuit represents a continuous occupancy of that circuit.

A second term often used to represent traffic intensity is the call-second (CS). The quantity represented by one hundred call-seconds is known as 1 CCS. Here the first C represents the quantity 100 and comes from the French term 'cent'. Assuming a one-hour unit interval, the previously discussed terms can be related to the erlang as follows

$$1 \text{ erlang} = 60 \text{ call-minutes} = 36 \text{ CCS} = 3600 \text{ CS}$$

If a group of 20 trunks were measured and a call intensity of 10 erlangs determined over the group, then we would expect one-half of all trunks to be busy at the time of the measurement. Similarly, a traffic intensity of 600 CM or 360 CCS offered to the 20 trunks would warrant the same conclusion. Table 7.1 is a traffic conversion table that will facilitate the conversion of erlangs to CCS and vice versa. Since the use of many dimensioning tables is based upon traffic intensity in erlangs or CCS, the conversion of such terms frequently is required in the process of sizing facilities.

To illustrate the applicability of traffic measurements to a typical communications network configuration, assume your organization has a 10-position rotary. Further assume that you measured the number of calls and holding time per call during a one-hour period and determined the traffic distribution to be that illustrated in Figure 7.4. Note that the total holding time is 266 minutes or 4.43 hours. Thus, the average traffic intensity during this one-hour period is 4.43/1 or 4.43 erlangs.

During the busy hour illustrated in Figure 7.4, a total of 45 calls resulted in a cumulative holding time of 266 minutes. Thus, the average holding time per call is 266/45 or 5.91 minutes, which is equivalent to 0.0985 hours. Multiplying the average holding time (0.0985 hours) per call by the number of calls (45) results

Table 7.1 Traffic conversion table.

Dimension		Erlangs (intensity) call-hours (quantity)	CCS (quantity)
Minutes	Hours		
12	.2	0.2	6
24	.4	0.4	12
36	.6	0.6	18
48	.8	0.8	24
60	1.0	1.0	36
120	2.0	2.0	72
180	3.0	3.0	108
240	4.0	4.0	144
300	5.0	5.0	180
360	6.0	6.0	210
420	7.0	7.0	252
480	8.0	8.0	288
540	9.0	9.0	324
600	10.0	10.0	360
900	15.0	15.0	540
1200	20.0	20.0	720
1500	25.0	25.0	900
1800	30.0	30.0	1080
2100	35.0	35.0	1260
2400	40.0	40.0	1440
2700	45.0	45.0	1620
3000	50.0	50.0	1800
6000	100.0	100.0	3600

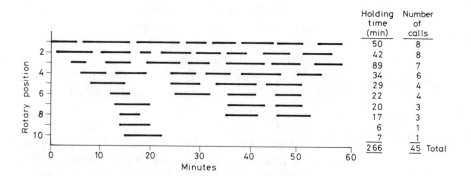

Figure 7.4 Traffic distribution example

in the average traffic intensity of 4.43 erlangs. Note that this tells us that if we know the average holding time and the number of calls we can easily determine the traffic intensity. The previously noted relationship between the average traffic intensity (E) and the holding times on each rotary position (H_i) during time period (T) can be expressed mathematically as follows

$$E = \frac{\sum_{i=1}^{n} H_i}{T}$$

Substituting the data contained in Figure 7.4 we obtain for the one-hour period

$$E = \frac{266}{1} = 266 \text{ call-minutes or } 4.43 \text{ CH}$$

The average call holding time or average call duration (D) can be expressed in terms of the total holding time ($\sum H_i$) and the number of calls (C) as:

$$D = \frac{\sum_{i=1}^{n} H_i}{C} = \frac{266}{45} = 5.91$$

Since $\sum H_i = C * D$ and as we previously noted, $E = \sum H_i / T$, we can express the traffic intensity (E) in terms of the number of calls, average call duration, and time period. Doing so we obtain

$$E = \frac{C * D}{T}$$

Using the data contained in Figure 7.4, we can compute the traffic intensity in erlangs as follows using a call duration expressed in minutes

$$E = \frac{45 * 5.91}{60} = 4.43 \text{ erlangs}$$

To find the traffic intensity when call duration is expressed in hours, our substitution would become

$$E = \frac{45 * 5.91/60}{1} = 4.43 \text{ erlangs}$$

As indicated, knowledge of the average call duration and number of calls permits the computation of traffic intensity. Since many types of network management systems as well as multiplexers and computer systems collect statistics to include the number of calls and call duration it is often possible to obtain traffic intensity information. Even when you cannot obtain such information directly, it is often possible to obtain information indirectly. As an example, consider a ten-position rotary connected to modems which in turn are connected to ports on a multiplexer. If the telephone company cannot provide the required information and your organization lacks monitoring equipment the statistics you require may be obtainable from the multiplexer.

7.3.3 Grade of service

One important concept in the dimensioning process is what is known as the grade of service. To understand this concept, let us return to our intercity calling example illustrated in Figure 7.2, again assuming 50 trunks are used to connect the telephone exchanges in each city. If a subscriber attempts to originate a call from one city to the other when all trunks are in use, that call is said to be blocked. Based upon mathematical formulas, the probability of a call being blocked can be computed given the traffic intensity and number of available trunks. The concept of determining the probability of blockage can be adapted easily to the sizing of data communications equipment.

From a logical analysis of traffic intensity, it follows that if a call were to be blocked, such blockage would occur during the busy hour since that is the period when the largest amount of activity occurs. Thus, telephone exchange capacity is engineered to service a portion of the busy hour traffic, the exact amount of service being dependent upon economics as well as the political process of determining the level of service one desires to provide to customers.

One could over-dimension the route between cities and provide a trunk for every subscriber. This would insure that a lost call could never occur and would be equivalent to providing a dial-in line for every terminal in a network. Since a 1 : 1 subscriber-to-trunk ratio is not economical and will result in most trunks being idle a large portion of the day, we can expect a lesser number of trunks between cities than subscribers. As the number of trunks decreases and the subscriber-to-trunk ratio correspondingly increases, we can intuitively expect some sizings to result in some call blockage. We can specify the number of calls we are willing to have blocked during the busy hour. This specification is known as the grade of service and represents the probability (P) of having a call blocked. If we specify a grade of service of 0.05 between the cities, we require a sufficient number of trunks so that only one call in every 20, or 5 calls in every 100, will be blocked during the busy hour.

7.3.4 Route dimensioning parameters

To determine the number of trunks required to service a particular route one can consider the use of several formulas. Each formula's utilization depends upon the call arrival and holding time distribution, the number of traffic sources, and the handling of lost or blocked calls. Regardless of the formula employed, the resulting computation will provide one with the probability of call blockage or grade of service based upon a given number of trunks and level of traffic intensity.

Concerning the number of traffic sources, one can consider the calling population as infinite or finite. If calls occur from a large subscriber population and subscribers tend to redial if blockage is encountered, the calling population can be considered as infinite. The consideration of an infinite traffic source results in the probability of a call arrival becoming constant and does not make the call dependent upon the state of traffic in the system. The two most commonly employed traffic dimensioning equations are both based upon an infinite calling population.

Concerning the handling of lost calls, such calls can be considered cleared, delayed, or held. When such calls are considered held, it is assumed that the telephone subscriber, upon encountering a busy signal, immediately redials the desired party. The lost call-delayed concept assumes each subscriber is placed in a waiting mechanism for service and forms the basis for queuing analysis. Since we can assume a service or non-service condition, we can disregard the lost call-delayed concept unless access to a network resource occurs through a data PBX or port selector that has queuing capability.

7.3.5 Traffic dimensioning formulas

The principal traffic dimensioning formula used in North America is based upon the lost call concept and is commonly known as the Poisson formula. In Europe, traffic formulas are based upon the assumption that a subscriber encountering a busy signal will hang up the telephone and wait a certain amount of time prior to redialing. The erlang B formula is based upon this lost call-cleared concept.

7.4 THE ERLANG TRAFFIC FORMULA

The most commonly used telephone traffic dimensioning equation is the erlang B formula. This formula is predominantly used outside the North American continent. In addition to assuming that data traffic originates from an infinite number of sources, this formula is based upon the lost call-cleared concept. This assumption is equivalent to stating that traffic offered to but not carried by one or more trunks vanishes and this is the key difference between this formula and the Poisson formula. The latter formula assumes that lost calls are held, and it is used for telephone dimensioning mainly in North America. Since data communications system users can be characterized by either the lost call-cleared or lost call-held concept, both traffic formulas and their application to data networks will be covered in this chapter.

If E is used to denote the traffic intensity in erlangs and T represents the number of trunks, channels, or ports designed to support the traffic, the probability $P(T,E)$ represents the probability that T trunks are busy when a traffic intensity of E erlangs is offered to those trunks. The probability is equivalent to specifying a grade of service and can be expressed by the erlang traffic formula as follows

$$P(T,E) = \frac{\frac{(E^T)}{T!}}{1 + \frac{E^1}{1!} + \frac{E^2}{2!} + \frac{E^3}{3!} + \ldots + \frac{E^T}{T!}} = \frac{\frac{E^T}{T!}}{\sum\limits_{i=0}^{T} \frac{E^i}{i!}}$$

where

$$T! = T * (T-1) * (T-2) \ldots 3 * 2 * 1$$

and

$$0! = 1$$

In Table 7.2, a list of factorials and their values is presented to assist the reader in computing specific grades of service based upon a given traffic intensity and trunk quantity.

To illustrate the use of the erlang traffic formula, assume that a traffic intensity of 3 erlangs is offered to a three-position rotary. The grade of service is calculated as follows

$$P(T,E) = \frac{\frac{E^T}{T!}}{\sum\limits_{i=0}^{T} \frac{E^i}{i!}} = \frac{\frac{3^3}{3*2*1}}{\frac{3^0}{0!} + \frac{3^1}{1!} + \frac{3^2}{2!} + \frac{3^3}{3!}} = 0.346$$

Table 7.2 Factorial values.

N	Factorial N	N	Factorial N
1	1	51	1.551118753287382E+66
2	2	52	8.065817517094390E+67
3	6	53	4.274883284060024E+69
4	24	54	2.308436973392413E+71
5	120	55	1.269640335365826E+73
6	720	56	7.109985878048632E+74
7	5040	57	4.052691950487723E+76
8	40320	58	2.350561331282879E+78
9	362880	59	1.386831185456898E+80
10	3628800	60	8.320987112741390E+81
11	39916800	61	5.075802138772246E+83
12	479001600	62	3.146997326038794E+85
13	6227020800	63	1.982608315404440E+87
14	87178291200	64	1.268869321858841E+89
15	1307674368000	65	8.247650592082472E+90
16	209222789888000	66	5.443449390774432E+92
17	355687428096000	67	3.647111091818871E+94
18	6402373705728000	68	2.480035542436830E+96
19	1.216451004088320E+17	69	1.711224524281413E+98
20	2.432902008176640E+18	70	1.197857166996989E+100
21	5.109094217170944E+19	71	8.504785885678624E+101
22	1.124000727777608E+21	72	6.123445837688612E+103
23	2.585201673888498E+22	73	4.470115461512686E+105
24	6.204484017332394E+23	74	3.307885441519387E+107
25	1.551121004333098E+25	75	2.480914081139540E+109
26	4.032914611266057E+26	76	1.885494701666051E+111
27	1.088886945041835E+28	77	1.451830920282859E+113
28	3.048883446117138E+29	78	1.132428117820629E+115
29	8.841761993739701E+30	79	8.946182130782980E+116
30	2.652528598121911E+32	80	7.156945704626380E+118
31	8.222838654177924E+33	81	5.797126020747369E+120
32	2.631308369336936E+35	82	4.753643337012843E+122
33	8.683317618811889E+36	83	3.045523969720660E+124
34	2.952327990396041E+38	84	3.314240134565354E+126
35	1.033314796638614E+40	85	2.817104114380549E+128
36	3.719933267899013E+41	86	2.422709538367274E+130
37	1.376375309122635E+43	87	2.107757298379527E+132
38	5.230226174666010E+44	88	1.854826422573984E+134
39	2.039788208119745E+46	89	1.650795516090847E+136
40	8.159152832478980E+47	90	1.485715964481761E+138
41	3.345252661316380E+49	91	1.352001527678403E+140
42	1.405006117752880E+51	92	1.243841405464131E+142
43	6.041526306837884E+52	93	1.156772507081641E+144
44	2.658271574788450E+54	94	1.087366156656743E+146
45	1.196222208654802E+56	95	1.032997848823906E+148
46	5.502622159812089E+57	96	9.916779348709491E+149
47	2.586232415111683E+59	97	9.619275968248216E+151
48	1.241391559253607E+61	98	9.426890448883248E+153
49	6.082818640342679E+62	99	9.332621544394415E+155
50	3.041409320171338E+64	100	9.332621544394418E+157

This means that on the average during the busy hour 37.5 out of every 100 calls will encounter a busy signal and for most organizations will represent an undesirable grade of service.

7.4.1 Computing lost traffic

Based upon the computed grade of service, we can compute the traffic lost during the busy hour. Here the traffic lost (e) is the traffic intensity multiplied by the grade of service. Thus, the traffic lost by position 3 is

$$e_3 = E * P(3, 3) = 3 * 0.346 = 1.038 \text{ erlangs}$$

Now, let us assume the rotary is expanded to four positions. The grade of service then becomes

$$P(4, 3) = \frac{\frac{3^4}{4*3*2*1}}{\frac{3^0}{0!} + \frac{3^1}{1!} + \frac{3^2}{2!} + \frac{3^3}{3!} + \frac{3^4}{4!}} = 0.2061$$

This expansion improves the grade of service so that approximately one in five calls now receives a busy signal during the busy hour. The traffic lost by position four now becomes

$$e_4 = E * P(4, 3) = 3 * 0.2061 = 0.6183 \text{ erlangs}$$

Note that the traffic carried by the fourth position is equal to the difference between the traffic lost by the three-position rotary and the traffic lost by the four-position rotary. That is

traffic carried by position 4 = $1.038 - 0.6183 = 0.4197$ erlangs

Based upon the preceding, we can calculate both the traffic carried and the traffic lost by each position of an n-position rotary. The results of the traffic computations are obtainable once we know the number of positions on the rotary and the traffic intensity offered to the rotary group. As noted before, the traffic lost by position $n(e_n)$ can be expressed in terms of the grade of service and traffic intensity as follows

$$e_n = E * P(T_n, E)$$

Substituting the preceding in the erlang formula gives

$$e_n = E * \frac{\frac{E^n}{n!}}{\sum_{i=0}^{n} \frac{E^i}{i!}}$$

where e_n is the traffic lost by the nth position on the rotary.

Since the traffic carried by any rotary position is the difference between the traffic offered to the position and the traffic lost by the position, we can easily compute the traffic carried by each rotary position. To do so, let us proceed as follows.

Let e_{n-1} equal the traffic lost by position $n - 1$.

Then, e_{n-1} becomes the traffic that is offered to position n on the rotary. Thus, the traffic carried by position n is equivalent to $e_{n-1} - e_n$. In the case of the first rotary position on a four-position rotary the traffic lost becomes

$$e_1 = E * \frac{\frac{E^1}{1!}}{1 + \frac{E^1}{1!}} = \frac{E^2}{1 + E}$$

Then, the traffic carried by the first rotary position is the difference between the traffic intensity offered to the rotary group (E) and the traffic lost by the first position. That is, if T_{Cn} is the traffic carried by position n, then

$$T_{C1} = E - e_1 = E - \frac{E^2}{1 + E} = \frac{E}{1 + E}$$

For the second rotary position traffic lost by that position is

$$e_2 = E * \frac{\frac{E^2}{2!}}{1 + \frac{E^1}{1!} + \frac{E^2}{2!}} = \frac{E^3}{2 + 2E + E^2}$$

Then, the traffic carried by the second position on the rotary is $e_1 - e_2$ or

$$e_1 - e_2 = \frac{E^2}{1 + E} - \frac{E^3}{2 + 2E + E^2}$$

We can continue this process to compute both the traffic carried as well as the traffic lost by each rotary position. Table 7.3 summarizes the formulas used to obtain the traffic lost and traffic carried for each position of a four-position rotary group.

7.4.2 Traffic analysis program

To assist readers in performing the computations required to determine the grade of service and traffic distribution over each port on a rotary group, a program was developed using the Microsoft Quick Basic compiler. Figure 7.5 contains the listing of this traffic analysis program that can be used to analyze rotaries containing up to 60 positions. For rotaries beyond 60 positions the program can be altered, however, execution time will considerably increase. This program is contained on the file TRAFFIC.BAS on the convenience diskette that can be purchased from the publisher of this book.

For readers not familiar with the Microsoft Basic compiler, several entries in the program listing contained in Figure 7.5 may warrant an explanation. Due to this, we will examine the

Table 7.3 Traffic lost and traffic carried by rotary position.

Rotary position	Traffic lost	Traffic carried
1	$e_1 = \dfrac{E^2}{1+E}$	$E - e_1 = \dfrac{E}{1+E}$
2	$e_2 = \dfrac{E^3}{2+2E+E^2}$	$e_1 - e_2 = \dfrac{E^2}{1+E} - \dfrac{E^3}{2+2E+E^2}$
3	$e_3 = \dfrac{E^4}{6+6E+3E^2+E^3}$	$e_2 - e_3 = \dfrac{E^3}{2+2E+E^2} - \dfrac{E^4}{6+6E+3E^2+E3}$
4	$e_4 = \dfrac{E^5}{24+24E+12E^2+4E^3+E^4}$	$e_3 - e_4 = \dfrac{E^4}{6+6E+3E^2+E^3} - \dfrac{E^5}{24+24E+12E^2+4E^3+E^4}$

program listing to provide all readers with a firm understanding of statements that may be different from the Basic interpreter or compiler they are using, as well as to obtain a better understanding of the logical construction of the program.

The $DYNAMIC statement in the second program line allocates memory to arrays as required. The FACTORIAL# statement allocates 61 elements (0 through 60) for the array that will contain the values of factorial 0 through factorial 60. Note that the variable suffix # (pound sign) is used in Microsoft Basic to denote a double precision variable. Similar to FACTORIAL#, TL#, and TC# are arrays that are used to hold the double precision values of traffic lost and traffic carried by each port.

After the traffic intensity in erlangs (assigned to the variable E#) and the number of ports (assigned to the variable PORT) are entered, the program branches to the subroutine beginning at statement number 100. This subroutine computes the values of factorial 0 through the number assigned to PORT and stores those factorial values in the array FACTORIAL#.

After computing the factorial values, the program computes the grade of service using the equations previously described in this chapter. Similarly, the traffic lost and carried by each port is computed by computerizing the previously described equations to Basic language statements.

To illustrate the equivalency of a grade of service (stored in the variable GOS#) to 1 in N calls obtaining a busy signal GOS# is first divided into one. Next, 0.5 is added to the result to raise its value to the next highest number prior to taking the integer value of the computation. This is necessary since the INT function rounds down the result obtained by dividing GOS# into unity.

The result of the execution of the traffic analyzer program using a traffic intensity of 3 erlangs being presented to a four-position rotary is contained in Figure 7.6. Note that the grade of service is 0.2061, which is approximately equivalent to one in five calls receiving a busy signal.

Through the use of the traffic analyzer program you can vary the traffic intensity and/or the number of ports on the rotary group to study the resulting traffic distribution and grade of service. To illustrate this, assume you want to analyze the effect of increasing the rotary group to five positions. Here you could simply rerun the traffic analyzer program as illustrated in Figure 7.7. Note that when the rotary group is expanded to five positions, the grade of service is approximately equivalent to one in nine calls receiving a busy signal. In addition, you can use multiple executions of the traffic analyzer program to determine the change in the traffic lost

```
REM Traffic Analyzer Program
REM $DYNAMIC
DIM FACTORIAL#(60)
DIM TL#(60), TC#(60)
REM E is the offered load in Erlangs
REM PORT is the number of ports, dial in lines or trunks
REM GOS is the grade of service for port or channel PORT with traffic E
REM TL# is an array that holds traffic lost by port number
REM TC# is an array that holds traffic carried by port number
CLS
PRINT TAB(25); "Traffic Analyzer"
PRINT
PRINT "This program computes the grade of service and the traffic carried"
PRINT "and lost by each port or channel in an n position rotary type group"
PRINT
INPUT "Enter traffic intensity in Erlangs"; E#
1 INPUT "Enter number of ports -maximum 60"; PORT
IF PORT > 60 OR PORT < 1 GOTO 1
GOSUB 100 T compute factorial 1 TO PORT
REM Compute the grade of service
                PORT# = PORT
                N# = (E# ^ PORT#) / FACTORIAL#(PORT)
                        D# = O
                        FOR S = O TO PORT
                        S# = S
                        D# = D# + (E# ^ S#) / FACTORIAL#(S)
                        NEXT S
                GOS# = N# / D#
REM Compute the traffic lost by port
        FOR S = 1 TO PORT
                S# = S
                LN# = E# * (E# ^ S# / FACTORIAL#(S))
                LD# = O
                        FOR S1 = O TO S
                        S1# = S1
                        LD# = LD# + E# ^ S1# / FACTORIAL#(S1)
                        NEXT S1
                        TL#(S) = LN# / LD#
                NEXT S
REM Compute the traffic carried by port
        FOR I = 1 TO PORT
                IF I = 1 THEN
                        TC#(I) = E# - TL#(1)
                        ELSE
                        TC#(I) = TL#(I - 1) - TL#(I)
```

Figure 7.5 Traffic analyzer program listing

```
                        END IF
            NEXT I
REM Output results
PRINT
PRINT "TOTAL TRAFFIC OFFERED"; E#; "ERLANGS TO"; PORT; "PORTS PROVIDES A";
PRINT USING "##.####"; GOS#;
PRINT " GRADE OF SERVICE"
PRINT
PRINT TAB(25); "TRAFFIC DISTRIBUTION"
PRINT
PRINT "PORT#    TRAFFIC OFFERED  TRAFFIC CARRIED   TRAFFIC LOST"
PRINT
FOR I = 1 TO PORT
        PRINT USING "##"; I;
        PRINT USING "       ###.#####"; E#;
        PRINT USING "       ###.#####"; TL#(I);
        E# = E# - TC#(I)
NEXT I
PRINT
PRINT "TRAFFIC LOST BY LAST PORT IS ";
PRINT USING "###.##### "; TL#(PORT);
PRINT "ERLANGS"
PRINT
PRINT "GRADE OF SERVICE IS EQUIVALENT TO 1 IN ";
PRINT USING "##### "; INT((1 / GOS#) + .5);
PRINT "CALLS RECEIVING A BUSY SIGNAL"
END
REM subroutine to compute factorials
100 FOR I = 1 TO PORT
        p# = 1
                FOR J = I TO 1 STEP -1
                p# = p# * J
                NEXT J
        FACTORIAL#(I) = p#
        NEXT I
        FACTORIAL#(0) = 1
        RETURN
```

Figure 7.5   (_continued_)

```
                              Traffic Analyzer

This program computes the grade of service and the traffic carried
and lost by each port or channel in an n position rotary type group

Enter traffic intensity in Erlangs? 3
Enter number of ports -maximum 60? 4

TOTAL TRAFFIC OFFERED 3 ERLANGS TO 4 PORTS PROVIDES A 0.2061 GRADE OF SERVICE

                          TRAFFIC DISTRIBUTION

PORT#      TRAFFIC OFFERED    TRAFFIC CARRIED    TRAFFIC LOST

   1            3.00000           0.75000           2.25000
   2            2.25000           0.66176           1.58824
   3            1.58824           0.54977           1.03846
   4            1.03846           0.42014           0.61832

TRAFFIC LOST BY LAST PORT IS    0.61832 ERLANGS

GRADE OF SERVICE IS EQUIVALENT TO 1 IN      5 CALLS RECEIVING A BUSY SIGNAL
```

Figure 7.6 Traffic analyzer program execution

```
                              Traffic Analyzer

This program computes the grade of service and the traffic carried
and lost by each port or channel in an n position rotary type group

Enter traffic intensity in Erlangs? 3
Enter number of ports -maximum 60? 5

TOTAL TRAFFIC OFFERED 3 ERLANGS TO 5 PORTS PROVIDES A 0.1101 GRADE OF SERVICE

                          TRAFFIC DISTRIBUTION

PORT#      TRAFFIC OFFERED    TRAFFIC CARRIED    TRAFFIC LOST

   1            3,00000           0.75000           2.25000
   2            2.25000           0.66176           1.58824
   3            1.58824           0.54977           1.03846
   4            1.03846           0.42014           0.61832
   5            0.61832           0.28816           0.33016

TRAFFIC LOST BY LAST PORT IS    0.33016 ERLANGS

GRADE OF SERVICE IS EQUIVALENT TO 1 IN      9   CALLS RECEIVING A BUSY SIGNAL
```

Figure 7.7 Analyzing the effect of port expansion

by the last port in a port grouping as you increase or decrease the number of ports to service a given traffic intensity. In comparing the executions of the program displayed in Figure 7.6 and 7.7, note that an increase in the number of ports from three to five decreased the traffic lost by the last port from 0.618 32 to 0.330 16 erlangs. Thus, you can use this program as a 'devil's advocate' to determine 'what-if' information without having to actually install or remove equipment and perform the line measurements normally associated with sizing such equipment.

7.4.3 Traffic capacity planning

There are three methods by which the erlang distribution equation can be used for capacity planning purposes. The first method as previously illustrated uses the erlang distribution equation to compute a grade of service based upon a defined traffic intensity and number of ports or channels. Using the value of the computed grade of service the reader can then accept it or alter the traffic intensity and/or number of ports to obtain a desired grade of service.

A second method by which the erlang formula can be used is to determine the amount of traffic that can be serviced by a given number of ports or channels to provide a prdefined grade of service. Using the erlang formula in this manner involves a trial and error process since different traffic intensity values must be substituted into the formula to determine if it results in the desired grade of service. Since this process can be quite laborious, a computer program was developed to generate a table of traffic intensities that can be serviced by a varying number of ports or channels to provide predefined grades of service.

Figure 7.8 contains a program listing of a Traffic Capacity Planner Program which was also developed using the Microsoft Quick Basic compiler. Readers that have purchased the convenience diskette sold by the publisher of this book will find this program on the file CAPACITY.BAS. This program computes and displays the traffic intensity that can be offered to 1 to 40 ports to obtain 0.01, 0.02, 0.04, and 0.08 grades of service. Readers can easily vary both the grades of service and/or number of ports.

To vary the grades of service the DATA statement should be changed. To increase the number of ports the variable MAXPORT's value of 40 should be changed. When the number of grades of service and/or number of ports are increased, the DIM E#(4,40) statement should be increased to reflect the revised number of

```
REM Traffic Capacity Planner Program
REM $DYNAMIC
DIM FACTORIAL#(60)
DIM E#(4, 40)
DIM GOS(10)
REM E is the offered load in Erlangs
REM E#(I,S) contains resulting traffic for GOS of I when S ports used
REM PORT is the number of ports, dial in lines or trunks
REM GOS is the grade of service for port or channel PORT with traffic E
MAXPORT = 40
CLS
FOR I = 1 TO 4
READ GOS(I)
NEXT I
DATA .01,.02,.04,.08
LPRINT TAB(25); "Capacity Planner"
LPRINT
LPRINT "This program computes and displays a table containing the traffic"
LPRINT "carrying capacity for a group of ports that will result in"
LPRINT "                                 a predefined grade of service"
LPRINT
        LPRINT
        LPRINT " NUMBER OF PORT"          TRAFFIC SUPPORTED IN ERLANGS PER PORT"
        LPRINT "                          FOR INDICATED GRADE OF SERVICE"
        LPRINT TAB(30);
        LPRINT USING "#.###  #.###    "; GOS(1); GOS(2);
        LPRINT USING "#.###  #.### "; GOS(3); GOS(4)
        LPRINT
GOSUB 100  "compute factorial 1 TO factorial MAXPORT
REM vary grade of service from .01 to .08 or 1 in 100 to 1 in 12.5 calls busy
        FOR I = 1 TO 4

        GOS# = GOS(I)
        REM Vary ports from 1 to MAXPORT
            FOR PORT = 1 TO MAXPORT
                    REM Find traffic in Erlangs that provides GOS
                    LOW# = 1
                    HIGH# = 100000
                      TRY# = (LOW# + HIGH#) / 2
1 E# = TRY# / 1000
PORT# = PORT

                    N# = (E# ^ PORT#) / FACTORIAL#(PORT)
                    D# = O
                    FOR S = O TO PORT
                    S# = S
```

Figure 7.8 Traffic capacity planner program

```
                          D# = D# + (E# ^ S#) / FACTORIAL#(S)
                          NEXT S
                          IF ABS(GOS# - N# / D#) < .0005 THEN GOTO 5
                          IF GOS# - N# / D# < O THEN
                                      OLD# = TRY#
                                      TRY# = TRY# - ((TRY# - LOW#) / 2)
                                      GOTO 1
                          ELSEIF GOS# - N# / D# > O THEN
                                  TRY# = (TRY# + OLD#) / 2
                                  GOTO 1
                          END IF
5 E#(I, PORT) = TRY# / 1000
NEXT PORT
                          NEXT I
REM output results
        FOR S = 1 TO MAXPORT
                LPRINT TAB(4); S;
                 LPRINT TAB(29);
                LPRINT USING "##.### ##.### "; E#1(1, S); E#(2, S);
                LPRINT USING "##.### ##.###"; E#(3, S); E#(4, S)
                NEXT S
        END
REM subroutine to compute factorials
100 FOR I = 1 TO MAXPORT
        p# = 1
                FOR J = I TO 1 STEP -1
                p# = p# * J
                NEXT j
        FACTORIAL#(I) = p#
        NEXT I
        FACTORIAL#(0) = 1
        RETURN
```

Figure 7.8   (*continued*)

grades of service and/or ports for which the traffic intensity is to be computed. If the number of ports increases beyond 60, you should both increase the size of the FACTORIAL#(60) array as well as have patience as the computations become lengthy. A word of caution if in order for readers that may require an expansion of the size of arrays. If the total number of elements in your program will exceed 64K, you must use the /AH option when invoking Microsoft's QuickBasic compiler. The reader is referred to Microsoft's QuickBasic manual for information concerning the use of the /AH option.

The modifications required to change the program to compute the traffic supported by 1 to 44 ports or channels for grades of service ranging from 0.01 to 0.55 or 1 in 100 to 55 in 100 calls receiving a busy signal in increments of 0.005 are contained in Figure 7.9. This illustration contains the revised Traffic Capacity Planner Program listing that readers can compare to the program listing contained in Figure 7.8 to denote the use of two additional FOR—NEXT statements which permit the use of only one DATA statement. Since the execution of this program can take a considerable amount of time, a significant portion of the series of tables generated by its use are contained in Appendix C. Readers are referred to that appendix for specific information concerning the traffic in erlangs up to 44 ports or channels can support based upon grades of service ranging from 0.01 to 0.325.

To speed up the computations of the trial and error procedure, the program was written to increment or decrement trials by one-half of the previously used value. When the grade of service and the computed grade of service differ by less than 0.0005 a match is considered to have occurred and the traffic intensity used to compute the grade of service is placed into the E# array.

Figure 7.10 illustrates the output produced from the execution of the Capacity Planner Program that was listed in Figure 7.8. In examining the traffic support by grade of service, you will note that a large group of ports is more efficient with respect to their traffic capacity support for a given grade of service than small groups of ports. Similarly, a small reduction in the number of ports from a large group of ports has a much more pronounced effect upon traffic capacity support than a similar reduction in the number of ports from a smaller group of ports. To illustrate the preceding consider the 0.01 grade of service. Four groups of 10 ports supports a total traffic intensity of 17.684 (4.471 times 4) erlangs. In comparison, one 40-port group supports a total of 28.877 erlangs. Based upon this, it is more efficient to have one large rotary group than several smaller rotary groups, and readers may wish to consider this important concept of equipment sizing prior to breaking rotary or port groups into subgroups designed to service individual groups of end-users. This concept also explains why it would be better to have one rotary group connected to V.22bis modems operating at 2400 bps that can also service end-user 1200 bps transmission requirements than separate 1200 and 2400 bps rotary groups.

7.4.4 Traffic tables

A third method by which the erlang formula can be used is through the generation of a series of tables that indicate grades of service based upon specific traffic loads and a given number of ports or channels. Once again, a computer program was developed to facilitate the required computations.

Figure 7.11 contains the Microsoft QuickBasic program listing of a program that was written to compute a table of grades of service based upon a given traffic intensity and port or channel size using the erlang distribution. This program is stored on the file ERLANG.BAS on the convenience disk.

The execution of the ERLANG.BAS program results in the generation of a data file named ERLANG.DAT that contains the grades of service for traffic intensities ranging from 0.5 to 40 erlangs for groups of up to 60 ports or channels. This program like other programs developed to assist in traffic computations can be easily modified to obtain grades of service for a different range of traffic intensities or larger number of ports or channels. In Appendix A, the reader will find a subset of tables generated by the execution of this program. This subset lists the grade of service based upon traffic intensity varying from 0.5 to 37.5 erlangs in increments of 0.5 erlangs. A more comprehensive table is contained on the convenience diskette on the file ERLANG.DAT which lists grades of service based upon traffic intensities up to 77.5 erlangs in increments of 0.5 erlangs. Since the data file is in ASCII format, readers can use any data processor capable of reading ASCII files to manipulate the entries to meet their specific requirements or they can use the DOS redirect feature to print the file. Concerning the latter, you can enter the DOS command

```
TYPE ERLANG.DAT>LPT1:
```

to direct the contents of the file ERLANG.DAT to your printer. These tables can be used to reduce many sizing problems to a simple look-up procedure to determine equipment and/or facility size once the

```
REM Traffic Capacity Planner Program
REM $DYNAMIC
DIM FACTORIAL#(60)
DIM E#(4, 44)
DIM GOS(4)
REM E is the offered load in Erlangs
REM E#(I,S) contains resulting traffic for GOS of I when S ports used
REM PORT is the number of ports, dial in lines or trunks
REM GOS is the grade of service for port or channel PORT with traffic E
MAXPORT = 44
CLS
FOR I = 1 TO 4
READ GOS(I)
NEXT I
DATA -.01,-.005,.00,.005
FOR TT = 1 TO 25
FOR K = 1 TO 4
GOS(K) = GOS(K) + 2 / 100
NEXT K
LPRINT TAB(30); "Capacity Planner"
LPRINT
LPRINT "    THE FOLLOWING TABLE DISPLAYS THE TRAFFIC CARRYING CAPACITY FOR THE "
LPRINT "INDICATED NUMBER OF PORTS THAT WILL RESULT IN A PREDEFINED GRADE OF SERVICE"
LPRINT
        LPRINT
        LPRINT " NUMBER OF PORTS          TRAFFIC SUPPORTED IN ERLANGS PER PORT"
        LPRINT "                          FOR INDICATED GRADE OF SERVICE"
        LPRINT TAB(30);
        LPRINT USING "#.###  #.###   "; GOS(1); GOS(2);
        LPRINT USING "#.###  #.### "; GOS(3); GOS(4)
        LPRINT
GOSUB 100   'compute factorial 1 TO factorial MAXPORT
REM vary grade of service
        FOR I = 1 TO 4
        GOS# = GOS(I)
        REM Vary ports from 1 to MAXPORT
            FOR PORT = 1 TO MAXPORT
                    REM Find traffic in Erlangs that provides GOS
                    LOW# = 1
                    HIGH# = 100000
                      TRY# = HIGH#
1 E# = TRY# / 1000
PORT# = PORT
                    N# = (E# ^ PORT#) / FACTORIAL#(PORT)
                    D# = O
```

Figure 7.9   Revised traffic capacity planner program

```
                          FOR S = O TO PORT
                          S# = S
                          D# = D# + (E# ^ S#) / FACTORIAL#(S)
                          NEXT S

                          IF ABS(GOS# - N# / D#) < .0005 THEN GOTO 5
                          IF GOS# - (N# / D#) < O THEN
                                  HIGH# = TRY#
                                  TRY# = (TRY# - LOW#) / 2
                              GOTO 1
                          ELSEIF GOS# - N# / D# > O THEN
                              LOW# = TRY#
                              TRY# = (TRY# + HIGH#) / 2
                            GOTO 1
                          END IF
5 E#(I, PORT) = TRY# / 1000
NEXT PORT
                          NEXT I
REM output results
     FOR S = 1 TO MAXPORT
                LPRINT TAB(4); S;
                 LPRINT TAB(29);
                LPRINT USING "##.### ##.###   "; E#(1, S); E#(2, S);
                LPRINT USING "##.### ##.###"; E#(3, S); E#(4, S)
                NEXT S
     REM Skip to next page
     FOR I = 1 TO 12
     LPRINT
     NEXT I
NEXT TT
END
REM subroutine to compute factorials
100 FOR I = 1 TO MAXPORT
     p# = 1
                FOR J = I TO 1 STEP -1
                p# = p# * J
                NEXT J
     FACTORIAL#(I) = p#
     NEXT I
     FACTORIAL#(O) = 1
RETURN
```

Figure 7.9   (*continued*)

Capacity Planner

This program computes and displays a table containing the traffic
carrying capacity for a roup of ports that will result in
a predefined grade of service

| NUMBER OF PORTS | TRAFFIC SUPPORTED IN ERLANGS PER PORT | | | |
| | FOR INDICATED GRADE OF SERVICE | | | |
	0.010	0.020	0.040	0.080
1	0.010	0.020	0.042	0.086
2	0.151	0.221	0.332	0.514
3	0.450	0.599	0.812	1.127
4	0.880	1.100	1.398	1.849
5	1.368	1.649	2.052	2.629
6	1.924	2.271	2.773	3.462
7	2.484	2.931	3.517	4.327
8	3.126	3.610	4.293	5.216
9	3.786	4.327	5.088	6.105
10	4.471	5.088	5.891	7.032
11	5.128	5.860	6.733	7.966
12	5.860	6.593	7.571	8.906
13	6.593	7.393	8.449	9.857
14	7.335	8.204	9.303	10.832
15	8.076	9.012	10.175	11.782
16	8.871	9.857	11.045	12.772
17	9.614	10.683	11.969	13.763
18	10.431	11.491	12.877	14.727
19	11.176	12.306	13.735	15.739
20	12.016	13.184	14.668	16.731
21	12.772	14.063	15.585	17.741
22	13.624	14.901	16.480	18.751
23	14.420	15.770	17.442	19.751
24	15.262	16.633	18.386	20.780
25	16.151	17.510	19.252	21.790
26	17.030	18.386	20.188	22.802
27	17.881	19.227	21.192	23.795
28	18.604	20.188	22.090	24.805
29	19.557	21.027	23.072	25.855
30	20.348	21.876	24.030	26.876
31	21.192	22.892	24.903	27.906
32	21.973	23.748	25.855	28.936
33	22.892	24.610	26.821	29.987
34	23.841	25.544	27.797	30.986
35	24.610	26.368	28.712	32.048
36	25.544	27.363	29.685	33.070
37	26.368	28.263	30.642	34.069
38	27.247	29.106	31.664	35.157
39	28.126	30.045	32.557	36.187
40	28.877	31.047	33.526	37.208

Figure 7.10 Capacity planner program execution

```
REM $DYNAMIC
DIM FACTORIAL#(60)
DIM E#(80), B#(80, 80)
REM E is the offered load in Erlangs
REM S is the number of ports, dial in lines or trunks
REM B(i,j) contains grade of service for port or channel i with traffic j
OPEN "D:ERLANG.DAT" FOR OUTPUT AS #1
GOSUB 100  'compute factorial 1 TO 60
C = O
FOR I = 5 TO 400 STEP 5
        C = C + 1
        E# = I / 10
        E#(C) = E#
                FOR S = 1 TO 60
                        SX# = S
                        N# = (E# ^ SX#) / FACTORIAL#(S)
                        D# = 1
                        FOR D1 = 1 TO S
                        D1X# = D1
                        D# = D# + (E# ^ D1X#) / FACTORIAL#(D1)
                        NEXT D1
                B#(S, C) = N# / D#
                NEXT S
NEXT i
FOR I = 1 TO 80 STEP 5  'print 16 pages 5 entries per page
        PRINT #1, "                    ERLANG B DISTRIBUTION"
        PRINT #1, "        PROBABILITY ALL PORTS ARE BUSY WHEN CALL ATTEMPTED"
        PRINT #1, "                 WHICH IS THE GRADE OF SERVICE"
        PRINT #1,
        PRINT #1, "PORT #                     TRAFFIC IN ERLANGS"
        PRINT #1,
        PRINT #1, USING "       ##.##       ##.##"; E#(I); E#(I + 1);
        PRINT #1, USING "       ##.## "; E#(I + 2);
        PRINT #1, USING "       ##.##       ##.##"; E#(I + 3); E#(I + 4)
        PRINT #1,
        FOR S = 1 TO 60

                IF B#(S, I + 4) < .00001# GOTO 50
                PRINT #1, USING "##    #.##### "; S; B#(S, I);
                PRINT #1, USING "  #.##### "; B#(S, I + 1);
                PRINT #1, USING "   #.##### "; B#(S, I + 2);
                PRINT #1, USING "    #.##### "; B#(S, I + 3);
                PRINT #1, USING "   #.##### "; B#(S, I + 4)
        NEXT S
50      REM space to top of page
        FOR LINECOUNT = 1 TO (66 - S)
        PRINT #1,
        NEXT LINECOUNT
NEXT I
CLOSE #1
END
REM subroutine to compute factorials
100 FOR I = 1 TO 60
    p# = 1
            FOR j = I TO 1 STEP -1
            p# = p# * j
            NEXT j
    FACTORIAL#(I) = p#
    NEXT I
    RETURN
```

Figure 7.11 Program to generate table of grades of service using the Erlang distribution

concepts involved in the use of the tables are understood. Thus, we will next focus our attention upon the use of traffic tables and their use in the equipment sizing process.

In examining the program listing contained in Figure 7.11, the reader should note that the program was written to store output on a file, however, the program can be easily modified to direct output to a printer. This can be accomplished by removing the statement OPEN "D:ERLANG.DAT" FOR OUTPUT AS #1 and changing all PRINT #1 entries to LPRINT.

Extracts from the execution of the ERLANG.BAS program are listed in Table 7.4. While the use of the erlang B formula is normally employed for telephone dimensioning, it can be easily adapted to sizing data communications equipment. As an example of the use of Table 7.4, consider the following situation. Suppose one desires to provide customers with a grade of service of 0.1 when the specific traffic intensity is 7.5 erlangs. From Table 7.4, 10 channels or trunks would be required since the use of the table requires one to interpolate and round to the highest port or channel. Thus, if it was desired to offer a 0.01 grade of service when the traffic intensity was 7 erlangs, one could read down the 7.0 erlang column and determine that between 13 and 14 channels are required. Since one cannot install a fraction of a trunk or channel, 14 channels would be required as we round to the highest channel number.

Multiplexer sizing

In applying the erlang B formula to multiplexer sizing, an analogy can be made between telephone network trunks and multiplexer channel adapters. Let us assume that a survey of terminal users in a geographic area indicated that during the busy hour normally 6 terminals would be active. This would represent a traffic intensity of 6 erlangs. Suppose we wish to size the multiplexer to insure that at most only 1 out of every 100 calls to the device encounters a busy signal. Then our desired grade of service becomes 0.01. From Table 7.4, the 6 erlang column indicates that to obtain a 0.011 36 grade of service would require 12 channels, while a 0.005 22 grade of service would result if the multiplexer had 13 channels. Based upon the preceding data, the multiplexer would be configured for 13 channels as illustrated in Figure 7.12.

From a practical consideration, the erlang B formula assumption that lost calls are cleared and traffic not carried vanishes can be interpreted as traffic overflowing one dial-in port is switched to the next port on the telephone company rotary as each dial-in port

Table 7.4 Erlang B distribution extracts.

	Probability all ports are busy when call attempted which is the grade of service				
Port no.	Traffic in erlangs				
	5.50	6.00	6.50	7.00	7.50
1	0.846 15	0.857 14	0.866 67	0.875 00	0.882 35
2	0.699 42	0.720 00	0.737 99	0.753 85	0.767 92
3	0.561 84	0.590 16	0.615 23	0.637 55	0.657 51
4	0.435 83	0.469 57	0.499 94	0.527 34	0.552 14
5	0.324 06	0.360 40	0.393 91	0.424 72	0.453 02
6	0.229 02	0.264 92	0.299 10	0.331 33	0.361 54
7	0.152 50	0.185 05	0.217 37	0.248 87	0.279 21
8	0.094 90	0.121 88	0.150 10	0.178 82	0.207 46
9	0.054 81	0.075 14	0.097 80	0.122 10	0.147 40
10	0.029 27	0.043 14	0.059 77	0.078 74	0.099 54
11	0.014 42	0.022 99	0.034 12	0.047 72	0.063 56
12	0.006 57	0.011 36	0.018 14	0.027 08	0.038 21
13	0.002 77	0.005 22	0.008 99	0.014 37	0.021 57
14	0.001 09	0.002 23	0.004 16	0.007 13	0.011 42
15	0.000 40	0.000 89	0.001 80	0.003 32	0.005 68

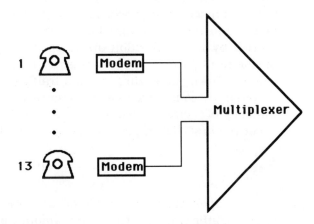

Figure 7.12 Multiplexer channel sizing. Based upon a busy hour traffic intensity of 6 erlangs, 13 dial-in lines, modems, and multiplexer ports would be required to provide a 0.01 grade of service

becomes busy. Thus, traffic overflowing dial-in port n is offered to port $n+1$ and the traffic lost by the nth dial-in port, e_n, is the total traffic offered to the entire group of dial-in ports multiplied by the probability that all dial-in ports are busy. Thus

$$e_n = E * P(T_{n;} E)$$

where E is the traffic intensity in erlangs and n the number of ports or channels.

For the first dial-in port, when n is 1, the proportion of traffic blocked becomes

$$e_1 = \frac{E}{1+E}$$

For the second dial-in port, the proportion of traffic lost by that port becomes

$$e_2 = \frac{E^2/2!}{1 + (E^1/1!) + (E^2/2!)}$$

In general, the proportion of traffic lost by the nth port can be expressed as

$$e_n = \frac{E^n/n!}{1 + (E^1/1!) + \ldots + (E^n/n!)}$$

From the preceding we note that we can analyze the traffic lost by each port on the multiplexer in the same manner as our previous discussion concerning the computation of lost traffic. In fact, the formulas contained in Table 7.4 for traffic lost and traffic carried by rotary position are applicable to each rotary position on the multiplexer. To verify this, let us reduce the complexity of calculations by analyzing the data traffic carried by a group of four dial-in ports connected to a four-channel multiplexer when a traffic intensity of 3 erlangs is offered to the group.

For the first dial-in port, the proportion of lost traffic becomes:

$$P_1 = \frac{3}{1+3} = 0.75$$

The proportion of lost traffic on the first port multiplied by the offered traffic provides the actual amount of lost traffic on port 1. Thus

$$e_1 = P_1 * E = \frac{E}{(1+E)} * E = \frac{E^2}{(1+E)} = 2.25 \text{ erlangs}$$

The total traffic carried on the first multiplexer port is the difference between the total traffic offered to that port and the traffic that overflows or is lost to the first port. Thus, the total traffic carried by port 1 is

$$3 - 2.25 = 0.75 \text{ erlangs}$$

Since we consider the rotary as a device that will pass traffic lost from port 1 to the remaining ports, we can compute the traffic lost by the second port in a similar manner. Substituting in the formula to determine the proportion of traffic lost, we obtain for the second port

$$P_2 = \frac{E^2/2!}{1 + (E^1/1!) + (E^2/2!)} = 0.5294$$

The amount of traffic lost by the second port, e_2, becomes

$$e_2 = P_2 * E = 0.5294 * 3 = 1.588 \text{ erlangs}$$

The traffic carried by the second port is the difference between the traffic lost by the first port and the traffic lost by the second port, thus

$$e_1 - e_2 = 2.25 - 1.588 = 0.662 \text{ erlangs}$$

A summary of individual port traffic statistics is presented in Table 7.5 for the four-port multiplexer based upon a traffic intensity of 3 erlangs offered to the device. Readers should note that the computation results contained in Table 7.5 are within a small fraction of the results computed by the traffic analyzer program execution displayed in Figure 7.6. The differences between the two can be attributed to the accuracy of the author's hand calculator versus the use of double precision in the program developed by the author. From Table 7.5, the traffic carried by all 4 ports totaled 2.3817 erlangs. Since 3 erlangs were offered to the multiplexer

Table 7.5 Individual port traffic statistics.

Port	Proportion of lost traffic	Amount of lost traffic	Traffic carried
1	0.7500	2.2500	0.7500
2	0.5294	1.5880	0.6620
3	0.3462	1.0380	0.5500
4	0.2061	0.6813	0.4197

ports, then 0.6183 erlangs were lost. The proportion of traffic lost to the group of 4 ports is e_4/E or 0.6183/3 which is 0.2061. If you examine Appendix A, at the column for a traffic intensity of 3 erlangs and a row of 4 channels you will note a similar 0.2061 grade of service. These calculations become extremely important from a financial standpoint if a table look-up results in a device dimensioning that causes a multiplexer expansion nest to be obtained to service one or only a few channel adapters. Under such circumstances, the user may wish to analyze a few of the individual high-order channels to see what the effect of the omission of one or more of those channels will have upon the system.

If data tables are available, the previous individual port calculations are greatly simplified. From such tables the grade of service for channels 1 through 4 with a traffic intensity of 3 erlangs is the proportion of traffic lost to each port. Thus, if tables are available, one only has to multiply the grade of service by the traffic intensity to determine the traffic lost to each port.

7.5 THE POISSON FORMULA

The number of arrivals per unit time at a service location can vary randomly according to one of many probability distributions. The Poisson distribution is a discrete probability distribution since it relates to the number of arrivals per unit time. The general model or formula for this probability distribution is given by the following equation

$$P(r) = \frac{e^{-n}(n)^r}{r!}$$

where
      r = number of arrivals
   $P(r)$ = probability of arrivals
      n = mean of arrival rate
      e = base of natural logarithm (2.718 28)
    $r!$ = r factorial = $r * (r - 1) * (r - 2) \ldots 3 * 2 * 1$

The Poisson distribution corresponds to the assumption of random arrivals since each arrival is assumed to be independent of other arrivals and also independent of the state of the system. One interesting characteristic of the Poisson distribution is that its mean is equal to its variance. This means that by specifying the mean of the distribution, the entire distribution is specified.

7.5.1 Multiplexer sizing

As an example of the application of the Poisson distribution, let us consider a multiplexer location where user calls arrive at a rate of 2 per unit period of time. From the Poisson formula, we obtain

$$P(r) = \frac{2.71828 - 2 * 2r}{r!}$$

Substituting the values 0, 1, 2, ..., 9 for r, we obtain the probability of arrivals listed in Table 7.6, rounded to 4 decimal points. The probability of arrivals in excess of 9 per unit period of time can be computed but is a very small value and was thus eliminated from consideration.

Table 7.6 Poisson distribution arrival (rate of 2 per unit time).

Number of arrivals per period	Probability
0	0.1358
1	0.2707
2	0.2707
3	0.1805
4	0.0902
5	0.0361
6	0.0120
7	0.0034
8	0.0009
9	0.0002

The probability of the arrival rate being less than or equal to some specific number, n, is the sum of the probabilities of the arrival rate being 0, 1, 2, ..., n. This can be expressed mathematically as follows

$$P(r \leq n) = P(r = 0) + P(r = 1) + P(r = 2) + \ldots + P(r = n)$$

This can be expressed in sigma notation (the mathematical shorthand for expressing 'sums' of numbers) as

$$P(r \leq n) = \sum_{r=0}^{n} \frac{e^{-n} * n^r}{r!}$$

To determine the probability of 4 or less arrivals per unit period of time we obtain

$$P(r \leq 4) = \sum_{r=0}^{4} \left[\left(e^{-2}2^r \right) / r! \right]$$

$$P(r \leq 4) = P(r = 0) + P(r = 1) + P(r = 2) + P(r = 3) + P(r = 4)$$

$$= 0.1358 + 0.2707 + 0.2707 + 0.1804 + 0.0902$$

$$= 0.9478$$

From the preceding, almost 95% of the time 4 or fewer calls will arrive at the multiplexer at the same time, given an arrival rate or traffic intensity of 2. The probability that a number of calls in excess of 4 arrives during the period is equal to 1 minus the probability of 4 or less calls arriving, which is the grade of service. Thus, the grade of service when a traffic intensity of 2 erlangs if offered to 4 ports is

$$P(r > 4) = 1 - P(r < 4) = 1 - 0.9478 = 0.0522$$

If 4 calls arrive and are being processed, any additional calls are lost and cannot be handled by the multiplexer. The probability of this occurring is 0.0522 for a four-channel multiplexer, given a traffic intensity of 2 erlangs. In general, when E erlangs of traffic are offered to a service area containing n channels, the probability that the service area will fail to handle the traffic is given by the equation

$$P(r \geq n) = \sum_{r=n+1}^{\infty} \frac{e^{-E} * E^r}{r!}$$

Although commonly known as the Poisson traffic formula, the preceding equation is also known as the Molina equation after the American who first applied it to traffic theory. Since the number of channels or ports is always finite, it is often easier to compute the probability that the number of channels cannot support the traffic intensity in terms of their support. This is because the probability of support plus the probability of not supporting a given traffic intensity must equal unity. Thus, we can rewrite the Molina or Poisson traffic formula as

$$P(r > n) = 1 - \sum_{r=0}^{n} \frac{e^{-E} * E^r}{r!}$$

To facilitate equipment and facility sizing using the Poisson traffic formula, another program was written in Microsoft QuickBasic. Figure 7.13 contains the program listing of the file labeled POISSON.BAS which is contained on the convenience diskette. This program generates a data file labeled POISSON.DAT which contains a table of grades of service for traffic intensities ranging from 0.5 to 80 erlangs when lost calls are assumed to be held and thus follow the Poisson distribution.

To execute the POISSON.BAT program using Microsoft's QuickBasic, you must execute that compiler using its /AH option. That option allows dynamic arrays to exceed 64K.

If you require the generation of a smaller set of tables or wish to alter the increments of traffic in erlangs both modifications can be easily accomplished. Altering the number of tables requires changing the size of the E# and B# arrays, the statements FOR I=5 TO 800 STEP 5, E#=I/10 and the statement I=1 TO 160 STEP 5. The FOR I=5 TO 800 STEP 5 statement controls the number of different traffic loads that will be computed. Since E# is set to I divided by 10, the program listing computes traffic from 0.5 to 80 erlangs in increments of 0.5 erlangs. Thus, you can change the FOR statement or the statement E#=I/10 or both to alter the number of traffic loads and their values. Lastly, you must alter the statement I=1 TO 160 STEP 5 if you change the previously referenced FOR statement. This is because the FOR I=1 TO 160 STEP 5 statement controls the printing of output. As included in the POISSON.BAS listing the FOR I=1 TO 160 STEP 5 statement results in the printing of 32 pages with 5 entries per page.

Similar to ERLANG.DAT, the file POISSON.DAT on the convenience diskette is in ASCII format and can be directed to your printer by the command TYPE POISSON.DAT>LPT1: or it can be imported into a word processor that is capable of reading ASCII files. The POISSON.DAT file contains grade of service computations based upon a traffic intensity of 0.5 to 80 erlangs in increments of 0.5 erlangs. For those readers that do not have the convenience diskette, a subset of the contents of POISSON.DAT is printed in Appendix B. This subset is limited to approximately the first half of the traffic table contained on the convenience diskette. By changing the values of the FOR I loop in the program, different traffic intensities can be computed easily.

7.5.2 Formula comparison and utilization

In order to contrast the difference between erlang B and Poisson formulas, let us return to the multiplexer examples previously

```
'$DYNAMIC
OPEN "A:POISSON.DAT" FOR OUTPUT AS #1
DIM FACTORIAL#(60)
DIM E#(180), B#(160, 160)
REM E is the offered load in Erlangs
REM S is the number of ports, dial in lines or trunks
REM B( i, j ) contains grade of service for port or channel i with traffic j
GOSUB 100   'compute factorial 1 TO 60
C = O
FOR I = 5 TO 800 STEP 5
       C = C + 1
       E# = I / 10
       E#(C) = E#
              K = O
              FOR S = O TO 59     'vary port number
                     K = K + 1
                     SX# = S
                     D# = O
                     FOR X = O TO S
                     D1X# = X
                     D# = D# + (E# ^ D1X#) / (FACTORIAL#(X) * 2.71828 ^ E#)
                     NEXT X
              B#(K, C) = 1# - D#
              B#(X, C) = ABS(B#(K, C))
              NEXT S
NEXT I
FOR I = 1 TO 160 STEP 5   ' print 32 pages 5 entries per page
       PRINT #1, "                      POISSON DISTRIBUTION"
       PRINT #1, "        PROBABILITY ALL PORTS ARE BUSY WHEN CALL ATTEMPTED"
       PRINT #1, "                  WHICH IS THE GRADE OF SERVICE"
       PRINT #1,
       PRINT #1, "PORT #               TRAFFIC IN ERLANGS"
       PRINT #1,
       PRINT #1, USING "        ##.##        ##.##"; E#(I); E#(I + 1);
       PRINT #1, USING "      ##.##"; E#(I + 2);
       PRINT #1, USING "      ##.##        ##.##"; E#(I + 3); E#(I + 4)
       PRINT #1,
       FOR S = 1 TO 60

              IF B#(S, I + 4) < .00001# GOTO 50
              PRINT #1, USING "##  #.##### "; S; B#(S, I);
              PRINT #1, USING "   #.#####"; B#(S, I + 1);
              PRINT #1, USING "   #.#####"; B#(S, I + 2);
              PRINT #1, USING "   #.#####"; B#(S, I + 3);
              PRINT #1, USING "   #.#####"; B#(S, I + 4)
       NEXT S
50     REM space to top of page
       FOR LINECOUNT = 1 TO (66 - S)
       PRINT #1,
       NEXT LINECOUNT
NEXT I
CLOSE #1
END
REM subroutine to compute factorials
100 FOR I = 1 TO 60
       p# = 1
              FOR j = I TO 1 STEP -1
              p# = p# * j
              NEXT j
       FACTORIAL#(I) = p#
       NEXT I
       FACTORIAL#(0) = 1#
       RETURN
```

Figure 7.13 POISSON.BAS program listing

considered. When 6 erlangs of traffic are offered and it is desired that the grade of service should be 0.01, 13 multiplexer channels are required when the erlang B formula is employed. If the Poisson formula is used, an excerpt of one of the tables in Appendix B produced by executing the POISSON.BAS program would appear as indicated in Table 7.7. By using this table a grade of service of 0.01 for a traffic intensity of 6 erlangs results in a required channel capacity somewhere between 9 and 10. Rounding to the next highest number results in a requirement for 10 multiplexer channels. Now let us compare what happens at a higher traffic intensity. For a traffic intensity of 10 erlangs and the same 0.01 grade of service, from Appendix A you will note that 19 channels will be required when the erlang B formula is used. If the Poisson formula is used, from Appendix B you will note that a 0.01 grade of service based upon 10 erlangs of traffic requires between 18 and 19 channels. Rounding to the next highest channel results in the Poisson formula providing the same value as provided through the use of the erlang B formula.

In general, the Poisson formula produces a more conservative sizing at lower traffic intensities than the erlang B formula. At higher traffic intensities the results are reversed. The selection

Table 7.7 Poisson distribution extracts.

Port no.	Probability all ports are busy when call attempted which is the grade of service				
	Traffic in erlangs				
	5.50	6.00	6.50	7.00	7.50
1	0.995 91	0.997 52	0.998 50	0.999 09	0.999 45
2	0.973 44	0.982 65	0.988 72	0.992 70	0.995 30
3	0.911 62	0.938 03	0.956 96	0.970 36	0.079 74
4	0.798 30	0.848 80	0.888 15	0.918 23	0.940 85
5	0.642 48	0.714 94	0.776 33	0.827 01	0.867 94
6	0.471 08	0.554 32	0.630 96	0.699 29	0.758 56
7	0.313 96	0.393 69	0.473 47	0.550 29	0.621 84
8	0.190 51	0.256 02	0.327 24	0.401 28	0.475 36
9	0.105 64	0.152 76	0.208 42	0.270 91	0.338 03
10	0.053 77	0.083 92	0.122 61	0.169 50	0.223 59
11	0.025 25	0.042 62	0.066 83	0.098 52	0.137 76
12	0.010 98	0.020 09	0.033 88	0.053 35	0.079 24
13	0.004 45	0.008 82	0.016 02	0.027 00	0.042 66
14	0.001 68	0.003 62	0.007 10	0.012 81	0.021 56
15	0.000 60	0.001 40	0.002 95	0.005 71	0.010 26

of the appropriate formula depends upon how one visualizes the calling pattern of users of the communications network.

7.5.3 Economic constraints

In the previous dimensioning exercises, the number of ports or channels selected was based upon a defined level of grade of service. Although we want to size equipment to have a high efficiency and keep network users happy, we must also consider the economics of dimensioning. One method that can be used for economic analysis is the assignment of a dollar value to each erlang-hour of traffic.

For a company such as a time-sharing service bureau, the assignment of a dollar value to each erlang-hour of traffic may be a simple matter. Here the average revenue per one hour time-sharing session could be computed and used as the dollar value assigned to each erlang-hour of traffic. For other organizations, the average hourly usage of employees waiting service could be employed.

As an example of the economics involved in sizing, let us assume lost calls are held, resulting in traffic following a Poisson distribution, and that 7.5 erlangs of traffic can be expected during the busy hour. Let us suppose we desire initially to offer a 0.02 grade of service. From the extract of the execution of the Poisson distribution program presented in Table 7.6, between 14 and 15 channels would be required. Rounding to the highest number, 15 channels would be selected to provide the desired 0.02 grade of service which is equivalent to 1 call in 50 obtaining a busy signal.

Multiplexers normally consist of a base unit which contains a number of channels or ports and an expansion chassis into which dual port adapter cards are normally inserted to expand the capacity of the multiplexer. Many times one may desire to compare the potential revenue loss in comparison to expanding the multiplexer beyond a certain capacity. As an example of this, consider the data in Table 7.7 which indicates that when the traffic intensity is 5.5 erlangs a 12-channel multiplexer would provide an equivalent grade of service. This means that during the busy hour, 2 erlangs of traffic would be lost and the network designer could then compare the cost of three additional ports on the multiplexer and additional modems and dial-in lines—if access to the multiplexer is over the switched network—to the loss of revenue by not being able to service the busy hour traffic.

7.6 APPLYING THE EQUIPMENT SIZING PROCESS

Many methods are available for end-users to obtain data traffic statistics required for sizing communications equipment. Two of the most commonly used methods are based upon user surveys and computer accounting information.

Normally, end-user surveys require each terminal user to estimate the number of originated calls to the computer for average and peak traffic situations as well as the call duration in minutes or fractions of an hour, on a daily basis. By accumulating the terminal traffic data for a group of terminals in a particular geographic area one then can obtain the traffic that the multiplexer will be required to support.

Suppose a new application is under consideration at a geographic area currently not served by a firm's data communications network. For this application, 10 terminals with the anticipated data traffic denoted in Table 7.8 are to be installed at five small offices in the greater metropolitan area of a city. If each terminal will dial a centrally-located multiplexer, how many dial-in lines, auto-answer modems, and multiplexer ports are required to provide users with a 98% probability of accessing the computer upon dialing the multiplexer? What would happen if a 90% probability of access was acceptable?

For the 10 terminals listed in Table 7.8, the average daily and peak daily traffic is easily computed. These figures can be obtained through multiplying the number of calls originated each day by the call duration and summing the values for the appropriate average and peak periods. Doing so, one obtains 480 minutes of

Table 7.8 Terminal traffic survey.

Terminal	Calls originated per day		Call duration (minutes)	
	Average	Peak	Average	Peak
A	3	6	15	30
B	2	3	30	60
C	5	5	10	15
D	2	3	15	15
E	2	4	15	30
F	2	4	15	30
G	3	3	15	35
H	4	6	30	30
I	2	3	20	25
J	2	2	15	60

average daily traffic and 1200 minutes of peak traffic. Dividing those numbers by 60 results in 8 erlangs average daily traffic and 20 erlangs peak daily traffic.

Prior to sizing, some additional knowledge and assumptions concerning the terminal traffic will be necessary. First, from the data contained in most survey forms, information containing busy hour traffic is nonexistent although such information is critical for equipment sizing. Although survey forms can be tailored to obtain the number of calls and call duration by specific time intervals, for most users the completion of such precise estimates is a guess at best.

Normally, busy hour traffic can be estimated accurately from historical or computer billing and accounting type data or from the use of a network management system that logs usage data. Suppose that the use of one of those sources shows a busy hour traffic equal to twice the average daily traffic based upon an 8-hour normal operational shift. Then the traffic would be (8/8) * 2 or 2 erlangs while the busy hour peak traffic would be (20/8) * 2 or 5 erlangs.

The next process in the sizing procedure is to determine the appropriate sizing formula to apply to the problem. If we assume that users encountering a busy signal will tend to redial the telephone numbers associated with the multiplexer, the Poisson

Table 7.9 Poisson distribution program extract.

Port no.	Probability all ports are busy when call attempted which is the grade of service				
	Traffic in erlangs				
	5.50	6.00	6.50	7.00	7.50
1	0.393 47	0.632 12	0.776 87	0.864 66	0.917 91
2	0.090 20	0.264 24	0.442 17	0.593 99	0.712 70
3	0.014 39	0.080 30	0.191 15	0.323 32	0.456 19
4	0.001 75	0.018 99	0.065 64	0.142 88	0.242 42
5	0.000 17	0.003 66	0.018 57	0.052 65	0.108 82
6	0.000 01	0.000 59	0.004 46	0.016 56	0.042 02
7	0.000 00	0.000 08	0.000 93	0.004 53	0.014 19
8	0.000 00	0.000 01	0.000 17	0.001 10	0.004 25
9	0.000 00	0.000 00	0.000 03	0.000 24	0.001 14
10	0.000 00	0.000 00	0.000 00	0.000 05	0.000 28
11	0.000 00	0.000 00	0.000 00	0.000 01	0.000 06
12	0.000 00	0.000 00	0.000 00	0.000 00	0.000 01

formula will be applicable. From Table 7.9 the 2.0-erlang traffic column shows a 0.016 56 probability (1.65%) of all channels busy for a device containing 6 channels, 0.052 65 for 5 channels, and 0.142 88 for 4 channels. Thus, to obtain a 98% probability of access based upon the daily average traffic would require 6 channels, while a 90% probability of access would require 5 channels.

If we want to size the equipment based upon the daily peak traffic load, how would sizing differ? We now would use a 5-erlang traffic column contained in the sizing tables in Appendix B. From the table, 11 channels would provide a 0.013 69 probability (1.37%) of encountering a busy signal, while 10 channels would provide a 0.031 82 probability. To obtain a 98% probability of access statistically would require 11 channels. Since there are only 10 terminals, logic would override statistics and 10 channels or 1 channel per terminal would suffice. It should be noted that the statistical approach is based upon a level of traffic that can be generated from an infinite number of terminals. Thus, one must also use logic and recognize the limits of the statistical approach when sizing equipment. Since a 0.068 09 probability of encountering a busy signal is associated with 9 channels and a 0.133 37 probability with 8 channels, 9 channels would be required to obtain a 90% probability of access.

In Table 7.10 the sizing required for average and peak daily traffic is listed for both 90% and 98% probability of obtaining access. Note that the difference between supporting the average and peak traffic loads is 4 channels for both the 90% and 98% probability of access scenarios, even though peak traffic is $2\frac{1}{2}$ times average traffic.

Table 7.10 Channel requirements summary.

Probability of access (%)	Daily average	Traffic peak
90	5	9
98	6	10

The last process in the sizing procedure is to determine the number of channels and associated equipment to install. Whether to support the average or peak load will depend upon the critical nature of the application, funds availability, how often peak daily traffic can be expected, and perhaps organizational politics. If peak traffic only occurs once per month, we could normally size equipment for the average daily traffic expected. If peak traffic was expected to occur twice each day, we would normally size equipment based upon peak traffic. Traffic between these extremes may require that the final step in the sizing procedure be one of human judgement, incorporating knowledge of economics, and the application into the decision process.

APPENDIX A

ERLANG B DISTRIBUTION TABLES

The tables in this appendix represent a subset of the tables generated by the program ERLANG.BAT. The reader is referred to the file ERLANG.DAT on the convenience diskette for the full set of ERLANG B distribution tables generated by that program. The file ERLANG.DAT is in ASCII format and can be directed to your printer by the DOS command TYPE ERLANG.DAT>LPT1. As an alternative, you can import that file into any word processor that accepts ASCII input files.

ERLANG B DISTRIBUTION

Probability all ports are busy when call attempted
which is the grade of service

Port no.	Traffic in erlangs				
	0.50	1.00	1.50	2.00	2.50
1	0.3333333	0.50000000	0.60000000	0.66666667	0.71428571
2	0.0769231	0.20000000	0.31034483	0.40000000	0.47169811
3	0.0126582	0.06250000	0.13432836	0.21052632	0.28216704
4	0.0015798	0.01538462	0.04795737	0.09523810	0.14991605
5	0.0001580	0.00306748	0.01418316	0.03669725	0.06973112
6	0.0000132	0.00051099	0.00353326	0.01208459	0.02823429
7	0.0000009	0.00007299	0.00075655	0.00344086	0.00998301
8	0.0000001	0.00000912	0.00014183	0.00085948	0.00310999
9	0.0000000	0.00000101	0.00002364	0.00019096	0.00086314
10	0.0000000	0.00000010	0.00000355	0.00003819	0.00021574
11	0.0000000	0.00000001	0.00000048	0.00000694	0.00004903
12	0.0000000	0.00000000	0.00000006	0.00000116	0.00001021
13	0.0000000	0.00000000	0.00000001	0.00000018	0.00000196
14	0.0000000	0.00000000	0.00000000	0.00000003	0.00000035
15	0.0000000	0.00000000	0.00000000	0.00000000	0.00000006

Port no.	Traffic in erlangs				
	3.00	3.50	4.00	4.50	5.00
1	0.7500000	0.77777778	0.80000000	0.81818182	0.83333333
2	0.5294118	0.57647059	0.61538462	0.64800000	0.67567568
3	0.3461538	0.40211020	0.45070423	0.49290061	0.52966102
4	0.2061069	0.26027100	0.31067961	0.35671179	0.39834289
5	0.1100543	0.15411207	0.19906687	0.24302100	0.28486782
6	0.0521571	0.08248354	0.11716247	0.15416648	0.19184726
7	0.0218643	0.03960826	0.06274894	0.09017049	0.12051864
8	0.0081324	0.01703345	0.03042006	0.04827248	0.07004785
9	0.0027035	0.00658053	0.01333967	0.02356741	0.03745779
10	0.0008104	0.00229789	0.00530755	0.01049404	0.01838457
11	0.0002210	0.00073061	0.00192630	0.00427467	0.00828737
12	0.0000552	0.00021305	0.00064169	0.00160043	0.00344119
13	0.0000127	0.00005736	0.00019740	0.00055369	0.00132178
14	0.0000027	0.00001434	0.00005640	0.00017794	0.00047184
15	0.0000005	0.00000335	0.00001504	0.00005338	0.00015726
16	0.0000001	0.00000073	0.00000376	0.00001501	0.00004914
17	0.0000000	0.00000015	0.00000088	0.00000397	0.00001445
18	0.0000000	0.00000003	0.00000020	0.00000099	0.00000401
19	0.0000000	0.00000001	0.00000004	0.00000024	0.00000106
20	0.0000000	0.00000000	0.00000001	0.00000005	0.00000026
21	0.0000000	0.00000000	0.00000000	0.00000001	0.00000006
22	0.0000000	0.00000000	0.00000000	0.00000000	0.00000001

Port no.	Traffic in erlangs				
	5.50	6.00	6.50	7.00	7.50
1	0.8461538	0.85714286	0.86666667	0.87500000	0.88235294
2	0.6994220	0.72000000	0.73799127	0.75384615	0.76791809
3	0.5618404	0.59016393	0.61523383	0.63754647	0.65751023
4	0.4358348	0.46956522	0.49993874	0.52734461	0.55213821
5	0.3240587	0.36040044	0.39391014	0.42471950	0.45301608
6	0.2290219	0.26492232	0.29909947	0.33133003	0.36154052
7	0.1525035	0.18505474	0.21736524	0.24887145	0.27920906
8	0.0948966	0.12187578	0.15010018	0.17882183	0.20745531
9	0.0548136	0.07514496	0.09780326	0.12210134	0.14739744
10	0.0292652	0.04314184	0.05977227	0.07874088	0.09954371
11	0.0144216	0.02299089	0.03411503	0.04771685	0.06355705
12	0.0065665	0.01136480	0.01814370	0.02708103	0.03820551
13	0.0027704	0.00521792	0.00899029	0.01437251	0.02156629
14	0.0010872	0.00223126	0.00415671	0.00713498	0.01142141
15	0.0003985	0.00089171	0.00179800	0.00331861	0.00567828
16	0.0001370	0.00033428	0.00072991	0.00144979	0.00265463
17	0.0000443	0.00011797	0.00027900	0.00059661	0.00116979
18	0.0000135	0.00003932	0.00010074	0.00023196	0.00048717
19	0.0000039	0.00001242	0.00003446	0.00008545	0.00019227
20	0.0000011	0.00000373	0.00001120	0.00002991	0.00007210
21	0.0000003	0.00000106	0.00000347	0.00000997	0.00002575
22	0.0000001	0.00000029	0.00000102	0.00000317	0.00000878
23	0.0000000	0.00000008	0.00000029	0.00000097	0.00000286
24	0.0000000	0.00000002	0.00000008	0.00000028	0.00000089
25	0.0000000	0.00000000	0.00000002	0.00000008	0.00000027
26	0.0000000	0.00000000	0.00000001	0.00000002	0.00000008
27	0.0000000	0.00000000	0.00000000	0.00000001	0.00000002

Port no.	Traffic in erlangs				
	8.00	8.50	9.00	9.50	10.00
1	0.8888889	0.89473684	0.90000000	0.90476190	0.90909091
2	0.7804878	0.79178082	0.80198020	0.81123596	0.81967213
3	0.6754617	0.69167957	0.70639535	0.71980271	0.73206442
4	0.5746352	0.59511205	0.61380859	0.63093250	0.64666322
5	0.4790083	0.50290564	0.52490800	0.54520063	0.56395218
6	0.3897519	0.41604122	0.44051624	0.46329886	0.48451490
7	0.3081647	0.33563333	0.36158451	0.38603703	0.40904078
8	0.2355703	0.26286870	0.28915810	0.31432598	0.33831843
9	0.1731408	0.19888798	0.22429995	0.24913004	0.27320794
10	0.1216611	0.14460809	0.16796323	0.19137916	0.21458234
11	0.0812883	0.10051123	0.12082073	0.14183863	0.16323233
12	0.0514064	0.06646355	0.08308661	0.10095301	0.11973919
13	0.0306646	0.04164708	0.05439275	0.06870477	0.08433886
14	0.0172209	0.02466213	0.03378540	0.04454439	0.05681914

Port no.	Traffic in erlangs				
	8.00	8.50	9.00	9.50	10.00
15	0.0091009	0.01378259	0.01986848	0.02743740	0.03649695
16	0.0045298	0.00726878	0.01105250	0.01602981	0.02230187
17	0.0021272	0.00362123	0.00581728	0.00887831	0.01294888
18	0.0009445	0.00170711	0.00290021	0.00466392	0.00714244
19	0.0003975	0.00076312	0.00137190	0.00232653	0.00374510
20	0.0001590	0.00032422	0.00061697	0.00110388	0.00186905
21	0.0000606	0.00013122	0.00026435	0.00049913	0.00088923
22	0.0000220	0.00005069	0.00010813	0.00021549	0.00040403
23	0.0000077	0.00001873	0.00004231	0.00008900	0.00017564
24	0.0000026	0.00000664	0.00001587	0.00003523	0.00007318
25	0.0000008	0.00000226	0.00000571	0.00001339	0.00002927
26	0.0000003	0.00000074	0.00000198	0.00000489	0.00001126
27	0.0000001	0.00000023	0.00000066	0.00000172	0.00000417
28	0.0000000	0.00000007	0.00000021	0.00000058	0.00000149
29	0.0000000	0.00000002	0.00000007	0.00000019	0.00000051
30	0.0000000	0.00000001	0.00000002	0.00000006	0.00000017
31	0.0000000	0.00000000	0.00000001	0.00000002	0.00000006
32	0.0000000	0.00000000	0.00000000	0.00000001	0.00000002

Port no.	Traffic in erlangs				
	10.50	11.00	11.50	12.00	12.50
1	0.9130435	0.91666667	0.92000000	0.92307692	0.92592593
2	0.8273921	0.83448276	0.84101749	0.84705882	0.85266030
3	0.7433181	0.75368063	0.76325199	0.77211796	0.78035259
4	0.6611559	0.67454504	0.68694721	0.69846403	0.70918413
5	0.5813145	0.59742336	0.61239988	0.62635172	0.63937457
6	0.5042880	0.52273594	0.53996898	0.55608893	0.57118912
7	0.4306640	0.45098450	0.47008410	0.48804464	0.50494573
8	0.3611230	0.38275556	0.40325081	0.42265511	0.44102154
9	0.2964238	0.31871400	0.34004940	0.36042576	0.37985647
10	0.2373660	0.25958033	0.28112210	0.30192504	0.32195142
11	0.1847228	0.20608477	0.22714297	0.24776555	0.26785727
12	0.1391425	0.15889418	0.17876529	0.19856739	0.21815017
13	0.1010301	0.11851474	0.13654543	0.15490075	0.17338961
14	0.0704355	0.08518629	0.10085067	0.11720988	0.13405830
15	0.0469881	0.05879690	0.07176970	0.08572925	0.10048909
16	0.0299135	0.03885235	0.04905404	0.06041259	0.07279238
17	0.0181408	0.02452325	0.03211783	0.04090003	0.05080456
18	0.0104713	0.01476515	0.02010713	0.02654295	0.03407862
19	0.0057535	0.00847579	0.01202378	0.01648757	0.02192850
20	0.0030115	0.00464006	0.00686620	0.00979564	0.01352002
21	0.0015035	0.00242461	0.00374598	0.00556635	0.00798338
22	0.0007171	0.00121084	0.00195430	0.00302700	0.00451553
23	0.0003272	0.00057876	0.00097619	0.00157681	0.00244808

24	0.0001431	0.00026520	0.00046754	0.00078779	0.00127342
25	0.0000601	0.00011667	0.00021502	0.00037799	0.00063631
26	0.0000243	0.00004936	0.00009510	0.00017443	0.00030582
27	0.0000094	0.00002011	0.00004050	0.00007752	0.00014156
28	0.0000035	0.00000790	0.00001663	0.00003322	0.00006319
29	0.0000013	0.00000300	0.00000660	0.00001375	0.00002724
30	0.0000004	0.00000110	0.00000253	0.00000550	0.00001135
31	0.0000002	0.00000039	0.00000094	0.00000213	0.00000458
32	0.0000000	0.00000013	0.00000034	0.00000080	0.00000179
33	0.0000000	0.00000004	0.00000012	0.00000029	0.00000068
34	0.0000000	0.00000001	0.00000004	0.00000010	0.00000025
35	0.0000000	0.00000000	0.00000001	0.00000004	0.00000009
36	0.0000000	0.00000000	0.00000000	0.00000001	0.00000003
37	0.0000000	0.00000000	0.00000000	0.00000000	0.00000001

Port no.	Traffic in erlangs				
	13.00	13.50	14.00	14.50	15.00
1	0.9285714	0.93103448	0.93333333	0.93548387	0.93750000
2	0.8578680	0.86272189	0.86725664	0.87150259	0.87548638
3	0.7880201	0.79517634	0.80187025	0.80814474	0.81403763
4	0.7191852	0.72853530	0.73729464	0.74551629	0.75324733
5	0.6515535	0.66296436	0.67367451	0.68374419	0.69322726
6	0.5853546	0.59866272	0.61118348	0.62298037	0.63411084
7	0.5208633	0.53586893	0.55002931	0.56340635	0.57605723
8	0.4584064	0.47486682	0.49045918	0.50523805	0.51925557
9	0.3983669	0.41599027	0.43276459	0.44873045	0.46392940
10	0.3411851	0.35962576	0.37728475	0.39418141	0.41034054
11	0.2873527	0.30621026	0.32440676	0.34193329	0.35879157
12	0.2373973	0.25622164	0.27456042	0.29237075	0.30962563
13	0.1918521	0.21015820	0.22820477	0.24591237	0.26322168
14	0.1512105	0.16850465	0.18580352	0.20299353	0.21998293
15	0.1158651	0.13168379	0.14778776	0.16403832	0.18031640
16	0.0860405	0.09999764	0.11450691	0.12942016	0.14460212
17	0.0617339	0.07356787	0.08617365	0.09941372	0.11315292
18	0.0426825	0.05229072	0.06281391	0.07414547	0.08616888
19	0.0283752	0.03582297	0.04423650	0.05355434	0.06369501
20	0.0181098	0.02360961	0.03003548	0.03737571	0.04559322
21	0.0110866	0.01495069	0.01963058	0.02515779	0.03153945
22	0.0065085	0.00909089	0.01233806	0.01631082	0.02105148
23	0.0036652	0.00530763	0.00745414	0.01017825	0.01354328
24	0.0019814	0.00297666	0.00432942	0.00611177	0.00839351
25	0.0010293	0.00160482	0.00241861	0.00353231	0.00501087
26	0.0005144	0.00083258	0.00130064	0.00196607	0.00288255
27	0.0002476	0.00041611	0.00067395	0.00105474	0.00159886
28	0.0001149	0.00020059	0.00033686	0.00054591	0.00085580
29	0.0000515	0.00009337	0.00016260	0.00027288	0.00044246
30	0.0000223	0.00004201	0.00007587	0.00013187	0.00022118
31	0.0000094	0.00001830	0.00003426	0.00006168	0.00010701
32	0.0000038	0.00000772	0.00001499	0.00002795	0.00005016

Port no.	Traffic in erlangs				
	13.00	13.50	14.00	14.50	15.00
33	0.0000015	0.00000316	0.00000636	0.00001228	0.00002280
34	0.0000006	0.00000125	0.00000262	0.00000524	0.00001006
35	0.0000002	0.00000048	0.00000105	0.00000217	0.00000431
36	0.0000001	0.00000018	0.00000041	0.00000087	0.00000180
37	0.0000000	0.00000007	0.00000015	0.00000034	0.00000073
38	0.0000000	0.00000002	0.00000006	0.00000013	0.00000029
39	0.0000000	0.00000001	0.00000002	0.00000005	0.00000011
40	0.0000000	0.00000000	0.00000001	0.00000002	0.00000004
41	0.0000000	0.00000000	0.00000000	0.00000001	0.00000002

Port no.	Traffic in erlangs				
	15.50	16.00	16.50	17.00	17.50
1	0.9393939	0.94117647	0.94285714	0.94444444	0.94594595
2	0.8792315	0.88275862	0.88608625	0.88923077	0.89220685
3	0.8195824	0.82480870	0.82974302	0.83440897	0.83882770
4	0.7605296	0.76740047	0.77389326	0.78003792	0.78586133
5	0.7021719	0.71062148	0.71861485	0.72618710	0.73336993
6	0.6446269	0.65457574	0.66400004	0.67293863	0.68142676
7	0.5880346	0.59938676	0.61015818	0.62038956	0.63011827
8	0.5325611	0.54520100	0.55721869	0.56865462	0.57954640
9	0.4784029	0.49219148	0.50533437	0.51786907	0.52983122
10	0.4257904	0.44056144	0.45468477	0.46819187	0.48111374
11	0.3749912	0.39054738	0.40547928	0.41980863	0.43355877
12	0.3263106	0.34242100	0.35795944	0.37293417	0.38735746
13	0.2800901	0.29648868	0.31239963	0.32781385	0.34272913
14	0.2366993	0.25308711	0.26910484	0.28472295	0.29992158
15	0.1965221	0.21257336	0.22840419	0.24396267	0.25920906
16	0.1599327	0.17530763	0.19063848	0.20585150	0.22088642
17	0.1272633	0.14162752	0.15614055	0.17071049	0.18525844
18	0.0987645	0.11181466	0.12520797	0.13884162	0.15262307
19	0.0745634	0.08605664	0.09806979	0.11049970	0.12324838
20	0.0546297	0.06441092	0.07485152	0.08586033	0.09734448
21	0.0387591	0.04677930	0.05554519	0.06498887	0.07503364
22	0.0265817	0.03290194	0.03999284	0.04781735	0.05632410
23	0.0175985	0.02237615	0.02789033	0.03413675	0.04109419
24	0.0112380	0.01469818	0.01881385	0.02360932	0.02909276
25	0.0069193	0.00931917	0.01226485	0.01580067	0.01995848
26	0.0041080	0.00570217	0.00772335	0.01022556	0.01325552
27	0.0023528	0.00336769	0.00469765	0.00639713	0.00851836
28	0.0013007	0.00192070	0.00276062	0.00386895	0.00529578
29	0.0006947	0.00105857	0.00156823	0.00226287	0.00318555
30	0.0003588	0.00056425	0.00086178	0.00128065	0.00185479
31	0.0001794	0.00029114	0.00045848	0.00070180	0.00104596
32	0.0000869	0.00014555	0.00023635	0.00037269	0.00057168

33	0.0000408	0.00007056	0.00011816	0.00019196	0.00030307
34	0.0000186	0.00003321	0.00005734	0.00009597	0.00015597
35	0.0000082	0.00001518	0.00002703	0.00004661	0.00007798
36	0.0000035	0.00000675	0.00001239	0.00002201	0.00003790
37	0.0000015	0.00000292	0.00000552	0.00001011	0.00001793
38	0.0000006	0.00000123	0.00000240	0.00000452	0.00000826
39	0.0000002	0.00000050	0.00000101	0.00000197	0.00000370
40	0.0000001	0.00000020	0.00000042	0.00000084	0.00000162
41	0.0000000	0.00000008	0.00000017	0.00000035	0.00000069
42	0.0000000	0.00000003	0.00000007	0.00000014	0.00000029
43	0.0000000	0.00000001	0.00000003	0.00000006	0.00000012
44	0.0000000	0.00000000	0.00000001	0.00000002	0.00000005
45	0.0000000	0.00000000	0.00000000	0.00000001	0.00000002

Port no.	Traffic in erlangs				
	18.00	18.50	19.00	19.50	20.00
1	0.9473684	0.94871795	0.95000000	0.95121951	0.95238095
2	0.8950276	0.89770492	0.90024938	0.90267062	0.90497738
3	0.8430182	0.84699764	0.85078144	0.85438361	0.85781686
4	0.7913877	0.79663902	0.80163500	0.80639366	0.81093135
5	0.7401920	0.74667924	0.75285532	0.75874171	0.76435799
6	0.6894965	0.69717718	0.70449538	0.71147553	0.71813995
7	0.6393786	0.64820192	0.65661720	0.66465095	0.67232758
8	0.5899289	0.59983464	0.60929348	0.61833324	0.62697966
9	0.5412545	0.55217065	0.56260945	0.57259880	0.58216481
10	0.4934806	0.50532168	0.51666490	0.52753696	0.53796317
11	0.4467539	0.45941831	0.47157641	0.48325198	0.49446818
12	0.4012445	0.41461241	0.42747960	0.43986517	0.45178854
13	0.3571485	0.37107921	0.38453125	0.39751696	0.41005014
14	0.3146887	0.32901878	0.34291100	0.35636862	0.36939785
15	0.2741138	0.28865611	0.30282200	0.31660342	0.32999693
16	0.2356949	0.25023915	0.26449017	0.27842661	0.29203347
17	0.1997179	0.21403364	0.22816080	0.24206348	0.25571358
18	0.1664707	0.18031377	0.19409199	0.20775477	0.22126034
19	0.1362251	0.14934786	0.16254358	0.17574854	0.18890791
20	0.1092128	0.12137870	0.13376144	0.14628772	0.15889196
21	0.0855981	0.09659957	0.10795705	0.11959322	0.13143603
22	0.0654510	0.07512865	0.08528412	0.09584339	0.10673395
23	0.0487266	0.05698593	0.06581527	0.07515180	0.08492963
24	0.0352565	0.04207830	0.04952340	0.05754697	0.06609672
25	0.0247562	0.03019765	0.03627257	0.04295838	0.05022178
26	0.0168501	0.02103482	0.02582240	0.03121314	0.03719521
27	0.0111086	0.01420797	0.01784702	0.02204585	0.02681325
28	0.0070906	0.00930010	0.01196557	0.01512120	0.01879240
29	0.0043818	0.00589783	0.00777853	0.01006536	0.01279446
30	0.0026222	0.00362382	0.00490225	0.00649996	0.00845750
31	0.0015202	0.00215793	0.00299561	0.00407203	0.00542684
32	0.0008544	0.00124600	0.00177548	0.00247525	0.00338031
33	0.0004658	0.00069803	0.00102120	0.00146051	0.00204448

Port no.	Traffic in erlangs				
	18.00	18.50	19.00	19.50	20.00
34	0.0002466	0.00037967	0.00057035	0.00083695	0.00120119
35	0.0001268	0.00020064	0.00030952	0.00046608	0.00068593
36	0.0000634	0.00010310	0.00016333	0.00025240	0.00038092
37	0.0000308	0.00005155	0.00008387	0.00013300	0.00020586
38	0.0000146	0.00002509	0.00004193	0.00006825	0.00010834
39	0.0000067	0.00001190	0.00002043	0.00003412	0.00005555
40	0.0000030	0.00000551	0.00000970	0.00001663	0.00002778
41	0.0000013	0.00000248	0.00000450	0.00000791	0.00001355
42	0.0000006	0.00000109	0.00000203	0.00000367	0.00000645
43	0.0000002	0.00000047	0.00000090	0.00000167	0.00000300
44	0.0000001	0.00000020	0.00000039	0.00000074	0.00000136
45	0.0000000	0.00000008	0.00000016	0.00000032	0.00000061
46	0.0000000	0.00000003	0.00000007	0.00000014	0.00000026
47	0.0000000	0.00000001	0.00000003	0.00000006	0.00000011
48	0.0000000	0.00000000	0.00000001	0.00000002	0.00000005
49	0.0000000	0.00000000	0.00000000	0.00000001	0.00000002

Port no.	Traffic in erlangs				
	20.50	21.00	21.50	22.00	22.50
1	0.9534884	0.95454545	0.95555556	0.95652174	0.95744681
2	0.9071775	0.90927835	0.91128635	0.91320755	0.91504745
3	0.8610927	0.86422172	0.86721349	0.87007681	0.87281975
4	0.8152630	0.81940214	0.82336127	0.82715178	0.83078413
5	0.7697221	0.77485028	0.77975768	0.78445804	0.78896402
6	0.7245091	0.73060170	0.73643508	0.74202510	0.74738640
7	0.6796696	0.68669766	0.69343094	0.69988706	0.70608234
8	0.6352566	0.64318610	0.65078869	0.65808335	0.66508773
9	0.5913319	0.60012277	0.60855876	0.61665969	0.62444408
10	0.5479675	0.55757260	0.56679977	0.57566909	0.58419944
11	0.5052474	0.51561107	0.52557977	0.53517303	0.54440946
12	0.4632691	0.47432591	0.48497777	0.49524281	0.50513858
13	0.4221456	0.43381873	0.44508525	0.45596091	0.46646131
14	0.3820072	0.39420671	0.40600780	0.41742256	0.42846364
15	0.3430028	0.35562418	0.36786658	0.37973716	0.39124444
16	0.3053010	0.31822369	0.33079961	0.34302960	0.35491674
17	0.2690898	0.28217636	0.29496247	0.30744117	0.31960882
18	0.2345748	0.24767103	0.26052802	0.27312979	0.28546472
19	0.2019752	0.21491145	0.22768474	0.24026911	0.25264396
20	0.1715164	0.18411106	0.19663299	0.20904600	0.22131992
21	0.1434196	0.15548462	0.16757867	0.17965584	0.19167652
22	0.1178865	0.12923626	0.14072373	0.15229513	0.16390253
23	0.0950822	0.10554428	0.11625341	0.12715105	0.13818322
24	0.0751155	0.08454354	0.09432077	0.10438815	0.11468916
25	0.0580209	0.06630764	0.07502976	0.08413299	0.09356268

26	0.0437460	0.05083371	0.05841928	0.06645832	0.07490298
27	0.0321468	0.03803358	0.04445123	0.05136950	0.05875191
28	0.0229948	0.02773407	0.03300564	0.03879588	0.04508293
29	0.0159950	0.01968789	0.02388523	0.02858992	0.03379601
30	0.0108117	0.01359418	0.01682966	0.02053540	0.02472042
31	0.0070989	0.00912493	0.01153752	0.01436417	0.01762599
32	0.0045272	0.00595259	0.00769214	0.00977880	0.01224156
33	0.0028044	0.00377372	0.00498656	0.00647697	0.00827743
34	0.0016881	0.00232540	0.00314335	0.00417349	0.00544787
35	0.0009877	0.00139330	0.00192720	0.00261647	0.00348998
36	0.0005621	0.00081210	0.00114964	0.00159640	0.00217649
37	0.0003114	0.00046071	0.00066759	0.00094831	0.00132179
38	0.0001679	0.00025454	0.00037757	0.00054872	0.00078203
39	0.0000883	0.00013704	0.00020811	0.00030944	0.00045097
40	0.0000452	0.00007194	0.00011184	0.00017016	0.00025360
41	0.0000226	0.00003685	0.00005865	0.00009130	0.00013915
42	0.0000110	0.00001842	0.00003002	0.00004782	0.00007454
43	0.0000053	0.00000900	0.00001501	0.00002447	0.00003900
44	0.0000025	0.00000429	0.00000733	0.00001223	0.00001994
45	0.0000011	0.00000200	0.00000350	0.00000598	0.00000997
46	0.0000005	0.00000091	0.00000164	0.00000286	0.00000488
47	0.0000002	0.00000041	0.00000075	0.00000134	0.00000233
48	0.0000001	0.00000018	0.00000034	0.00000061	0.00000109
49	0.0000000	0.00000008	0.00000015	0.00000028	0.00000050
50	0.0000000	0.00000003	0.00000006	0.00000012	0.00000023
51	0.0000000	0.00000001	0.00000003	0.00000005	0.00000010
52	0.0000000	0.00000001	0.00000001	0.00000002	0.00000004
53	0.0000000	0.00000000	0.00000000	0.00000001	0.00000002

Port no.	Traffic in erlangs				
	23.00	23.50	24.00	24.50	25.00
1	0.9583333	0.95918367	0.96000000	0.96078431	0.96153846
2	0.9168111	0.91850312	0.92012780	0.92168906	0.92319055
3	0.8754497	0.87797350	0.88039740	0.88272721	0.88496828
4	0.8342679	0.83761210	0.84082477	0.84391350	0.84688530
5	0.7932873	0.79743869	0.80142808	0.80526471	0.80895710
6	0.7525325	0.75747590	0.76222815	0.76679998	0.77120132
7	0.7120319	0.71774972	0.72324879	0.72854117	0.73363808
8	0.6718182	0.67829003	0.68451734	0.69051337	0.69629040
9	0.6319292	0.63913125	0.64606526	0.65274532	0.65918463
10	0.5924086	0.60031311	0.60792872	0.61527009	0.62235102
11	0.5533067	0.56188142	0.57014945	0.57812570	0.58582428
12	0.5146820	0.52388913	0.53277554	0.54135593	0.54964434
13	0.4766018	0.48639732	0.49586244	0.50501120	0.51385710
14	0.4391439	0.44947643	0.45947404	0.46914952	0.47851534
15	0.4023978	0.41320743	0.42368376	0.43383756	0.44367968
16	0.3664659	0.37768313	0.38857577	0.39915176	0.40941958
17	0.3314644	0.34300922	0.35424610	0.36517937	0.37581441
18	0.2975248	0.30930526	0.32080358	0.33201951	0.34295444

Port no.	Traffic in erlangs				
	23.00	23.50	24.00	24.50	25.00
19	0.2647933	0.27670501	0.28837048	0.29978384	0.31094162
20	0.2334300	0.24535614	0.25708255	0.26859695	0.27989015
21	0.2036070	0.21541872	0.22708817	0.23859594	0.24992643
22	0.1755038	0.18706217	0.19854619	0.20992905	0.22118823
23	0.1493009	0.16046018	0.17162219	0.18275287	0.19382274
24	0.1251706	0.13578335	0.14648253	0.15722777	0.16798312
25	0.1032653	0.11318928	0.12328631	0.13351136	0.14382324
26	0.0837037	0.09281064	0.10217496	0.11174969	0.12149047
27	0.0665574	0.07474200	0.08326030	0.09206670	0.10111647
28	0.0518380	0.05902713	0.06661213	0.07455253	0.08280657
29	0.0394894	0.04564884	0.05224705	0.05925210	0.06662869
30	0.0293856	0.03452375	0.04012069	0.04615577	0.05260317
31	0.0213370	0.02550376	0.03012544	0.03519414	0.04069553
32	0.0151043	0.01838499	0.02209487	0.02623850	0.03081371
33	0.0104176	0.01292315	0.01581487	0.01910788	0.02281122
34	0.0069979	0.00885310	0.01104019	0.01358190	0.01649627
35	0.0045776	0.00590910	0.00751354	0.00941779	0.01164582
36	0.0029160	0.00384251	0.00498406	0.00636851	0.00802250
37	0.0018094	0.00243457	0.00322248	0.00419928	0.00539138
38	0.0010940	0.00150333	0.00203112	0.00270012	0.00353442
39	0.0006447	0.00090503	0.00124836	0.00169336	0.00226054
40	0.0003706	0.00053142	0.00074846	0.00103611	0.00141084
41	0.0002078	0.00030450	0.00043793	0.00061875	0.00085953
42	0.0001138	0.00017035	0.00025018	0.00036081	0.00051136
43	0.0000609	0.00009309	0.00013962	0.00020554	0.00029722
44	0.0000318	0.00004972	0.00007615	0.00011443	0.00016884
45	0.0000163	0.00002596	0.00004061	0.00006230	0.00009379
46	0.0000081	0.00001326	0.00002119	0.00003318	0.00005097
47	0.0000040	0.00000663	0.00001082	0.00001730	0.00002711
48	0.0000019	0.00000325	0.00000541	0.00000883	0.00001412
49	0.0000009	0.00000156	0.00000265	0.00000441	0.00000720
50	0.0000004	0.00000073	0.00000127	0.00000216	0.00000360
51	0.0000002	0.00000034	0.00000060	0.00000104	0.00000177
52	0.0000001	0.00000015	0.00000028	0.00000049	0.00000085
53	0.0000000	0.00000007	0.00000013	0.00000023	0.00000040
54	0.0000000	0.00000003	0.00000006	0.00000010	0.00000019
55	0.0000000	0.00000001	0.00000002	0.00000005	0.00000008
56	0.0000000	0.00000001	0.00000001	0.00000002	0.00000004
57	0.0000000	0.00000000	0.00000000	0.00000001	0.00000002

Port no.	Traffic in erlangs				
	25.50	26.00	26.50	27.00	27.50
1	0.9622642	0.96296296	0.96363636	0.96428571	0.96491228
2	0.9246356	0.92602740	0.92736877	0.92866242	0.92991085

3	0.8871256	0.88920368	0.89120688	0.89313912	0.89500412
4	0.8497466	0.85250354	0.85516158	0.85772596	0.86020151
5	0.8125132	0.81594025	0.81924520	0.82243436	0.82551368
6	0.7754414	0.77952886	0.78347165	0.78727725	0.79095261
7	0.7385499	0.74328649	0.74785677	0.75226926	0.75653187
8	0.7018599	0.70723262	0.71241853	0.71742702	0.72226684
9	0.6653955	0.67138951	0.67717742	0.68276940	0.68817495
10	0.6291845	0.63578257	0.64215682	0.64831794	0.65427605
11	0.5932585	0.60044092	0.60738341	0.61409716	0.62059273
12	0.5576541	0.56539791	0.57288778	0.58013512	0.58715076
13	0.5224131	0.53069178	0.53870490	0.54646387	0.55397955
14	0.4875837	0.49636639	0.50487486	0.51312010	0.52111273
15	0.4532209	0.46247206	0.47144357	0.48014578	0.48858871
16	0.4193881	0.42906638	0.43846359	0.44758889	0.45645139
17	0.3861574	0.39621518	0.40599494	0.41550427	0.42475087
18	0.3536111	0.36399343	0.37410606	0.38395438	0.39354426
19	0.3218423	0.33248616	0.34287458	0.35301018	0.36289644
20	0.2909556	0.30178910	0.31238813	0.32275189	0.33288085
21	0.2610673	0.27200915	0.28274489	0.29326960	0.30358014
22	0.2323051	0.24326431	0.25405370	0.26466359	0.27508663
23	0.2048065	0.21568285	0.22643371	0.23704427	0.24750242
24	0.1787169	0.18940154	0.20001316	0.21053139	0.22093899
25	0.1541847	0.16456248	0.17492699	0.18525235	0.19551606
26	0.1313560	0.14130842	0.15131319	0.16133938	0.17135942
27	0.1103666	0.11977625	0.12930750	0.13892527	0.14859759
28	0.0913324	0.10008884	0.10903640	0.11813752	0.12735706
29	0.0743393	0.08234556	0.09060875	0.09909107	0.10775598
30	0.0594330	0.06661229	0.07410642	0.08187976	0.08989665
31	0.0466097	0.05291225	0.05957502	0.06656740	0.07385714
32	0.0358120	0.04121914	0.04701600	0.05317936	0.05968285
33	0.0269277	0.03145419	0.03638167	0.04169617	0.04737927
34	0.0197960	0.02348824	0.02757440	0.03205042	0.03690713
35	0.0142177	0.01714918	0.02045079	0.02412805	0.02818125
36	0.0099705	0.01223399	0.01483079	0.01777439	0.02107368
37	0.0068247	0.00852358	0.01051041	0.01280442	0.01542133
38	0.0045588	0.00579811	0.00727630	0.00901586	0.01103700
39	0.0029719	0.00385052	0.00491983	0.00620303	0.00772240
40	0.0018910	0.00249659	0.00324880	0.00416959	0.00528111
41	0.0011747	0.00158070	0.00209543	0.00273831	0.00352971
42	0.0007127	0.00097757	0.00132037	0.00175725	0.00230579
43	0.0004225	0.00059074	0.00081306	0.00110217	0.00147246
44	0.0002448	0.00034895	0.00048944	0.00067588	0.00091944
45	0.0001387	0.00020158	0.00028814	0.00040536	0.00056157
46	0.0000769	0.00011392	0.00016597	0.00023787	0.00033561
47	0.0000417	0.00006302	0.00009357	0.00013663	0.00019633
48	0.0000222	0.00003413	0.00005166	0.00007685	0.00011247
49	0.0000115	0.00001811	0.00002794	0.00004234	0.00006311
50	0.0000059	0.00000942	0.00001481	0.00002287	0.00003471
51	0.0000029	0.00000480	0.00000769	0.00001210	0.00001872

Port no.	Traffic in erlangs				
	25.50	26.00	26.50	27.00	27.50
52	0.0000014	0.00000240	0.00000392	0.00000629	0.00000990
53	0.0000007	0.00000118	0.00000196	0.00000320	0.00000514
54	0.0000003	0.00000057	0.00000096	0.00000160	0.00000262
55	0.0000002	0.00000027	0.00000046	0.00000079	0.00000131
56	0.0000001	0.00000012	0.00000022	0.00000038	0.00000064
57	0.0000000	0.00000006	0.00000010	0.00000018	0.00000031
58	0.0000000	0.00000003	0.00000005	0.00000008	0.00000015
59	0.0000000	0.00000001	0.00000002	0.00000004	0.00000007
60	0.0000000	0.00000000	0.00000001	0.00000002	0.00000003

Port no.	Traffic in erlangs				
	28.00	28.50	29.00	29.50	30.00
1	0.9655172	0.96610169	0.96666667	0.96721311	0.96774194
2	0.9311164	0.93228121	0.93340733	0.93449664	0.93555094
3	0.8968053	0.89854587	0.90022885	0.90185703	0.90343305
4	0.8625928	0.86490392	0.86713893	0.86930147	0.87139501
5	0.8284887	0.83136458	0.83414618	0.83683802	0.83944435
6	0.7945042	0.79793823	0.80126027	0.80447569	0.80758951
7	0.7606520	0.76463658	0.76849209	0.77222464	0.77583993
8	0.7269462	0.73147282	0.73585391	0.74009626	0.74420626
9	0.6934030	0.69846191	0.70335958	0.70810343	0.71270044
10	0.6600407	0.66562078	0.67102480	0.67626070	0.68133597
11	0.6268801	0.63296865	0.63886732	0.64458449	0.65012811
12	0.5939449	0.60052739	0.60690732	0.61309347	0.61909409
13	0.5612623	0.56832187	0.57516774	0.58180877	0.58825348
14	0.5288629	0.53638045	0.54367464	0.55075446	0.55762844
15	0.4967821	0.50473544	0.51245776	0.51995786	0.52724418
16	0.4650601	0.47342369	0.48155091	0.48945007	0.49712932
17	0.4337426	0.44248723	0.45099264	0.45926650	0.46731641
18	0.4028819	0.41197390	0.42082681	0.42944739	0.43784243
19	0.3725375	0.38193807	0.39110326	0.40003849	0.40874938
20	0.3427765	0.35244139	0.36187852	0.37109164	0.38008488
21	0.3136749	0.32355341	0.33321643	0.34266547	0.35190279
22	0.2853174	0.29535222	0.30518877	0.31482598	0.32426380
23	0.2577985	0.26792482	0.27787575	0.28764707	0.29723599
24	0.2312216	0.24136717	0.25136618	0.26121086	0.27089523
25	0.2056987	0.21578381	0.22575736	0.23560773	0.24532532
26	0.1813490	0.19128676	0.20115435	0.21093589	0.22061789
27	0.1582956	0.16799358	0.17766856	0.18730043	0.19687164
28	0.1366625	0.14602427	0.15541529	0.16481142	0.17419110
29	0.1165688	0.12549697	0.13451033	0.14358118	0.15268432
30	0.0981221	0.10652230	0.11506512	0.12372032	0.13245979
31	0.0814112	0.08919661	0.09718086	0.10533263	0.11362204
32	0.0664979	0.07359434	0.08094162	0.08850899	0.09626631

33	0.0534090	0.05976045	0.06640695	0.07332044	0.08047231
34	0.0421308	0.04770368	0.05360497	0.05981129	0.06629752
35	0.0326057	0.03739196	0.04252670	0.04799293	0.05377084
36	0.0247327	0.02875088	0.03312291	0.03783941	0.04288730
37	0.0183728	0.02166613	0.02530427	0.02928573	0.03360492
38	0.0133570	0.01598977	0.01894530	0.02222959	0.02584454
39	0.0094986	0.01154988	0.01389183	0.01653663	0.01949289
40	0.0066051	0.00816212	0.00997115	0.01204882	0.01440901
41	0.0044905	0.00564166	0.00700337	0.00859476	0.01043318
42	0.0029848	0.00381367	0.00481239	0.00600057	0.00739715
43	0.0019398	0.00252129	0.00323507	0.00409979	0.00513430
44	0.0012329	0.00163045	0.00212767	0.00274119	0.00348845
45	0.0007665	0.00103155	0.00136928	0.00179378	0.00232024
46	0.0004664	0.00063870	0.00086250	0.00114904	0.00151091
47	0.0002778	0.00038715	0.00053190	0.00072068	0.00096348
48	0.0001620	0.00022982	0.00032125	0.00044272	0.00060181
49	0.0000926	0.00013365	0.00019009	0.00026647	0.00036832
50	0.0000518	0.00007618	0.00011024	0.00015719	0.00022094
51	0.0000285	0.00004257	0.00006268	0.00009092	0.00012995
52	0.0000153	0.00002333	0.00003496	0.00005157	0.00007497
53	0.0000081	0.00001254	0.00001913	0.00002871	0.00004243
54	0.0000042	0.00000662	0.00001027	0.00001568	0.00002357
55	0.0000021	0.00000343	0.00000542	0.00000841	0.00001286
56	0.0000011	0.00000175	0.00000280	0.00000443	0.00000689
57	0.0000005	0.00000087	0.00000143	0.00000229	0.00000363
58	0.0000003	0.00000043	0.00000071	0.00000117	0.00000188
59	0.0000001	0.00000021	0.00000035	0.00000058	0.00000095
60	0.0000001	0.00000010	0.00000017	0.00000029	0.00000048

Port no.	Traffic in erlangs				
	30.50	31.00	31.50	32.00	32.50
1	0.9682540	0.96875000	0.96923077	0.96969697	0.97014925
2	0.9365719	0.93756098	0.93851974	0.93944954	0.94035166
3	0.9049594	0.90643826	0.90787195	0.90926245	0.91061167
4	0.8734228	0.87538780	0.87729296	0.87914093	0.88093424
5	0.8419692	0.84441620	0.84678898	0.84909082	0.85132483
6	0.8106064	0.81353084	0.81636693	0.81911860	0.82178954
7	0.7793434	0.78273997	0.78603452	0.78923151	0.79233515
8	0.7481899	0.75205284	0.75580041	0.75943762	0.76296923
9	0.7171572	0.72147983	0.72567426	0.72974599	0.73370024
10	0.6862577	0.69103260	0.69566696	0.70016675	0.70453763
11	0.6555057	0.66072431	0.66579073	0.67071129	0.67549203
12	0.6249171	0.63056978	0.63605934	0.64139242	0.64657537
13	0.5945099	0.60058576	0.60648833	0.61222456	0.61780106
14	0.5643048	0.57079122	0.57709527	0.58322400	0.58918421
15	0.5343248	0.54120763	0.54790001	0.55440914	0.56074188
16	0.5045965	0.51185932	0.51892504	0.52580077	0.53249334
17	0.4751498	0.48277392	0.49019585	0.49742244	0.50446034
18	0.4460187	0.45398275	0.46174131	0.46930079	0.47666753

Port no.	Traffic in erlangs				
	30.50	31.00	31.50	32.00	32.50
19	0.4172417	0.42552134	0.43359415	0.44146601	0.44914275
20	0.3888627	0.39742995	0.40579144	0.41395226	0.42191753
21	0.3609312	0.36975411	0.37837509	0.38679815	0.39502746
22	0.3335030	0.34254522	0.35139244	0.36004730	0.36851277
23	0.3066409	0.31586106	0.32489673	0.33374880	0.34241873
24	0.2804148	0.28976627	0.29894763	0.30795771	0.31679617
25	0.2549024	0.26433273	0.27361163	0.28273552	0.29170194
26	0.2301890	0.23963968	0.24896226	0.25815043	0.26719925
27	0.2063670	0.21577353	0.22508011	0.23427746	0.24335785
28	0.1835353	0.19282722	0.20205240	0.21119825	0.22025402
29	0.1617970	0.17089898	0.17997210	0.18900047	0.19797016
30	0.1412577	0.15009032	0.15893639	0.16777665	0.17659397
31	0.1220209	0.13050307	0.13904425	0.14762227	0.15621701
32	0.1041844	0.11223550	0.12039325	0.12863316	0.13693248
33	0.0878340	0.09537739	0.10307533	0.11090182	0.11883229
34	0.0730375	0.08000441	0.08717169	0.09451308	0.10200318
35	0.0598384	0.06617203	0.07274718	0.07953885	0.08652210
36	0.0482503	0.05390962	0.05984445	0.06603262	0.07245106
37	0.0382525	0.04321558	0.04847873	0.05402402	0.05983179
38	0.0297881	0.03405424	0.03863377	0.04351427	0.04868083
39	0.0227654	0.02635535	0.03025996	0.03447319	0.03898581
40	0.0170625	0.02001655	0.02327508	0.02683839	0.03070341
41	0.0125337	0.01490883	0.01756792	0.02051726	0.02375980
42	0.0090198	0.01088436	0.01300459	0.01539159	0.01805363
43	0.0063571	0.00778577	0.00943672	0.01132450	0.01346150
44	0.0043873	0.00545550	0.00671050	0.00816872	0.00984526
45	0.0029648	0.00374416	0.00467539	0.00577532	0.00706027
46	0.0019619	0.00251689	0.00319141	0.00400154	0.00496347
47	0.0012715	0.00165733	0.00213436	0.00271705	0.00342045
48	0.0008073	0.00106921	0.00139871	0.00180809	0.00231058
49	0.0005023	0.00067598	0.00089836	0.00117940	0.00153018
50	0.0003063	0.00041893	0.00056565	0.00075425	0.00099363
51	0.0001831	0.00025458	0.00034925	0.00047303	0.00063279
52	0.0001074	0.00015175	0.00021152	0.00029101	0.00039534
53	0.0000618	0.00008875	0.00012570	0.00017567	0.00024237
54	0.0000349	0.00005095	0.00007332	0.00010409	0.00014585
55	0.0000194	0.00002871	0.00004199	0.00006056	0.00008618
56	0.0000105	0.00001590	0.00002362	0.00003460	0.00005001
57	0.0000056	0.00000864	0.00001305	0.00001943	0.00002851
58	0.0000030	0.00000462	0.00000709	0.00001072	0.00001598
59	0.0000015	0.00000243	0.00000378	0.00000581	0.00000880
60	0.0000008	0.00000125	0.00000199	0.00000310	0.00000477

Port no.	Traffic in erlangs				
	33.00	33.50	34.00	34.50	35.00
1	0.9705882	0.97101449	0.97142857	0.97183099	0.97222222
2	0.9412273	0.94207765	0.94290375	0.94370664	0.94448728
3	0.9119214	0.91319344	0.91442930	0.91563051	0.91679853
4	0.8826753	0.88436626	0.88600935	0.88760652	0.88915967
5	0.8534940	0.85560096	0.85764848	0.85963898	0.86157479
6	0.8243832	0.82690293	0.82935177	0.83173267	0.83404839
7	0.7953494	0.79827815	0.80112484	0.80389288	0.80658545
8	0.7663997	0.76973327	0.77297393	0.77612549	0.77919151
9	0.7375419	0.74127571	0.74490601	0.74843702	0.75187269
10	0.7087849	0.71291374	0.71692883	0.72083475	0.72463582
11	0.6801387	0.68465663	0.68905104	0.69332678	0.69748850
12	0.6516142	0.65651474	0.66128233	0.66592217	0.67043920
13	0.6232241	0.62849972	0.63363356	0.63863106	0.64349740
14	0.5949824	0.60062463	0.60611690	0.61146480	0.61667370
15	0.5669048	0.57290419	0.57874605	0.58443614	0.58997998
16	0.5390093	0.54535497	0.55153640	0.55755941	0.56342958
17	0.5113160	0.51799565	0.52450528	0.53085070	0.53703748
18	0.4838477	0.49084734	0.49767226	0.50432817	0.51082054
19	0.4566301	0.46393383	0.47105939	0.47801225	0.48479772
20	0.4296924	0.43728203	0.44469155	0.45192600	0.45899039
21	0.4030674	0.41092231	0.41859680	0.42609539	0.43342262
22	0.3767921	0.38488891	0.39280683	0.40054971	0.40812152
23	0.3509085	0.35922043	0.36735726	0.37532193	0.38311759
24	0.3254634	0.33396023	0.34228821	0.35044912	0.35844514
25	0.3005093	0.30915692	0.31764460	0.32597286	0.33414266
26	0.2761049	0.28486470	0.29347666	0.30193966	0.31025322
27	0.2523150	0.26114375	0.26984019	0.27840129	0.28682485
28	0.2292106	0.23806032	0.24679687	0.25541508	0.26391083
29	0.2068690	0.21568671	0.22441423	0.23304406	0.24156990
30	0.1853732	0.19410092	0.20276553	0.21135689	0.21986629
31	0.1648103	0.17338582	0.18192914	0.19042746	0.19886953
32	0.1452704	0.15362779	0.16198756	0.17033421	0.17865391
33	0.1268437	0.13491478	0.14302580	0.15115881	0.15929750
34	0.1096177	0.11733351	0.12512911	0.13298436	0.14088072
35	0.0936724	0.10096596	0.10837998	0.11589282	0.12348418
36	0.0790764	0.08588514	0.09285439	0.09996180	0.10718595
37	0.0658811	0.07215040	0.07861756	0.08526068	0.09205815
38	0.0541164	0.05980246	0.06571921	0.07184627	0.07816293
39	0.0437858	0.04885895	0.05418898	0.05975830	0.06554826
40	0.0348639	0.03931080	0.04403247	0.04901521	0.05424360
41	0.0272953	0.03112022	0.03522838	0.03961078	0.04425621
42	0.0209960	0.02422087	0.02772747	0.03151210	0.03556840
43	0.0158577	0.01852028	0.02145370	0.02465950	0.02813645
44	0.0117535	0.01390460	0.01630751	0.01896853	0.02189131
45	0.0085456	0.01024515	0.01217127	0.01433409	0.01674152

Port no.	Traffic in erlangs				
	33.00	33.50	34.00	34.50	35.00
46	0.0060932	0.00740589	0.00891594	0.01063622	0.01257790
47	0.0042599	0.00525095	0.00640850	0.00774695	0.00927960
48	0.0029202	0.00365134	0.00451884	0.00553729	0.00672090
49	0.0019628	0.00249011	0.00312572	0.00388356	0.00477771
50	0.0012938	0.00166559	0.00212098	0.00267250	0.00333325
51	0.0008364	0.00109287	0.00141199	0.00180460	0.00228230
52	0.0005305	0.00070357	0.00092237	0.00119585	0.00153381
53	0.0003302	0.00044451	0.00059136	0.00077783	0.00101187
54	0.0002018	0.00027568	0.00037220	0.00049670	0.00065541
55	0.0001210	0.00016789	0.00023003	0.00031147	0.00041691
56	0.0000713	0.00010042	0.00013964	0.00019185	0.00026050
57	0.0000413	0.00005902	0.00008329	0.00011611	0.00015993
58	0.0000235	0.00003409	0.00004882	0.00006906	0.00009650
59	0.0000131	0.00001935	0.00002813	0.00004038	0.00005724
60	0.0000072	0.00001081	0.00001594	0.00002322	0.00003339

Port no.	Traffic in erlangs				
	35.50	36.00	36.50	37.00	37.50
1	0.9726027	0.97297297	0.97333333	0.97368421	0.97402597
2	0.9452466	0.94598540	0.94670457	0.94740484	0.94808697
3	0.9179347	0.91904030	0.92011656	0.92116462	0.92218557
4	0.8906706	0.89214099	0.89357245	0.89496651	0.89632460
5	0.8634581	0.86529111	0.86707570	0.86881379	0.87050716
6	0.8363016	0.83849468	0.84063010	0.84271004	0.84473664
7	0.8092056	0.81175614	0.81423984	0.81665924	0.81901680
8	0.7821754	0.78508039	0.78790954	0.79066574	0.79335177
9	0.7552168	0.75847287	0.76164432	0.76473438	0.76774608
10	0.7283361	0.73193959	0.73544986	0.73887048	0.74220477
11	0.7015406	0.70548724	0.70933244	0.71307996	0.71673342
12	0.6748381	0.67912329	0.68329904	0.68736940	0.69133820
13	0.6482375	0.65285602	0.65735747	0.66174609	0.66602597
14	0.6217487	0.62669471	0.63151638	0.63621818	0.64080436
15	0.5953828	0.60064971	0.60578547	0.61079471	0.61568186
16	0.5691523	0.57473263	0.58017557	0.58548583	0.59066794
17	0.5430710	0.54895646	0.55469881	0.56030286	0.56577320
18	0.5171547	0.52333579	0.52936878	0.53525846	0.54100947
19	0.4914210	0.49788701	0.50420073	0.51036686	0.51638999
20	0.4658896	0.47262853	0.47921178	0.48564399	0.49192961
21	0.4405830	0.44758106	0.45442118	0.46110773	0.46764499
22	0.4155262	0.42276789	0.42985053	0.43677817	0.44355479
23	0.3907475	0.39821522	0.40552415	0.41267787	0.41967999
24	0.3662787	0.37395248	0.38146930	0.38883215	0.39604408
25	0.3421554	0.35001269	0.35771663	0.36526941	0.37267345
26	0.3184174	0.32643284	0.33430042	0.34202149	0.34959763

27	0.2951094	0.30325426	0.31125902	0.31912396	0.32684967
28	0.2722809	0.28052291	0.28863513	0.29661649	0.30446642
29	0.2499865	0.25828973	0.26647613	0.27454314	0.28248885
30	0.2282863	0.23661073	0.24483427	0.25295264	0.26096237
31	0.2072456	0.21554707	0.22376677	0.23189846	0.23993693
32	0.1869344	0.19516484	0.20333578	0.21143893	0.21946717
33	0.1674271	0.17553455	0.18360795	0.19163693	0.19961230
34	0.1488012	0.15673022	0.16465386	0.17255947	0.18043577
35	0.1311351	0.13882801	0.14654683	0.15427683	0.16200465
36	0.1145065	0.12190428	0.12936140	0.13686126	0.14438857
37	0.0989890	0.10603304	0.11317113	0.12038519	0.12765828
38	0.0846485	0.09128278	0.09804589	0.10491887	0.11188363
39	0.0715396	0.07771286	0.08404853	0.09052745	0.09713102
40	0.0597009	0.06536953	0.07123125	0.07726766	0.08346040
41	0.0491515	0.05428198	0.05963175	0.06518411	0.07092186
42	0.0398876	0.04445885	0.04926954	0.05430564	0.05955207
43	0.0318806	0.03588565	0.04014297	0.04464207	0.04937087
44	0.0250768	0.02852351	0.03222724	0.03618167	0.04037842
45	0.0193991	0.02230973	0.02547398	0.02888991	0.03255331
46	0.0147502	0.01716017	0.01981258	0.02270982	0.02585196
47	0.0110184	0.01297344	0.01515321	0.01756394	0.02020971
48	0.0080831	0.00963632	0.01139149	0.01335801	0.01554342
49	0.0058220	0.00702997	0.00841410	0.00998594	0.01175564
50	0.0041166	0.00503609	0.00610480	0.00733539	0.00873967
51	0.0028573	0.00354229	0.00435011	0.00529358	0.00638520
52	0.0019469	0.00244636	0.00304415	0.00375245	0.00458360
53	0.0013023	0.00165892	0.00209206	0.00261279	0.00323263
54	0.0008554	0.00110473	0.00141208	0.00178705	0.00223986
55	0.0005518	0.00072257	0.00093623	0.00120075	0.00152485
56	0.0003497	0.00046429	0.00060985	0.00079273	0.00102006
57	0.0002178	0.00029315	0.00039036	0.00051431	0.00067064
58	0.0001333	0.00018192	0.00024560	0.00032799	0.00043342
59	0.0000802	0.00011099	0.00015192	0.00020564	0.00027540
60	0.0000474	0.00006659	0.00009241	0.00012680	0.00017210

Port no.	Traffic in erlangs				
	38.00	38.50	39.00	39.50	40.00
1	0.9743590	0.97468354	0.97500000	0.97530864	0.97560976
2	0.9487516	0.94939952	0.95003123	0.95064737	0.95124851
3	0.9231805	0.92415026	0.92509591	0.92601830	0.92691829
4	0.8976481	0.89893831	0.90019646	0.90142374	0.90262127
5	0.8721575	0.87376646	0.87533554	0.87686621	0.87835986
6	0.8467119	0.84863777	0.85051604	0.85234845	0.85413666
7	0.8213149	0.82355560	0.82574115	0.82787350	0.82995456
8	0.7959702	0.79852363	0.80101435	0.80344465	0.80581668
9	0.7706823	0.77354594	0.77633950	0.77906555	0.78172646
10	0.7454559	0.74862699	0.75172083	0.75474019	0.75768771
11	0.7202963	0.72377175	0.72716300	0.73047300	0.73370459

Port no.	Traffic in erlangs				
	38.00	38.50	39.00	39.50	40.00
12	0.6952091	0.69898567	0.70267118	0.70626884	0.70978169
13	0.6702010	0.67427484	0.67825108	0.68213308	0.68592409
14	0.6452790	0.64964598	0.65390903	0.65807170	0.66213741
15	0.6204511	0.62510657	0.62965205	0.63409130	0.63842785
16	0.5957262	0.60066492	0.60548796	0.61019920	0.61480232
17	0.5711143	0.57633032	0.58142544	0.58640356	0.59126846
18	0.5466262	0.55211310	0.55747417	0.56271346	0.56783479
19	0.5222745	0.52802482	0.53364497	0.53913900	0.54451079
20	0.4980730	0.50407841	0.50994990	0.51569148	0.52130700
21	0.4740372	0.48028831	0.48640246	0.49238350	0.49823522
22	0.4501843	0.45667072	0.46301774	0.46922914	0.47530861
23	0.4265341	0.43324379	0.43981264	0.44624417	0.45254186
24	0.4031082	0.41002785	0.41680609	0.42344620	0.42995141
25	0.3799313	0.38704566	0.39401927	0.40085498	0.40755565
26	0.3570307	0.36432273	0.37147591	0.37849257	0.38537514
27	0.3344371	0.34188758	0.34920251	0.35638364	0.36343283
28	0.3121848	0.31977204	0.32722870	0.33455575	0.34175438
29	0.2903119	0.29801160	0.30558747	0.31303961	0.32036839
30	0.2688607	0.27664560	0.28431549	0.29186937	0.29930666
31	0.2478778	0.25571757	0.26345333	0.27108287	0.27860449
32	0.2274144	0.23527534	0.24304572	0.25072188	0.25830088
33	0.2075260	0.21537113	0.22314159	0.23083224	0.23843873
34	0.1882727	0.19606143	0.20379410	0.21146390	0.21906490
35	0.1697182	0.17740670	0.18506043	0.19267081	0.20023026
36	0.1519293	0.15947076	0.16700135	0.17451067	0.18198942
37	0.1349747	0.14231984	0.14968043	0.15704428	0.16440032
38	0.1189231	0.12602116	0.13316298	0.14033469	0.14752358
39	0.1038413	0.11064114	0.11751441	0.12444588	0.13142136
40	0.0897914	0.09624298	0.10279828	0.10944106	0.11615598
41	0.0768276	0.08288391	0.08907376	0.09538048	0.10178800
42	0.0649930	0.07061204	0.07639280	0.08231882	0.08837390
43	0.0543160	0.05946301	0.06479694	0.07030230	0.07596346
44	0.0448074	0.04945689	0.05431419	0.05936559	0.06459678
45	0.0364579	0.04059540	0.04495611	0.04952886	0.05430141
46	0.0292368	0.03286011	0.03671555	0.04079519	0.04508955
47	0.0230924	0.02621177	0.02956535	0.03314880	0.03695594
48	0.0179533	0.02059112	0.02345834	0.02655433	0.02987652
49	0.0137318	0.01592115	0.01832871	0.02095743	0.02380833
50	0.0103284	0.01211082	0.01409489	0.01628672	0.01869067
51	0.0076369	0.00905965	0.01066351	0.01245709	0.01444756
52	0.0055498	0.00666293	0.00793418	0.00937389	0.01099135
53	0.0039633	0.00481674	0.00580447	0.00693774	0.00822711
54	0.0027813	0.00342241	0.00417461	0.00504920	0.00605725
55	0.0019179	0.00238996	0.00295144	0.00361314	0.00438595
56	0.0012997	0.00164040	0.00205125	0.00254208	0.00312304
57	0.0008657	0.00110676	0.00140152	0.00175852	0.00218681
58	0.0005669	0.00073412	0.00094152	0.00119618	0.00150587
59	0.0003650	0.00047882	0.00062197	0.00080019	0.00101989
60	0.0002311	0.00030715	0.00040412	0.00052651	0.00067947

APPENDIX B

POISSON DISTRIBUTION TABLES

The tables in this appendix represent a subset of the tables generated by the program POISSON.BAS. The reader is referred to the file POISSON.DAT on the convenience diskette for the full set of POISSON distribution tables generated by that program. The file POISSON.DAT is in ASCII format and can be directed to your printer by the DOS command TYPE POISSON.DAT>LPT1. As an alternative, you can import that file into any word processor that accepts ASCII input files.

POISSON DISTRIBUTION

Probability all ports are busy when call attempted
which is the grade of service

Port no.	Traffic in erlangs				
	0.50	1.00	1.50	2.00	2.50
1	0.39347	0.63212	0.77687	0.86466	0.91791
2	0.09020	0.26424	0.44217	0.59399	0.71270
3	0.01439	0.08030	0.19115	0.32332	0.45619
4	0.00175	0.01899	0.06564	0.14288	0.24242
5	0.00017	0.00366	0.01857	0.05265	0.10882
6	0.00001	0.00059	0.00446	0.01656	0.04202
7	0.00000	0.00008	0.00093	0.00453	0.01419
8	0.00000	0.00001	0.00017	0.00110	0.00425
9	0.00000	0.00000	0.00003	0.00024	0.00114
10	0.00000	0.00000	0.00000	0.00005	0.00028
11	0.00000	0.00000	0.00000	0.00001	0.00006
12	0.00000	0.00000	0.00000	0.00000	0.00001

Port no.	Traffic in erlangs				
	3.00	3.50	4.00	4.50	5.00
1	0.95021	0.96980	0.98168	0.98889	0 99326
2	0.80085	0.86411	0.90842	0.93890	0.95957
3	0.57681	0.67915	0.76190	0.82642	0.87535
4	0.35277	0.46337	0.56653	0.65770	0.73497
5	0.18474	0.27455	0.37116	0.46789	0.55951
6	0.08392	0.14238	0.21487	0.29707	0.38404
7	0.03351	0.06529	0.11067	0.16895	0.23781
8	0.01190	0.02674	0.05113	0.08658	0.13337
9	0.00380	0.00987	0.02136	0.04025	0.06809
10	0.00110	0.00331	0.00813	0.01709	0.03182
11	0.00029	0.00102	0.00284	0.00667	0.01369
12	0.00007	0.00029	0.00091	0.00240	0.00545
13	0.00001	0.00007	0.00027	0.00080	0.00202
14	0.00000	0.00002	0.00007	0.00025	0.00069
15	0.00000	0.00000	0.00002	0.00007	0.00022
16	0.00000	0.00000	0.00000	0.00002	0.00007
17	0.00000	0.00000	0.00000	0.00000	0.00002

Port no.	Traffic in erlangs				
	5.50	6.00	6.50	7.00	7.50
1	0.99591	0.99752	0.99850	0.99909	0.99945
2	0.97344	0.98265	0.98872	0.99270	0.99530

3	0.91162	0.93803	0.95696	0.97036	0.97974
4	0.79830	0.84880	0.88815	0.91823	0.94085
5	0.64248	0.71494	0.77633	0.82701	0.86794
6	0.47108	0.55432	0.63096	0.69929	0.75856
7	0.31396	0.39369	0.47347	0.55029	0.62184
8	0.19051	0.25602	0.32724	0.40128	0.47536
9	0.10564	0.15276	0.20842	0.27091	0.33803
10	0.05377	0.08392	0.12261	0.16950	0.22359
11	0.02525	0.04262	0.06683	0.09852	0.13776
12	0.01098	0.02009	0.03388	0.05335	0.07924
13	0.00445	0.00882	0.01602	0.02700	0.04266
14	0.00168	0.00362	0.00710	0.01281	0.02156
15	0.00060	0.00140	0.00295	0.00571	0.01026
16	0.00020	0.00051	0.00116	0.00240	0.00460
17	0.00006	0.00017	0.00043	0.00095	0.00195
18	0.00002	0.00005	0.00015	0.00036	0.00079
19	0.00000	0.00001	0.00005	0.00013	0.00030
20	0.00000	0.00000	0.00001	0.00004	0.00011
21	0.00000	0.00000	0.00000	0.00001	0.00003

Port no.	Traffic in erlangs				
	8.00	8.50	9.00	9.50	10.00
1	0.99966	0.99980	0.99988	0.99993	0.99995
2	0.99698	0.99807	0.99877	0.99921	0.99950
3	0.98625	0.99072	0.99377	0.99584	0.99723
4	0.95762	0.96989	0.97877	0.98514	0.98966
5	0.90037	0.92564	0.94504	0.95974	0.97075
6	0.80876	0.85040	0.88431	0.91147	0.93291
7	0.68662	0.74382	0.79322	0.83505	0.86986
8	0.54704	0.61440	0.67610	0.73134	0.77978
9	0.40745	0.47689	0.54434	0.60817	0.66718
10	0.28337	0.34702	0.41259	0.47817	0.54207
11	0.18411	0.23663	0.29401	0.35467	0.41696
12	0.11192	0.15133	0.19699	0.24801	0.30322
13	0.06379	0.09091	0.12422	0.16357	0.20844
14	0.03418	0.05141	0.07385	0.10186	0.13553
15	0.01725	0.02742	0.04146	0.05999	0.08345
16	0.00823	0.01383	0.02203	0.03347	0.04873
17	0.00371	0.00661	0.01110	0.01772	0.02704
18	0.00159	0.00300	0.00531	0.00892	0.01427
19	0.00065	0.00129	0.00242	0.00428	0.00718
20	0.00025	0.00053	0.00105	0.00196	0.00345
21	0.00009	0.00021	0.00043	0.00085	0.00158
22	0.00003	0.00007	0.00017	0.00035	0.00069
23	0.00001	0.00002	0.00006	0.00014	0.00029
24	0.00000	0.00000	0.00002	0.00005	0.00011
25	0.00000	0.00000	0.00000	0.00001	0.00004
26	0.00000	0.00000	0.00000	0.00000	0.00001

Port no.	Traffic in erlangs				
	10.50	11.00	11.50	12.00	12.50
1	0.99997	0.99998	0.99999	0.99999	1.00000
2	0.99968	0.99980	0.99987	0.99992	0.99995
3	0.99817	0.99879	0.99920	0.99948	0.99966
4	0.99285	0.99508	0.99664	0.99771	0.99845
5	0.97891	0.98490	0.98925	0.99240	0.99465
6	0.94962	0.96248	0.97227	0.97966	0.98518
7	0.89837	0.92139	0.93973	0.95418	0.96543
8	0.82149	0.85681	0.88626	0.91049	0.93017
9	0.72059	0.76801	0.80941	0.84497	0.87508
10	0.60286	0.65949	0.71120	0.75761	0.79857
11	0.47926	0.54011	0.59827	0.65277	0.70292
12	0.36127	0.42073	0.48020	0.53840	0.59424
13	0.25803	0.31130	0.36705	0.42403	0.48102
14	0.17465	0.21870	0.26695	0.31846	0.37216
15	0.11211	0.14595	0.18473	0.22797	0.27496
16	0.06833	0.09260	0.12170	0.15558	0.19396
17	0.03960	0.05592	0.07639	0.10128	0.13068
18	0.02186	0.03218	0.04574	0.06296	0.08416
19	0.01150	0.01768	0.02616	0.03741	0.05184
20	0.00578	0.00928	0.01431	0.02127	0.03059
21	0.00278	0.00466	0.00750	0.01159	0.01730
22	0.00128	0.00224	0.00376	0.00606	0.00939
23	0.00056	0.00104	0.00181	0.00304	0.00490
24	0.00024	0.00046	0.00084	0.00147	0.00246
25	0.00009	0.00019	0.00037	0.00068	0.00118
26	0.00003	0.00007	0.00016	0.00030	0.00055
27	0.00001	0.00003	0.00006	0.00013	0.00024
28	0.00000	0.00001	0.00002	0.00005	0.00010
29	0.00000	0.00000	0.00000	0.00001	0.00004
30	0.00001	0.00001	0.00000	0.00000	0.00001

Port no.	Traffic in erlangs				
	13.00	13.50	14.00	14.50	15.00
1	1.00000	1.00000	1.00000	1.00000	1.00000
2	0.99997	0.99998	0.99999	0.99999	1.00000
3	0.99978	0.99986	0.99991	0.99994	0.99996
4	0.99895	0.99929	0.99953	0.99968	0.99979
5	0.99626	0.99740	0.99819	0.99875	0.99914
6	0.98927	0.99227	0.99447	0.99606	0.99721
7	0.97411	0.98075	0.98577	0.98955	0.99237
8	0.94597	0.95852	0.96838	0.97606	0.98200
9	0.90024	0.92100	0.93794	0.95162	0.96255
10	0.83419	0.86473	0.89060	0.91224	0.93015
11	0.74832	0.78877	0.82432	0.85514	0.88153

12	0.64683	0.69554	0.73996	0.77987	0.81525
13	0.53689	0.59066	0.64154	0.68891	0.73239
14	0.42695	0.48175	0.53555	0.58747	0.63678
15	0.32486	0.37672	0.42956	0.48240	0.53434
16	0.23639	0.28220	0.33063	0.38083	0.43190
17	0.16450	0.20245	0.24408	0.28879	0.33587
18	0.10953	0.13911	0.17279	0.21028	0.25113
19	0.06983	0.09161	0.11735	0.14703	0.18052
20	0.04266	0.05786	0.07650	0.09877	0.12477
21	0.02500	0.03508	0.04790	0.06378	0.08296
22	0.01407	0.02044	0.02884	0.03961	0.05310
23	0.00761	0.01145	0.01670	0.02369	0.03273
24	0.00396	0.00618	0.00932	0.01365	0.01946
25	0.00199	0.00321	0.00501	0.00759	0.01116
26	0.00096	0.00161	0.00260	0.00407	0.00618
27	0.00044	0.00077	0.00130	0.00211	0.00330
28	0.00020	0.00036	0.00063	0.00105	0.00171
29	0.00008	0.00016	0.00029	0.00051	0.00085
30	0.00003	0.00006	0.00013	0.00023	0.00041
31	0.00001	0.00002	0.00005	0.00010	0.00019
32	0.00000	0.00000	0.00002	0.00004	0.00008
33	0.00001	0.00000	0.00000	0.00001	0.00003

Port no.	Traffic in erlangs				
	15.50	16.00	16.50	17.00	17.50
1	1.00000	1.00000	1.00000	1.00000	1.00000
2	1.00000	1.00000	1.00000	1.00000	1.00000
3	0.99997	0.99998	0.99999	0.99999	1.00000
4	0.99986	0.99991	0.99994	0.99996	0.99997
5	0.99941	0.99960	0.99973	0.99982	0.99988
6	0.99803	0.99862	0.99903	0.99933	0.99953
7	0.99446	0.99599	0.99712	0.99794	0.99853
8	0.98654	0.99000	0.99261	0.99457	0.99603
9	0.97121	0.97801	0.98331	0.98740	0.99055
10	0.94481	0.95670	0.96626	0.97388	0.97990
11	0.90388	0.92260	0.93813	0.95088	0.96125
12	0.84622	0.87301	0.89593	0.91533	0.93160
13	0.77173	0.80688	0.83790	0.86497	0.88835
14	0.68292	0.72549	0.76425	0.79912	0.83013
15	0.58459	0.63247	0.67745	0.71916	0.75736
16	0.48298	0.53325	0.58198	0.62854	0.67245
17	0.38455	0.43403	0.48351	0.53226	0.57959
18	0.29481	0.34065	0.38795	0.43597	0.48400
19	0.21753	0.25764	0.30035	0.34503	0.39106
20	0.15448	0.18774	0.22427	0.26367	0.30546
21	0.10562	0.13182	0.16151	0.19451	0.23056
22	0.06956	0.08922	0.11219	0.13852	0.16814
23	0.04415	0.05823	0.07521	0.09526	0.11849

Port no.	Traffic in erlangs				
	15.50	16.00	16.50	17.00	17.50
24	0.02703	0.03668	0.04868	0.06329	0.08071
25	0.01597	0.02231	0.03043	0.04064	0.05317
26	0.00912	0.01311	0.01840	0.02523	0.03388
27	0.00503	0.00745	0.01076	0.01516	0.02090
28	0.00268	0.00409	0.00609	0.00882	0.01249
29	0.00138	0.00218	0.00333	0.00497	0.00724
30	0.00069	0.00112	0.00177	0.00272	0.00406
31	0.00033	0.00056	0.00091	0.00144	0.00221
32	0.00015	0.00027	0.00045	0.00074	0.00117
33	0.00006	0.00012	0.00021	0.00036	0.00060
34	0.00002	0.00005	0.00010	0.00017	0.00029
35	0.00000	0.00002	0.00004	0.00008	0.00014
36	0.00000	0.00000	0.00001	0.00003	0.00006
37	0.00001	0.00001	0.00000	0.00001	0.00002

Port no.	Traffic in erlangs				
	18.00	18.50	19.00	19.50	20.00
1	1.00000	1.00000	1.00000	1.00000	1.00000
2	1.00000	1.00000	1.00000	1.00000	1.00000
3	1.00000	1.00000	1.00000	1.00000	1.00000
4	0.99998	0.99999	0.99999	1.00000	1.00000
5	0.99992	0.99994	0.99996	0.99997	0.99998
6	0.99968	0.99978	0.99985	0.99989	0.99993
7	0.99896	0.99926	0.99948	0.99964	0.99974
8	0.99711	0.99790	0.99849	0.99891	0.99922
9	0.99294	0.99476	0.99613	0.99715	0.99791
10	0.98462	0.98830	0.99114	0.99333	0.99500
11	0.96963	0.97634	0.98168	0.98589	0.98919
12	0.94511	0.95624	0.96533	0.97269	0.97861
13	0.90833	0.92525	0.93944	0.95124	0.96099
14	0.85740	0.88114	0.90160	0.91908	0.93387
15	0.79192	0.82285	0.85025	0.87427	0.89513
16	0.71334	0.75097	0.78520	0.81602	0.84348
17	0.62495	0.66785	0.70796	0.74503	0.77892
18	0.53135	0.57740	0.62163	0.66360	0.70297
19	0.43775	0.48444	0.53051	0.57539	0.61857
20	0.34908	0.39392	0.43939	0.48485	0.52974
21	0.26927	0.31020	0.35282	0.39658	0.44090
22	0.20087	0.23644	0.27449	0.31461	0.35629
23	0.14490	0.17441	0.20685	0.24195	0.27938
24	0.10110	0.12452	0.15097	0.18036	0.21250
25	0.06825	0.08607	0.10673	0.13031	0.15676
26	0.04460	0.05761	0.07311	0.09127	0.11217
27	0.02822	0.03736	0.04855	0.06199	0.07787

28	0.01731	0.02348	0.03126	0.04085	0.05247
29	0.01029	0.01432	0.01952	0.02612	0.03432
30	0.00593	0.00847	0.01184	0.01622	0.02181
31	0.00332	0.00486	0.00697	0.00978	0.01346
32	0.00180	0.00271	0.00399	0.00573	0.00808
33	0.00095	0.00147	0.00221	0.00327	0.00471
34	0.00048	0.00077	0.00119	0.00181	0.00268
35	0.00024	0.00039	0.00062	0.00097	0.00148
36	0.00011	0.00019	0.00032	0.00051	0.00079
37	0.00005	0.00009	0.00015	0.00025	0.00041
38	0.00002	0.00003	0.00007	0.00012	0.00020
39	0.00000	0.00001	0.00003	0.00005	0.00010
40	0.00001	0.00000	0.00001	0.00002	0.00004
41	0.00001	0.00001	0.00000	0.00000	0.00001

Port no.	Traffic in erlangs				
	20.50	21.00	21.50	22.00	22.50
1	1.00000	1.00000	1.00000	1.00000	1.00000
2	1.00000	1.00000	1.00000	1.00000	1.00000
3	1.00000	1.00000	1.00000	1.00000	1.00000
4	1.00000	1.00000	1.00000	1.00000	1.00000
5	0.99999	0.99999	1.00000	1.00000	1.00000
6	0.99995	0.99997	0.99998	0.99998	0.99999
7	0.99982	0.99988	0.99991	0.99994	0.99996
8	0.99944	0.99961	0.99972	0.99980	0.99986
9	0.99848	0.99889	0.99920	0.99942	0.99959
10	0.99627	0.99723	0.99796	0.99850	0.99890
11	0.99176	0.99375	0.99528	0.99645	0.99735
12	0.98334	0.98710	0.99005	0.99237	0.99417
13	0.96897	0.97545	0.98069	0.98488	0.98823
14	0.94629	0.95664	0.96519	0.97221	0.97794
15	0.91310	0.92843	0.94140	0.95231	0.96140
16	0.86772	0.88892	0.90730	0.92311	0.93659
17	0.80959	0.83708	0.86148	0.88296	0.90170
18	0.73949	0.77303	0.80353	0.83100	0.85552
19	0.65966	0.69832	0.73431	0.76750	0.79780
20	0.57352	0.61573	0.65599	0.69397	0.72945
21	0.48523	0.52902	0.57178	0.61309	0.65256
22	0.39904	0.44231	0.48558	0.52835	0.57017
23	0.31872	0.35954	0.40133	0.44362	0.48590
24	0.24714	0.28396	0.32258	0.36257	0.40348
25	0.18600	0.21783	0.25203	0.28827	0.32620
26	0.13586	0.16229	0.19136	0.22289	0.25665
27	0.09633	0.11742	0.14119	0.16757	0.19646
28	0.06631	0.08253	0.10123	0.12249	0.14630
29	0.04434	0.05636	0.07056	0.08707	0.10600
30	0.02880	0.03741	0.04781	0.06020	0.07473
31	0.01819	0.02414	0.03151	0.04050	0.05128
32	0.01117	0.01515	0.02021	0.02652	0.03425

Port no.	Traffic in erlangs				
	20.50	21.00	21.50	22.00	22.50
33	0.00667	0.00926	0.01262	0.01690	0.02228
34	0.00388	0.00550	0.00767	0.01049	0.01412
35	0.00219	0.00318	0.00454	0.00635	0.00872
36	0.00120	0.00179	0.00262	0.00374	0.00525
37	0.00064	0.00098	0.00147	0.00215	0.00308
38	0.00033	0.00052	0.00080	0.00120	0.00176
39	0.00016	0.00027	0.00042	0.00065	0.00098
40	0.00008	0.00013	0.00022	0.00034	0.00053
41	0.00003	0.00006	0.00010	0.00017	0.00028
42	0.00001	0.00002	0.00004	0.00008	0.00014
43	0.00000	0.00000	0.00001	0.00003	0.00006
44	0.00001	0.00001	0.00000	0.00001	0.00002

Port no.	Traffic in erlangs				
	23.00	23.50	24.00	24.50	25.00
1	1.00000	1.00000	1.00000	1.00000	1.00000
2	1.00000	1.00000	1.00000	1.00000	1.00000
3	1.00000	1.00000	1.00000	1.00000	1.00000
4	1.00000	1.00000	1.00000	1.00000	1.00000
5	1.00000	1.00000	1.00000	1.00000	1.00000
6	0.99999	1.00000	1.00000	1.00000	1.00000
7	0.99997	0.99998	0.99999	0.99999	0.99999
8	0.99990	0.99993	0.99995	0.99997	0.99998
9	0.99970	0.99979	0.99985	0.99989	0.99992
10	0.99919	0.99941	0.99957	0.99969	0.99978
11	0.99802	0.99853	0.99891	0.99920	0.99941
12	0.99557	0.99665	0.99748	0.99811	0.99858
13	0.99088	0.99296	0.99460	0.99587	0.99686
14	0.98257	0.98630	0.98928	0.99166	0.99353
15	0.96893	0.97512	0.98017	0.98428	0.98760
16	0.94800	0.95759	0.96560	0.97224	0.97771
17	0.91792	0.93186	0.94374	0.95379	0.96225
18	0.87723	0.89628	0.91287	0.92722	0.93952
19	0.82523	0.84983	0.87172	0.89104	0.90796
20	0.76228	0.79238	0.81974	0.84439	0.86642
21	0.68989	0.72488	0.75736	0.78724	0.81450
22	0.61061	0.64934	0.68607	0.72057	0.75270
23	0.52773	0.56865	0.60830	0.64632	0.68246
24	0.44484	0.48621	0.52714	0.56723	0.60612
25	0.36541	0.40549	0.44599	0.48650	0.52659
26	0.29233	0.32960	0.36808	0.40737	0.44707
27	0.22769	0.26102	0.29617	0.33282	0.37060
28	0.17262	0.20132	0.23225	0.26516	0.29980
29	0.12738	0.15122	0.17745	0.20597	0.23659
30	0.09151	0.11062	0.13211	0.15595	0.18209

31	0.06400	0.07882	0.09583	0.11511	0.13668
32	0.04360	0.05471	0.06775	0.08283	0.10005
33	0.02893	0.03701	0.04669	0.05812	0.07144
34	0.01871	0.02440	0.03137	0.03977	0.04977
35	0.01179	0.01569	0.02055	0.02655	0.03383
36	0.00725	0.00983	0.01314	0.01730	0.02244
37	0.00434	0.00602	0.00820	0.01100	0.01454
38	0.00254	0.00359	0.00499	0.00683	0.00919
39	0.00145	0.00209	0.00297	0.00414	0.00568
40	0.00080	0.00119	0.00172	0.00245	0.00343
41	0.00043	0.00065	0.00097	0.00141	0.00202
42	0.00022	0.00035	0.00053	0.00079	0.00116
43	0.00011	0.00018	0.00028	0.00043	0.00065
44	0.00005	0.00009	0.00014	0.00023	0.00035
45	0.00002	0.00004	0.00007	0.00011	0.00018
46	0.00000	0.00001	0.00003	0.00005	0.00009
47	0.00001	0.00000	0.00001	0.00002	0.00004
48	0.00001	0.00001	0.00001	0.00000	0.00001

Port no.	Traffic in erlangs				
	25.50	26.00	26.50	27.00	27.50
1	1.00000	1.00000	1.00000	1.00000	1.00000
2	1.00000	1.00000	1.00000	1.00000	1.00000
3	1.00000	1.00000	1.00000	1.00000	1.00000
4	1.00000	1.00000	1.00000	1.00000	1.00000
5	1.00000	1.00000	1.00000	1.00000	1.00000
6	1.00000	1.00000	1.00000	1.00000	1.00000
7	1.00000	1.00000	1.00000·	1.00000	1.00000
8	0.99998	0.99999	0.99999	0.99999	1.00000
9	0.99995	0.99996	0.99997	0.99998	0.99999
10	0.99984	0.99989	0.99992	0.99994	0.99996
11	0.99957	0.99969	0.99977	0.99984	0.99988
12	0.99895	0.99922	0.99942	0.99957	0.99969
13	0.99762	0.99820	0.99865	0.99898	0.99924
14	0.99501	0.99616	0.99706	0.99776	0.99830
15	0.99026	0.99238	0.99407	0.99540	0.99645
16	0.98218	0.98583	0.98878	0.99116	0.99306
17	0.96932	0.97518	0.98002	0.98399	0.98723
18	0.95001	0.95889	0.96636	0.97261	0.97780
19	0.92267	0.93537	0.94626	0.95554	0.96339
20	0.88597	0.90318	0.91822	0.93128	0.94254
21	0.83918	0.86133	0.88107	0.89853	0.91387
22	0.78236	0.80951	0.83418	0.85642	0.87633
23	0.71650	0.74828	0.77771	0.80475	0.82939
24	0.64348	0.67906	0.71264	0.74408	0.77328
25	0.56590	0.60407	0.64080	0.67584	0.70898
26	0.48677	0.52608	0.56464	0.60213	0.63826
27	0.40916	0.44809	0.48702	0.52559	0.56345

Port no.	Traffic in erlangs				
	25.50	26.00	26.50	27.00	27.50
28	0.33586	0.37299	0.41084	0.44905	0.48726
29	0.26910	0.30325	0.33873	0.37524	0.41243
30	0.21040	0.24073	0.27285	0.30652	0.34147
31	0.16051	0.18654	0.21465	0.24468	0.27642
32	0.11947	0.14109	0.16490	0.19081	0.21872
33	0.08676	0.10417	0.12370	0.14536	0.16913
34	0.06149	0.07507	0.09061	0.10818	0.12780
35	0.04254	0.05283	0.06483	0.07865	0.09438
36	0.02873	0.03630	0.04530	0.05587	0.06812
37	0.01895	0.02436	0.03093	0.03878	0.04806
38	0.01221	0.01598	0.02064	0.02631	0.03315
39	0.00768	0.01024	0.01346	0.01746	0.02236
40	0.00472	0.00641	0.00858	0.01132	0.01475
41	0.00284	0.00393	0.00535	0.00718	0.00952
42	0.00167	0.00235	0.00326	0.00446	0.00601
43	0.00095	0.00137	0.00194	0.00270	0.00371
44	0.00053	0.00078	0.00113	0.00160	0.00224
45	0.00029	0.00043	0.00064	0.00093	0.00132
46	0.00015	0.00023	0.00035	0.00052	0.00076
47	0.00007	0.00012	0.00019	0.00029	0.00043
48	0.00003	0.00005	0.00009	0.00015	0.00023
49	0.00001	0.00002	0.00004	0.00007	0.00012
50	0.00000	0.00000	0.00001	0.00003	0.00006
51	0.00001	0.00001	0.00000	0.00001	0.00002

Port no.	Traffic in erlangs				
	28.00	28.50	29.00	29.50	30.00
1	1.00000	1.00000	1.00000	1.00000	1.00000
2	1.00000	1.00000	1.00000	1.00000	1.00000
3	1.00000	1.00000	1.00000	1.00000	1.00000
4	1.00000	1.00000	1.00000	1.00000	1.00000
5	1.00000	1.00000	1.00000	1.00000	1.00000
6	1.00000	1.00000	1.00000	1.00000	1.00000
7	1.00000	1.00000	1.00000	1.00000	1.00000
8	1.00000	1.00000	1.00000	1.00000	1.00000
9	0.99999	0.99999	1.00000	1.00000	1.00000
10	0.99997	0.99998	0.99999	0.99999	0.99999
11	0.99991	0.99994	0.99996	0.99997	0.99998
12	0.99977	0.99983	0.99988	0.99991	0.99994
13	0.99944	0.99958	0.99969	0.99977	0.99983
14	0.99871	0.99903	0.99927	0.99945	0.99959
15	0.99727	0.99791	0.99840	0.99879	0.99908
16	0.99457	0.99578	0.99672	0.99747	0.99805
17	0.98986	0.99198	0.99368	0.99504	0.99613

18	0.98209	0.98561	0.98849	0.99083	0.99273
19	0.97000	0.97553	0.98013	0.98394	0.98707
20	0.95219	0.96041	0.96737	0.97322	0.97813
21	0.92726	0.93886	0.94886	0.95742	0.96471
22	0.89401	0.90962	0.92331	0.93523	0.94556
23	0.85170	0.87174	0.88962	0.90547	0.91943
24	0.80019	0.82480	0.84715	0.86730	0.88535
25	0.74009	0.76906	0.79582	0.82038	0.84275
26	0.67278	0.70551	0.73629	0.76502	0.79164
27	0.60030	0.63585	0.66988	0.70220	0.73266
28	0.52513	0.56233	0.59856	0.63357	0.66712
29	0.44996	0.48749	0.52469	0.56126	0.59691
30	0.37738	0.41394	0.45082	0.48770	0.52427
31	0.30964	0.34407	0.37941	0.41537	0.45164
32	0.24845	0.27983	0.31261	0.34654	0.38135
33	0.19492	0.22262	0.25207	0.28309	0.31545
34	0.14949	0.17321	0.19887	0.22636	0.25554
35	0.11209	0.13179	0.15349	0.17715	0.20268
36	0.08216	0.09807	0.11590	0.13567	0.15737
37	0.05888	0.07137	0.08561	0.10167	0.11961
38	0.04127	0.05080	0.06187	0.07457	0.08900
39	0.02829	0.03538	0.04375	0.05353	0.06483
40	0.01897	0.02411	0.03028	0.03762	0.04623
41	0.01245	0.01608	0.02052	0.02588	0.03229
42	0.00799	0.01049	0.01361	0.01744	0.02209
43	0.00502	0.00671	0.00884	0.01150	0.01480
44	0.00309	0.00419	0.00562	0.00744	0.00972
45	0.00186	0.00257	0.00350	0.00471	0.00625
46	0.00109	0.00154	0.00213	0.00292	0.00394
47	0.00063	0.00090	0.00127	0.00177	0.00243
48	0.00035	0.00051	0.00074	0.00105	0.00147
49	0.00019	0.00028	0.00042	0.00061	0.00087
50	0.00009	0.00015	0.00023	0.00034	0.00050
51	0.00004	0.00007	0.00012	0.00019	0.00028
52	0.00001	0.00003	0.00006	0.00009	0.00015
53	0.00000	0.00001	0.00002	0.00004	0.00007
54	0.00001	0.00000	0.00000	0.00001	0.00003

Port no.	Traffic in erlangs				
	30.50	31.00	31.50	32.00	32.50
1	1.00000	1.00000	1.00000	1.00000	1.00000
2	1.00000	1.00000	1.00000	1.00000	1.00000
3	1.00000	1.00000	1.00000	1.00000	1.00000
4	1.00000	1.00000	1.00000	1.00000	1.00000
5	1.00000	1.00000	1.00000	1.00000	1.00000
6	1.00000	1.00000	1.00000	1.00000	1.00000
7	1.00000	1.00000	1.00000	1.00000	1.00000
8	1.00000	1.00000	1.00000	1.00000	1.00000
9	1.00000	1.00000	1.00000	1.00000	1.00000

Port no.	Traffic in erlangs				
	30.50	31.00	31.50	32.00	32.50
10	1.00000	1.00000	1.00000	1.00000	1.00000
11	0.99998	0.99999	0.99999	0.99999	1.00000
12	0.99995	0.99997	0.99998	0.99998	0.99999
13	0.99988	0.99991	0.99993	0.99995	0.99997
14	0.99970	0.99978	0.99983	0.99988	0.99991
15	0.99930	0.99948	0.99961	0.99971	0.99978
16	0.99851	0.99886	0.99913	0.99934	0.99950
17	0.99699	0.99766	0.99819	0.99861	0.99893
18	0.99426	0.99548	0.99646	0.99723	0.99784
19	0.98963	0.99172	0.99341	0.99478	0.99588
20	0.98221	0.98559	0.98837	0.99066	0.99252
21	0.97089	0.97608	0.98043	0.98406	0.98707
22	0.95444	0.96205	0.96852	0.97400	0.97862
23	0.93165	0.94228	0.95147	0.95938	0.96614
24	0.90142	0.91563	0.92812	0.93903	0.94851
25	0.86300	0.88120	0.89746	0.91190	0.92464
26	0.81613	0.83852	0.85884	0.87717	0.89360
27	0.76115	0.78762	0.81204	0.83443	0.85481
28	0.69905	0.72919	0.75745	0.78377	0.80811
29	0.63139	0.66450	0.69604	0.72587	0.75390
30	0.56024	0.59534	0.62932	0.66199	0.69316
31	0.48791	0.52388	0.55928	0.59384	0.62735
32	0.41674	0.45242	0.48810	0.52350	0.55836
33	0.34890	0.38319	0.41804	0.45316	0.48829
34	0.28621	0.31816	0.35116	0.38495	0.41928
35	0.22996	0.25886	0.28919	0.32075	0.35331
36	0.18095	0.20634	0.23343	0.26206	0.29206
37	0.13943	0.16112	0.18463	0.20988	0.23676
38	0.10520	0.12323	0.14309	0.16476	0.18819
39	0.07773	0.09232	0.10865	0.12676	0.14665
40	0.05624	0.06775	0.08084	0.09558	0.11203
41	0.03986	0.04871	0.05894	0.07064	0.08390
42	0.02768	0.03431	0.04211	0.05117	0.06161
43	0.01883	0.02369	0.02949	0.03634	0.04435
44	0.01255	0.01602	0.02024	0.02530	0.03131
45	0.00820	0.01063	0.01362	0.01728	0.02168
46	0.00525	0.00691	0.00899	0.01157	0.01473
47	0.00329	0.00440	0.00582	0.00760	0.00981
48	0.00202	0.00275	0.00369	0.00489	0.00641
49	0.00122	0.00168	0.00230	0.00309	0.00411
50	0.00072	0.00101	0.00140	0.00191	0.00259
51	0.00041	0.00059	0.00083	0.00116	0.00159
52	0.00023	0.00033	0.00048	0.00069	0.00096
53	0.00012	0.00018	0.00027	0.00040	0.00057
54	0.00006	0.00009	0.00015	0.00022	0.00032
55	0.00002	0.00004	0.00007	0.00012	0.00018

56	0.00000	0.00001	0.00003	0.00006	0.00009
57	0.00001	0.00000	0.00001	0.00002	0.00004
58	0.00001	0.00001	0.00001	0.00000	0.00001

Port no.	Traffic in erlangs				
	33.00	33.50	34.00	34.50	35.00
1	1.00000	1.00000	1.00000	1.00000	1.00000
2	1.00000	1.00000	1.00000	1.00000	1.00000
3	1.00000	1.00000	1.00000	1.00000	1.00000
4	1.00000	1.00000	1.00000	1.00000	1.00000
5	1.00000	1.00000	1.00000	1.00000	1.00000
6	1.00000	1.00000	1.00000	1.00000	1.00000
7	1.00000	1.00000	1.00000	1.00000	1.00000
8	1.00000	1.00000	1.00000	1.00000	1.00000
9	1.00000	1.00000	1.00000	1.00000	1.00000
10	1.00000	1.00000	1.00000	1.00000	1.00000
11	1.00000	1.00000	1.00000	1.00000	1.00000
12	0.99999	0.99999	1.00000	1.00000	1.00000
13	0.99998	0.99998	0.99999	0.99999	0.99999
14	0.99993	0.99995	0.99996	0.99997	0.99998
15	0.99984	0.99988	0.99991	0.99993	0.99995
16	0.99962	0.99972	0.99979	0.99984	0.99988
17	0.99918	0.99938	0.99953	0.99964	0.99973
18	0.99833	0.99871	0.99900	0.99923	0.99941
19	0.99676	0.99746	0.99802	0.99846	0.99880
20	0.99404	0.99526	0.99625	0.99704	0.99768
21	0.98955	0.99158	0.99325	0.99460	0.99570
22	0.98249	0.98571	0.98839	0.99060	0.99242
23	0.97190	0.97677	0.98088	0.98432	0.98719
24	0.95671	0.96375	0.96977	0.97489	0.97923
25	0.93582	0.94557	0.95404	0.96135	0.96763
26	0.90824	0.92122	0.93264	0.94265	0.95138
27	0.87325	0.88983	0.90466	0.91785	0.92951
28	0.83047	0.85090	0.86943	0.88616	0.90116
29	0.78006	0.80431	0.82665	0.84710	0.86572
30	0.72269	0.75049	0.77649	0.80065	0.82295
31	0.65959	0.69040	0.71964	0.74722	0.77305
32	0.59242	0.62546	0.65730	0.68776	0.71672
33	0.52314	0.55748	0.59105	0.62365	0.65510
34	0.45387	0.48846	0.52280	0.55664	0.58975
35	0.38663	0.42046	0.45455	0.48863	0.52247
36	0.32324	0.35538	0.38824	0.42160	0.45520
37	0.26513	0.29481	0.32563	0.35736	0.38979
38	0.21330	0.23998	0.26809	0.29746	0.32792
39	0.16829	0.19164	0.21660	0.24308	0.27093
40	0.13021	0.15011	0.17172	0.19497	0.21979
41	0.09879	0.11533	0.13357	0.15348	0.17504
42	0.07350	0.08692	0.10193	0.11856	0.13684

Port no.	Traffic in erlangs				
	33.00	33.50	34.00	34.50	35.00
43	0.05363	0.06425	0.07632	0.08988	0.10501
44	0.03838	0.04660	0.05607	0.06687	0.07910
45	0.02694	0.03315	0.04042	0.04883	0.05849
46	0.01855	0.02314	0.02859	0.03500	0.04246
47	0.01254	0.01586	0.01986	0.02463	0.03026
48	0.00831	0.01066	0.01353	0.01701	0.02118
49	0.00541	0.00704	0.00906	0.01154	0.01455
50	0.00345	0.00456	0.00595	0.00768	0.00982
51	0.00216	0.00290	0.00384	0.00502	0.00651
52	0.00133	0.00181	0.00243	0.00323	0.00424
53	0.00080	0.00110	0.00151	0.00203	0.00271
54	0.00047	0.00066	0.00092	0.00125	0.00170
55	0.00026	0.00038	0.00054	0.00076	0.00104
56	0.00014	0.00021	0.00031	0.00045	0.00063
57	0.00007	0.00011	0.00017	0.00026	0.00037
58	0.00003	0.00006	0.00009	0.00014	0.00021
59	0.00001	0.00002	0.00004	0.00007	0.00011
60	0.00001	0.00000	0.00001	0.00003	0.00005

Port no.	Traffic in erlangs				
	35.50	36.00	36.50	37.00	37.50
1	1.00000	1.00000	1.00000	1.00000	1.00000
2	1.00000	1.00000	1.00000	1.00000	1.00000
3	1.00000	1.00000	1.00000	1.00000	1.00000
4	1.00000	1.00000	1.00000	1.00000	1.00000
5	1.00000	1.00000	1.00000	1.00000	1.00000
6	1.00000	1.00000	1.00000	1.00000	1.00000
7	1.00000	1.00000	1.00000	1.00000	1.00000
8	1.00000	1.00000	1.00000	1.00000	1.00000
9	1.00000	1.00000	1.00000	1.00000	1.00000
10	1.00000	1.00000	1.00000	1.00000	1.00000
11	1.00000	1.00000	1.00000	1.00000	1.00000
12	1.00000	1.00000	1.00000	1.00000	1.00000
13	1.00000	1.00000	1.00000	1.00000	1.00000
14	0.99999	0.99999	0.99999	0.99999	1.00000
15	0.99996	0.99997	0.99998	0.99999	0.99999
16	0.99991	0.99993	0.99995	0.99996	0.99997
17	0.99980	0.99985	0.99988	0.99991	0.99994
18	0.99955	0.99966	0.99974	0.99980	0.99985
19	0.99907	0.99929	0.99945	0.99958	0.99968
20	0.99818	0.99858	0.99889	0.99914	0.99934
21	0.99659	0.99730	0.99787	0.99833	0.99869
22	0.99390	0.99512	0.99610	0.99690	0.99754
23	0.98957	0.99154	0.99317	0.99450	0.99558

24	0.98288	0.98595	0.98851	0.99063	0.99239
25	0.97299	0.97755	0.98142	0.98467	0.98740
26	0.95894	0.96547	0.97107	0.97585	0.97992
27	0.93976	0.94873	0.95654	0.96330	0.96913
28	0.91454	0.92642	0.93689	0.94610	0.95414
29	0.88257	0.89772	0.91129	0.92337	0.93406
30	0.84342	0.86211	0.87906	0.89436	0.90810
31	0.79711	0.81937	0.83985	0.85859	0.87564
32	0.74407	0.76974	0.79369	0.81590	0.83639
33	0.68522	0.71390	0.74103	0.76654	0.79038
34	0.62192	0.65299	0.68279	0.71119	0.73811
35	0.55583	0.58849	0.62026	0.65096	0.68045
36	0.48879	0.52216	0.55506	0.58729	0.61867
37	0.42269	0.45582	0.48895	0.52185	0.55432
38	0.35926	0.39127	0.42373	0.45641	0.48910
39	0.30001	0.33012	0.36109	0.39270	0.42473
40	0.24607	0.27368	0.30246	0.33225	0.36285
41	0.19820	0.22288	0.24896	0.27633	0.30483
42	0.15676	0.17827	0.20134	0.22587	0.25176
43	0.12173	0.14004	0.15995	0.18142	0.20438
44	0.09280	0.10803	0.12482	0.14316	0.16306
45	0.06947	0.08184	0.09567	0.11100	0.12784
46	0.05106	0.06089	0.07203	0.08455	0.09850
47	0.03685	0.04450	0.05328	0.06328	0.07457
48	0.02612	0.03194	0.03871	0.04653	0.05548
49	0.01819	0.02252	0.02763	0.03362	0.04057
50	0.01244	0.01560	0.01938	0.02388	0.02916
51	0.00835	0.01061	0.01336	0.01666	0.02060
52	0.00551	0.00710	0.00905	0.01143	0.01430
53	0.00357	0.00466	0.00602	0.00771	0.00977
54	0.00227	0.00301	0.00394	0.00511	0.00655
55	0.00142	0.00191	0.00253	0.00333	0.00432
56	0.00087	0.00118	0.00160	0.00213	0.00280
57	0.00052	0.00072	0.00099	0.00134	0.00179
58	0.00030	0.00043	0.00060	0.00082	0.00112
59	0.00017	0.00025	0.00035	0.00049	0.00068
60	0.00009	0.00013	0.00020	0.00029	0.00041

Port no.	Traffic in erlangs				
	38.00	38.50	39.00	39.50	40.00
1	1.00000	1.00000	1.00000	1.00000	1.00000
2	1.00000	1.00000	1.00000	1.00000	1.00000
3	1.00000	1.00000	1.00000	1.00000	1.00000
4	1.00000	1.00000	1.00000	1.00000	1.00000
5	1.00000	1.00000	1.00000	1.00000	1.00000
6	1.00000	1.00000	1.00000	1.00000	1.00000
7	1.00000	1.00000	1.00000	1.00000	1.00000
8	1.00000	1.00000	1.00000	1.00000	1.00000

Port no.	Traffic in erlangs				
	38.00	38.50	39.00	39.50	40.00
9	1.00000	1.00000	1.00000	1.00000	1.00000
10	1.00000	1.00000	1.00000	1.00000	1.00000
11	1.00000	1.00000	1.00000	1.00000	1.00000
12	1.00000	1.00000	1.00000	1.00000	1.00000
13	1.00000	1.00000	1.00000	1.00000	1.00000
14	1.00000	1.00000	1.00000	1.00000	1.00000
15	0.99999	0.99999	1.00000	1.00000	1.00000
16	0.99998	0.99999	0.99999	0.99999	0.99999
17	0.99995	0.99996	0.99997	0.99998	0.99999
18	0.99989	0.99992	0.99994	0.99995	0.99997
19	0.99976	0.99981	0.99986	0.99989	0.99992
20	0.99949	0.99961	0.99970	0.99977	0.99982
21	0.99898	0.99921	0.99938	0.99952	0.99963
22	0.99806	0.99847	0.99880	0.99906	0.99927
23	0.99647	0.99719	0.99776	0.99823	0.99860
24	0.99384	0.99503	0.99601	0.99680	0.99744
25	0.98968	0.99158	0.99315	0.99445	0.99552
26	0.98336	0.98627	0.98870	0.99074	0.99243
27	0.97413	0.97840	0.98203	0.98510	0.98769
28	0.96112	0.96717	0.97238	0.97685	0.98066
29	0.94348	0.95174	0.95895	0.96521	0.97062
30	0.92036	0.93125	0.94088	0.94935	0.95677
31	0.89107	0.90496	0.91740	0.92848	0.93830
32	0.85517	0.87231	0.88785	0.90188	0.91448
33	0.81254	0.83302	0.85184	0.86904	0.88469
34	0.76345	0.78718	0.80928	0.82974	0.84859
35	0.70859	0.73528	0.76047	0.78409	0.80612
36	0.64902	0.67819	0.70607	0.73256	0.75758
37	0.58614	0.61714	0.64714	0.67602	0.70365
38	0.52156	0.55361	0.58503	0.61566	0.64534
39	0.45699	0.48924	0.52128	0.55292	0.58397
40	0.39407	0.42570	0.45754	0.48938	0.52102
41	0.33429	0.36454	0.39538	0.42663	0.45807
42	0.27889	0.30711	0.33626	0.36617	0.39665
43	0.22876	0.25447	0.28136	0.30932	0.33817
44	0.18447	0.20733	0.23157	0.25709	0.28376
45	0.14621	0.16609	0.18744	0.21020	0.23430
46	0.11391	0.13080	0.14919	0.16904	0.19033
47	0.08722	0.10127	0.11676	0.13370	0.15210
48	0.06564	0.07708	0.08985	0.10400	0.11956
49	0.04856	0.05768	0.06799	0.07956	0.09245
50	0.03532	0.04243	0.05059	0.05986	0.07031
51	0.02525	0.03069	0.03701	0.04429	0.05260
52	0.01775	0.02183	0.02663	0.03224	0.03872
53	0.01227	0.01527	0.01885	0.02308	0.02803
54	0.00833	0.01050	0.01312	0.01625	0.01997
55	0.00557	0.00711	0.00898	0.01126	0.01400
56	0.00366	0.00473	0.00605	0.00768	0.00965
57	0.00236	0.00309	0.00401	0.00515	0.00655
58	0.00150	0.00199	0.00261	0.00339	0.00437
59	0.00093	0.00125	0.00167	0.00220	0.00287
60	0.00057	0.00078	0.00105	0.00140	0.00185

APPENDIX C

CAPACITY PLANNING TABLES

The tables in this appendix were generated by the revised capacity planner program contained in Chapter 7. Each table indicates the traffic in erlangs a given number of ports can support based upon a defined grade of service.

CAPACITY PLANNER

The following table displays the traffic carrying capacity for the indicated number of ports that will result in a predefined grade of service

Number of ports	Traffic supported in erlangs per port for indicated grade of service			
	0.010	0.015	0.020	0.025
1	0.010	0.016	0.020	0.025
2	0.150	0.188	0.225	0.254
3	0.463	0.538	0.603	0.663
4	0.877	0.987	1.093	1.172
5	1.366	1.513	1.653	1.777
6	1.915	2.099	2.282	2.416
7	2.497	2.733	2.929	3.100
8	3.124	3.402	3.610	3.832
9	3.773	4.075	4.341	4.565
10	4.442	4.833	5.072	5.309
11	5.150	5.507	5.858	6.104
12	5.858	6.323	6.616	6.912
13	6.616	7.018	7.421	7.723
14	7.320	7.784	8.210	8.550
15	8.150	8.616	8.989	9.374
16	8.886	9.374	9.836	10.184
17	9.667	10.224	10.619	11.010
18	10.456	11.010	11.451	11.922
19	11.189	11.830	12.304	12.745
20	12.015	12.646	13.135	13.611
21	12.844	13.507	14.038	14.528
22	13.611	14.329	14.850	15.329
23	14.440	15.211	15.807	16.239
24	15.329	16.051	16.673	17.100
25	16.051	16.836	17.503	17.979
26	16.968	17.773	18.361	18.905
27	17.773	18.627	19.265	19.827
28	18.627	19.521	20.135	20.750
29	19.521	20.293	21.076	21.631
30	20.293	21.239	21.874	22.554
31	21.239	22.030	22.815	23.437
32	22.021	22.904	23.661	24.323
33	22.904	23.846	24.609	25.292
34	23.846	24.804	25.490	26.168
35	24.609	25.688	26.464	27.119
36	25.490	26.464	27.329	28.076
37	26.464	27.435	28.216	28.944
38	27.224	28.326	29.171	29.953

39	28.076	29.284	30.070	30.776
40	28.881	30.187	31.016	31.730
41	29.953	31.016	31.854	32.714
42	30.659	31.854	32.842	33.593
43	31.616	32.842	33.673	34.600
44	32.604	33.673	34.735	35.546

Number of ports	Traffic supported in erlangs per port for indicated grade of service			
	0.030	0.035	0.040	0.045
1	0.031	0.036	0.042	0.047
2	0.280	0.307	0.331	0.360
3	0.715	0.768	0.814	0.857
4	1.258	1.327	1.398	1.464
5	1.871	1.975	2.052	2.137
6	2.536	2.654	2.775	2.862
7	3.259	3.376	3.509	3.631
8	3.981	4.137	4.274	4.409
9	4.763	4.918	5.072	5.227
10	5.529	5.725	5.891	6.054
11	6.323	6.519	6.727	6.912
12	7.164	7.371	7.576	7.784
13	7.963	8.210	8.418	8.649
14	8.818	9.060	9.313	9.526
15	9.667	9.913	10.184	10.415
16	10.497	10.778	11.059	11.320
17	11.364	11.674	11.969	12.208
18	12.208	12.548	12.844	13.135
19	13.135	13.454	13.771	14.038
20	13.984	14.329	14.642	14.976
21	14.850	15.270	15.568	15.865
22	15.807	16.176	16.485	16.796
23	16.673	17.100	17.435	17.773
24	17.569	17.979	18.361	18.688
25	18.505	18.905	19.265	19.673
26	19.357	19.827	20.214	20.605
27	20.293	20.750	21.158	21.557
28	21.239	21.716	22.119	22.466
29	22.119	22.641	23.083	23.437
30	23.083	23.569	24.032	24.418
31	24.032	24.513	24.902	25.391
32	24.902	25.391	25.874	26.367
33	25.874	26.367	26.805	27.329
34	26.805	27.329	27.754	28.271
35	27.754	28.216	28.770	29.227
36	28.659	29.171	29.687	30.187
37	29.586	30.187	30.659	31.137
38	30.541	31.137	31.616	32.103
39	31.496	32.103	32.604	33.099

Number of ports	Traffic supported in erlangs per port for indicated grade of service			
	0.030	0.035	0.040	0.045
40	32.354	32.971	33.593	34.068
41	33.346	33.936	34.532	35.070
42	34.333	34.938	35.546	36.100
43	35.276	35.890	36.523	37.011
44	36.241	36.867	37.499	38.033

Number of ports	Traffic supported in erlangs per port for indicated grade of service			
	0.050	0.055	0.060	0.065
1	0.052	0.058	0.064	0.069
2	0.384	0.404	0.425	0.451
3	0.902	0.943	0.980	1.018
4	1.525	1.580	1.641	1.694
5	2.221	2.294	2.362	2.439
6	2.957	3.051	3.136	3.221
7	3.743	3.846	3.951	4.043
8	4.547	4.656	4.779	4.899
9	5.368	5.504	5.638	5.770
10	6.225	6.372	6.519	6.649
11	7.081	7.235	7.396	7.546
12	7.963	8.119	8.303	8.450
13	8.818	9.024	9.216	9.374
14	9.722	9.913	10.107	10.302
15	10.619	10.857	11.059	11.233
16	11.541	11.784	11.969	12.208
17	12.450	12.695	12.937	13.135
18	13.402	13.611	13.877	14.108
19	14.329	14.585	14.843	15.064
20	15.270	15.508	15.778	16.051
21	16.176	16.485	16.734	17.000
22	17.133	17.435	17.705	17.979
23	18.050	18.361	18.688	18.979
24	19.053	19.335	19.673	19.942
25	19.981	20.293	20.605	20.913
26	20.913	21.306	21.631	21.938
27	21.874	22.249	22.554	22.904
28	22.859	23.214	23.569	23.892
29	23.846	24.218	24.561	24.902
30	24.804	25.194	25.539	25.874
31	25.773	26.168	26.545	26.909
32	26.753	27.119	27.542	27.863
33	27.754	28.106	28.547	28.881
34	28.659	29.114	29.486	29.895

35	29.687	30.070	30.541	30.896
36	30.659	31.077	31.496	31.916
37	31.616	32.103	32.479	32.906
38	32.604	33.099	33.531	33.936
39	33.593	34.068	34.532	34.938
40	34.600	35.070	35.546	35.960
41	35.546	36.100	36.523	37.011
42	36.581	37.110	37.499	37.959
43	37.542	38.107	38.530	39.043
44	38.530	39.043	39.578	40.037

Number of ports	Traffic supported in erlangs per port for indicated grade of service			
	0.070	0.075	0.080	0.085
1	0.075	0.081	0.086	0.093
2	0.471	0.493	0.612	0.534
3	1.060	1.093	1.132	1.163
4	1.747	1.804	1.855	1.901
5	2.506	2.575	2.634	2.694
6	3.307	3.389	3.456	3.540
7	4.137	4.225	4.324	4.409
8	4.994	5.111	5.207	5.309
9	5.868	6.007	6.104	6.225
10	6.779	6.912	7.026	7.164
11	7.693	7.828	7.963	8.088
12	8.616	8.751	8.920	9.060
13	9.559	9.722	9.874	10.028
14	10.497	10.653	10.815	11.010
15	11.451	11.629	11.784	11.969
16	12.401	12.597	12.794	12.962
17	13.350	13.559	13.771	13.957
18	14. 29	14.528	14.742	14.947
19	15.299	15.508	15.748	15.958
20	16.270	16.485	16.734	16.968
21	17.233	17.503	17.739	17.979
22	18.261	18.505	18.749	18.979
23	19.227	19.483	19.750	19.981
24	20.214	20.487	20.750	21.035
25	21.239	21.473	21.795	22.021
26	22.206	22.510	22.815	23.083
27	23.214	23.523	23.799	24.125
28	24.218	24.513	24.804	25.145
29	25.194	25.539	25.874	26.168
30	26.219	26.545	26.909	27.224
31	27.224	27.596	27.915	28.216
32	28.216	28.603	28.944	29.284
33	29.284	29.586	29.953	30.304
34	30.304	30.659	31.016	31.376
35	31.315	31.668	32.041	32.416

Number of ports	Traffic supported in erlangs per port for indicated grade of service			
	0.070	0.075	0.080	0.085
36	32.291	32.714	33.099	33.470
37	33.346	33.738	34.068	34.466
38	34.333	34.735	35.139	35.546
39	35.411	35.820	36.171	36.581
40	36.382	36.796	37.255	37.591
41	37.438	37.811	38.240	38.671
42	38.455	38.891	39.348	39.731
43	39.501	39.885	40.350	40.739
44	40.508	40.974	41.421	41.826

Number of ports	Traffic supported in erlangs per port for indicated grade of service			
	0.090	0.095	0.100	0.105
1	0.099	0.105	0.111	0.117
2	0.554	0.575	0.595	0.614
3	1.199	1.238	1.267	1.306
4	1.945	1.998	2.044	2.091
5	2.764	2.818	2.884	2.945
6	3.610	3.685	3.758	3.832
7	4.494	4.590	4.671	4.744
8	5.407	5.504	5.594	5.692
9	6.323	6.443	6.542	6.649
10	7.264	7.396	7.517	7.635
11	8.242	8.367	8.483	8.616
12	9.198	9.344	9.471	9.597
13	10.184	10.334	10.456	10.619
14	11.146	11.320	11.474	11.629
15	12.161	12.304	12.499	12.646
16	13.135	13.324	13.507	13.664
17	14.163	14.329	14.528	14.714
18	15.152	15.357	15.538	15.748
19	16.176	16.357	16.575	16.796
20	17.166	17.401	17.603	17.840
21	18.191	18.433	18.652	18.868
22	19.227	19.445	19.673	19.904
23	20.253	20.487	20.750	20.994
24	21.306	21.557	21.795	22.021
25	22.292	22.554	22.815	23.083
26	23.348	23.615	23.892	24.125
27	24.370	24.659	24.950	25.194
28	25.441	25.688	25.975	26.270
29	26.464	26.753	27.066	27.329
30	27.489	27.808	28.106	28.436

31	28.547	28.881	29.171	29.486
32	29.586	29.895	30.245	30.541
33	30.659	30.956	31.315	31.616
34	31.668	32.041	32.354	32.714
35	32.714	33.099	33.404	33.804
36	33.804	34.134	34.532	34.870
37	34.870	35.208	35.546	35.960
38	35.890	36.241	36.652	37.011
39	36.939	37.304	37.738	38.107
40	38.033	38.389	38.815	39.195
41	39.043	39.501	39.885	40.272
42	40.115	40.508	40.898	41.340
43	41.210	41.583	41.989	42. 98
44	42.234	42.697	43.115	43.506

Number of ports	Traffic supported in erlangs per port for indicated grade of service			
	0.110	0.115	0.120	0.125
1	0.124	0.130	0.136	0.142
2	0.636	0.658	0.678	0.696
3	1.336	1.375	1.409	1.442
4	2.137	2.187	2.229	2.273
5	3.003	3.063	3.112	3.173
6	3.906	3.966	4.043	4.105
7	4.833	4.918	4.994	5.072
8	5.792	5.868	5.961	6.054
9	6.753	6.858	6.965	7.053
10	7.738	7.843	7.963	8.072
11	8.734	8.852	8.989	9.095
12	9.741	9.874	10.009	10.146
13	10.757	10.897	11.038	11.189
14	11.784	11.922	12.085	12.232
15	12.819	12.987	13.135	13.298
16	13.850	14.011	14.190	14.357
17	14.889	15.064	15.240	15.417
18	15.927	16.113	16.302	16.485
19	16.968	17.166	17.367	17.569
20	18.050	18.226	18.433	18.627
21	19.082	19.300	19.521	19.750
22	20.135	20.369	20.605	20.832
23	21.199	21.431	21.673	21.895
24	22.292	22.510	22.770	22.993
25	23.348	23.569	23.846	24.078
26	24.418	24.659	24.902	25.194
27	25.490	25.773	26.026	26.270
28	26.545	26.805	27.119	27.382
29	27.650	27.915	28.216	28.492
30	28.714	29.000	29.284	29.586
31	29.778	30.070	30.364	30.659

Number of ports	Traffic supported in erlangs per port for indicated grade of service			
	0.110	0.115	0.120	0.125
32	30.836	31.193	31.496	31.792
33	31.916	32.228	32.573	32.906
34	33.035	33.346	33.673	34.001
35	34.134	34.466	34.802	35.070
36	35.208	35.546	35.890	36.241
37	36.311	36.652	36.939	37.304
38	37.377	37.738	38.107	38.455
39	38.455	38.815	39.195	39.539
40	39.578	39.885	40.272	40.660
41	40.660	40.974	41.421	41.745
42	41.745	42.112	42.480	42.864
43	42.780	43.179	43.591	43.959
44	43.876	44.326	44.673	45.109

Number of ports	Traffic supported in erlangs per port for indicated grade of service			
	0.130	0.135	0.140	0.145
1	0.149	0.156	0.162	0.170
2	0.715	0.736	0.756	0.777
3	1.472	1.507	1.537	1.568
4	2.318	2.362	2.407	2.458
5	3.234	3.283	3.337	3.402
6	4.175	4.241	4.307	4.375
7	5.150	5.227	5.309	5.388
8	6.151	6.237	6.323	6.409
9	7.164	7.264	7.357	7.459
10	8.178	8.287	8.398	8.516
11	9.216	9.344	9.452	9.578
12	10.263	10.395	10.517	10.653
13	11.320	11.451	11.584	11.718
14	12.377	12.523	12.670	12.819
15	13.454	13.611	13.771	13.904
16	14.528	14.685	14.843	15.005
17	15.596	15.778	15.927	16.113
18	16.673	16.869	17.033	17.233
19	17.773	17.945	18.155	18.326
20	18.832	19.053	19.265	19.445
21	19.942	20.135	20.369	20.566
22	21.035	21.239	21.473	21.673
23	22.119	22.336	22.597	22.815
24	23.214	23.473	23.707	23.938
25	24.323	24.561	24.804	25.048
26	25.441	25.688	25.924	26.168

27	26.545	26.805	27.066	27.329
28	27.650	27.915	28.161	28.436
29	28.770	29.000	29.284	29.586
30	29.837	30.129	30.423	30.716
31	30.956	31.254	31.556	31.854
32	32.103	32.384	32.683	32.971
33	33.216	33.531	33.804	34.134
34	34.333	34.600	34.938	35.276
35	35.411	35.751	36.100	36.382
36	36.523	36.867	37.183	37.542
37	37.664	38.033	38.314	38.671
38	38.777	39.119	39.501	39.809
39	39.885	40.272	40.586	40.974
40	41.054	41.381	41.745	42.112
41	42.153	42.480	42.864	43.263
42	43.263	43.670	44.042	44.412
43	44.412	44.759	45.195	45.541
44	45.541	45.898	46.294	46.697

Number of ports	Traffic supported in erlangs per port for indicated grade of service			
	0.150	0.155	0.160	0.165
1	0.177	0.184	0.190	0.197
2	0.796	0.817	0.837	0.857
3	1.605	1.635	1.668	1.701
4	2.497	2.545	2.593	2.634
5	3.456	3.509	3.568	3.617
6	4.442	4.512	4.572	4.638
7	5.468	5.540	5.616	5.692
8	6.493	6.591	6.675	6.753
9	7.546	7.649	7.754	7.843
10	8.616	8.717	8.835	8.937
11	9.683	9.798	9.932	10.048
12	10.778	10.897	11.016	11.146
13	11.876	12.015	12.137	12.280
14	12.962	13.109	13.246	13.402
15	14.080	14.218	14.385	14.528
16	15.181	15.329	15.508	15.657
17	16.302	16.453	16.640	16.796
18	17.401	17.569	17.773	17.945
19	18.518	18.719	18.905	19.082
20	19.635	19.827	20.057	20.253
21	20.791	20.994	21.199	21.390
22	21.895	22.119	22.336	22.554
23	23.038	23.260	23.473	23.707
24	24.171	24.418	24.609	24.853
25	25.292	25.539	25.773	26.026
26	26.416	26.701	26.909	27.171
27	27.596	27.808	28.076	28.326

Number of ports	Traffic supported in erlangs per port for indicated grade of service			
	0.150	0.155	0.160	0.165
28	28.714	29.000	29.227	29.486
29	29.837	30.129	30.423	30.659
30	31.016	31.254	31.556	31.854
31	32.165	32.416	32.714	33.035
32	33.281	33.593	33.870	34.201
33	34.400	34.735	35.070	35.342
34	35.546	35.890	36.206	36.523
35	36.724	37.038	37.377	37.664
36	37.885	38.202	38.530	38.891
37	39.043	39.348	39.731	40.037
38	40.193	40.508	40.898	41.210
39	41.340	41.664	42.030	42.398
40	42.480	42.864	43.179	43.591
41	43.627	44.001	44.369	44.759
42	44.759	45.195	45.541	45.898
43	45.898	46.339	46.697	47.093
44	47.093	47.508	47.878	48.251

Number of ports	Traffic supported in erlangs per port for indicated grade of service			
	0.170	0.175	0.180	0.185
1	0.205	0.212	0.220	0.226
2	0.877	0.898	0.917	0.939
3	1.734	1.763	1.797	1.830
4	2.678	2.723	2.764	2.807
5	3.678	3.729	3.787	3.846
6	4.707	4.779	4.838	4.908
7	5.770	5.847	5.926	5.996
8	6.845	6.938	7.018	7.109
9	7.932	8.041	8.135	8.226
10	9.042	9.145	9.252	9.374
11	10.146	10.263	10.395	10.497
12	11.276	11.407	11.541	11.651
13	12.401	12.548	12.670	12.819
14	13.533	13.691	13.824	13.984
15	14.685	14.843	14.976	15.152
16	15.834	15.989	16.145	16.302
17	16.968	17.133	17.333	17.503
18	18.120	18.290	18.505	18.652
19	19.265	19.483	19.673	19.865
20	20.449	20.629	20.832	21.035
21	21.589	21.795	22.021	22.206
22	22.770	22.993	23.214	23.392

23	23.938	24.171	24.370	24.609
24	25.096	25.341	25.539	25.773
25	26.270	26.494	26.753	26.988
26	27.435	27.700	27.915	28.161
27	28.603	28.881	29.114	29.371
28	29.778	30.041	30.304	30.600
29	30.956	31.224	31.496	31.792
30	32.103	32.416	32.714	32.971
31	33.281	33.593	33.870	34.201
32	34.466	34.802	35.070	35.411
33	35.681	35.960	36.276	36.581
34	36.867	37.183	37.499	37.811
35	38.033	38.314	38.671	38.967
36	39.195	39.501	39.885	40.193
37	40.350	40.739	41.054	41.421
38	41.583	41.907	42.234	42.614
39	42.780	43.115	43.432	43.790
40	43.959	44.326	44.673	45.021
41	45.109	45.458	45.898	46.249
42	46.339	46.697	47.047	47.415
43	47.508	47.878	48.251	48.647
44	48.647	49.075	49.464	49.902

Number of ports	Traffic supported in erlangs per port for indicated grade of service			
	0.190	0.195	0.200	0.205
1	0.235	0.242	0.250	0.258
2	0.957	0.980	0.999	1.021
3	1.864	1.897	1.930	1.960
4	2.857	2.901	2.945	2.991
5	3.898	3.951	4.012	4.067
6	4.975	5.043	5.111	5.177
7	6.080	6.151	6.225	6.310
8	7.192	7.278	7.371	7.459
9	8.336	8.418	8.516	8.616
10	9.471	9.578	9.678	9.798
11	10.619	10.736	10.857	10.968
12	11.784	11.899	12.038	12.161
13	12.937	13.084	13.232	13.350
14	14.108	14.273	14.413	14.557
15	15.299	15.447	15.596	15.778
16	16.485	16.640	16.796	16.968
17	17.671	17.840	18.014	18.191
18	18.868	19.016	19.227	19.407
19	20.057	20.214	20.409	20.605
20	21.239	21.431	21.631	21.835
21	22.422	22.641	22.859	23.038
22	23.615	23.846	24.078	24.275
23	24.805	25.048	25.292	25.490

Number of ports	Traffic supported in erlangs per port for indicated grade of service			
	0.190	0.195	0.200	0.205
24	26.026	26.270	26.494	26.753
25	27.224	27.489	27.700	27.969
26	28.436	28.686	28.944	29.171
27	29.637	29.895	30.187	30.423
28	30.836	31.137	31.376	31.668
29	32.041	32.354	32.604	32.906
30	33.281	33.531	33.837	34.134
31	34.466	34.769	35.070	35.342
32	35.681	35.960	36.311	36.581
33	36.867	37.183	37.499	37.811
34	38.107	38.455	38.733	39.081
35	39.348	39.655	39.962	40.350
36	40.508	40.898	41.210	41.583
37	41.745	42.071	42.480	42.780
38	42.948	43.348	43.670	44.042
39	44.153	44.542	44.933	45.284
40	45.371	45.809	46.166	46.520
41	46.606	47.001	47.415	47.784
42	47.831	48.251	48.647	49.028
43	49.028	49.416	49.853	50.291
44	50.291	50.684	51.079	51.497

Number of ports	Traffic supported in erlangs per port for indicated grade of service			
	0.210	0.215	0.220	0.225
1	0.266	0.275	0.282	0.290
2	1.041	1.064	1.085	1.106
3	1.998	2.029	2.064	2.099
4	3.039	3.082	3.124	3.173
5	4.121	4.183	4.241	4.291
6	5.248	5.309	5.378	5.448
7	6.384	6.468	6.542	6.616
8	7.546	7.635	7.723	7.813
9	8.717	8.818	8.920	9.007
10	9.894	10.009	10.126	10.224
11	11.102	11.211	11.320	11.451
12	12.280	12.426	12.548	12.670
13	13.507	13.637	13.771	13.904
14	14.714	14.843	15.005	15.152
15	15.927	16.082	16.239	16.389
16	17.133	17.299	17.469	17.638
17	18.361	18.518	18.719	18.905
18	19.597	19.750	19.942	20.135

19	20.791	20.994	21.199	21.390
20	22.021	22.249	22.466	22.641
21	23.260	23.473	23.707	23.892
22	24.513	24.707	24.950	25.170
23	25.723	25.975	26.219	26.416
24	26.962	27.224	27.435	27.700
25	28.216	28.436	28.714	28.944
26	29.428	29.687	29.953	30.245
27	30.716	30.956	31.224	31.496
28	31.916	32.228	32.479	32.778
29	33.151	33.470	33.738	34.035
30	34.400	34.735	35.006	35.276
31	35.681	35.960	36.241	36.581
32	36.939	37.219	37.542	37.848
33	38.165	38.455	38.815	39.119
34	39.424	39.731	40.037	40.390
35	40.660	40.974	41.340	41.664
36	41.907	42.234	42.614	42.948
37	43.115	43.506	43.876	44.239
38	44.412	44.759	45.109	45.458
39	45.630	45.988	46.430	46.786
40	46.874	47.277	47.692	48.065
41	48.157	48.552	48.932	49.320
42	49.416	49.804	50.193	50.586
43	50.684	51.079	51.447	51.849
44	51.900	52.337	52.735	53.195

Number of ports	Traffic supported in erlangs per port for indicated grade of service			
	0.230	0.235	0.240	0.245
1	0.299	0.307	0.316	0.325
2	1.127	1.151	1.171	1.194
3	2.128	2.166	2.200	2.238
4	3.221	3.259	3.307	3.356
5	4.350	4.409	4.459	4.521
6	5.507	5.583	5.649	5.725
7	6.701	6.779	6.858	6.938
8	7.903	7.994	8.088	8.178
9	9.112	9.216	9.313	9.415
10	10.334	10.456	10.558	10.674
11	11.562	11.696	11.807	11.922
12	12.794	12.937	13.058	13.208
13	14.038	14.190	14.329	14.472
14	15.299	15.447	15.596	15.748
15	16.549	16.702	16.869	17.033
16	17.805	17.979	18.155	18.326
17	19.053	19.227	19.426	19.597
18	20.329	20.527	20.710	20.913
19	21.589	21.795	21.979	22.206

Number of ports	Traffic supported in erlangs per port for indicated grade of service			
	0.230	0.235	0.240	0.245
20	22.859	23.083	23.260	23.473
21	24.125	24.323	24.561	24.780
22	25.391	25.638	25.849	26.076
23	26.649	26.909	27.119	27.382
24	27.942	28.161	28.436	28.659
25	29.227	29.486	29.702	29.982
26	30.481	30.776	31.016	31.285
27	31.792	32.041	32.291	32.604
28	33.035	33.346	33.593	33.870
29	34.333	34.600	34.904	35.208
30	35.612	35.890	36.206	36.523
31	36.867	37.183	37.499	37.811
32	38.165	38.455	38.815	39.119
33	39.424	39.770	40.115	40.429
34	40.739	41.054	41.421	41.745
35	41.989	42.357	42.697	43.031
36	43.263	43.670	44.042	44.369
37	44.586	44.933	45.284	45.675
38	45.898	46.249	46.606	46.953
39	47.139	47.508	47.878	48.297
40	48.437	48.837	49.218	49.609
41	49.707	50.096	50.488	50.931
42	50.981	51.376	51.849	52.235
43	52.286	52.735	53.091	53.558
44	53.610	54.029	54.448	54.871

Number of ports	Traffic supported in erlangs per port for indicated grade of service			
	0.250	0.255	0.260	0.265
1	0.333	0.343	0.351	0.360
2	1.214	1.238	1.263	1.282
3	2.273	2.303	2.343	2.376
4	3.402	3.449	3.496	3.547
5	4.581	4.638	4.698	4.763
6	5.792	5.858	5.926	6.007
7	7.018	7.095	7.178	7.264
8	8.258	8.350	8.450	8.533
9	9.526	9.613	9.722	9.836
10	10.778	10.897	11.010	11.124
11	12.062	12.185	12.304	12.426
12	13.324	13.454	13.611	13.744
13	14.613	14.764	14.918	15.064
14	15.896	16.051	16.207	16.357

15	17.199	17.367	17.535	17.705
16	18.505	18.652	18.832	19.016
17	19.788	19.981	20.175	20.329
18	21.076	21.265	21.473	21.673
19	22.379	22.597	22.815	22.993
20	23.707	23.892	24.125	24.323
21	24.999	25.243	25.441	25.688
22	26.316	26.545	26.779	27.014
23	27.623	27.863	28.106	28.354
24	28.944	29.171	29.428	29.687
25	30.245	30.481	30.776	31.016
26	31.556	31.85	32.103	32.354
27	32.842	33.151	33.437	33.738
28	34.201	34.466	34.769	35.070
29	35.479	35.820	36.100	36.382
30	36.796	37.110	37.438	37.738
31	38.107	38.455	38.777	39.119
32	39.424	39.809	40.115	40.429
33	40.739	41.132	41.421	41.826
34	42.071	42.439	42.780	43.115
35	43.432	43.749	44.153	44.499
36	44.759	45.109	45.458	45.809
37	46.077	46.430	46.786	47.185
38	47.369	47.784	48.157	48.552
39	48.694	49.123	49.512	49.902
40	50.000	50.390	50.832	51.277
41	51.376	51.748	52.153	52.633
42	52.633	53.091	53.506	53.924
43	53.977	54.448	54.871	55.300
44	55.300	55.726	56.152	56.653

Number of ports	Traffic supported in erlangs per port for indicated grade of service			
	0.270	0.275	0.280	0.285
1	0.370	0.379	0.390	0.398
2	1.306	1.331	1.351	1.375
3	2.412	2.449	2.487	2.521
4	3.596	3.646	3.690	3.743
5	4.816	4.880	4.937	5.004
6	6.068	6.151	6.213	6.286
7	7.342	7.421	7.517	7.605
8	8.632	8.734	8.818	8.920
9	9.932	10.028	10.146	10.243
10	11.233	11.364	11.474	11.584
11	12.548	12.670	12.819	12.937
12	13.877	14.011	14.163	14.301
13	15.211	15.357	15.508	15.657
14	16.517	16.673	16.836	17.000
15	17.875	18.014	18.191	18.361

Number of ports	Traffic supported in erlangs per port for indicated grade of service			
	0.270	0.275	0.280	0.285
16	19.194	19.366	19.559	19.750
17	20.527	20.710	20.913	21.117
18	21.874	22.076	22.292	22.466
19	23.214	23.437	23.661	23.846
20	24.561	24.804	24.999	25.243
21	25.924	26.117	26.367	26.597
22	27.275	27.489	27.754	27.969
23	28.603	28.854	29.114	29.371
24	29.953	30.216	30.481	30.746
25	31.315	31.556	31.854	32.103
26	32.651	32.938	33.216	33.531
27	34.001	34.300	34.600	34.870
28	35.342	35.681	35.960	36.276
29	36.724	37.011	37.341	37.664
30	38.070	38.389	38.714	39.043
31	39.424	39.731	40.115	40.429
32	40.819	41.132	41.502	41.826
33	42.153	42.480	42.864	43.179
34	43.506	43.876	44.239	44.586
35	44.846	45.195	45.630	45.988
36	46.249	46.606	46.948	47.369
37	47.600	47.971	48.344	48.742
38	48.932	49.320	49.707	50.145
39	50.291	50.684	51.079	51.547
40	51.648	52.052	52.490	52.930
41	52.988	53.403	53.871	54.343
42	54.343	54.818	55.300	55.726
43	55.726	56.152	56.653	57.096
44	57.096	57.541	58.002	58.456

Number of ports	Traffic supported in erlangs per port for indicated grade of service			
	0.290	0.295	0.300	0.305
1	0.408	0.418	0.428	0.438
2	1.401	1.425	1.447	1.472
3	2.555	2.593	2.634	2.673
4	3.787	3.839	3.891	3.944
5	5.063	5.131	5.187	5.248
6	6.360	6.443	6.519	6.591
7	7.678	7.769	7.858	7.947
8	9.024	9.112	9.216	9.313
9	10.355	10.476	10.578	10.694
10	11.718	11.830	11.945	12.085

11	13.058	13.208	13.324	13.454
12	14.440	14.585	14.714	14.850
13	15.807	15.958	16.113	16.270
14	17.166	17.333	17.503	17.671
15	18.555	18.719	18.905	19.082
16	19.942	20.096	20.293	20.487
17	21.306	21.515	21.716	21.895
18	22.685	22.904	23.124	23.303
19	24.078	24.275	24.513	24.732
20	25.441	25.688	25.924	26.168
21	26.857	27.066	27.329	27.569
22	28.216	28.492	28.714	29.000
23	29.637	29.895	30.129	30.423
24	31.016	31.285	31.556	31.854
25	32.416	32.714	32.971	33.281
26	33.804	34.068	34.400	34.667
27	35.208	35.479	35.820	36.100
28	36.581	36.867	37.183	37.542
29	37.959	38.314	38.601	38.967
30	39.348	39.731	40.037	40.390
31	40.739	41.132	41.462	41.826
32	42.153	42.531	42.864	43.263
33	43.591	43.959	44.326	44.673
34	44.933	45.371	45.719	46.077
35	46.339	46.786	47.139	47.508
36	47.784	48.157	48.552	48.932
37	49.123	49.561	50.000	50.390
38	50.586	50.981	51.376	51.849
39	51.951	52.388	52.832	53.246
40	53.351	53.819	54.238	54.658
41	54.765	55.193	55.618	56.152
42	56.152	56.653	57.096	57.541
43	57.541	58.002	58.456	58.972
44	58.972	59.404	59.907	60.375

Number of ports	Traffic supported in erlangs per port for indicated grade of service			
	0.310	0.315	0.320	0.325
1	0.449	0.460	0.471	0.482
2	1.498	1.525	1.549	1.574
3	2.714	2.752	2.786	2.829
4	3.997	4.043	4.097	4.151
5	5.316	5.378	5.448	5.507
6	6.662	6.740	6.818	6.898
7	8.025	8.119	8.210	8.303
8	9.415	9.508	9.613	9.722
9	10.794	10.917	11.038	11.146
10	12.208	12.329	12.450	12.572
11	13.611	13.744	13.877	14.011

Number of ports	Traffic supported in erlangs per port for indicated grade of service			
	0.310	0.315	0.320	0.325
12	15.005	15.152	15.299	15.447
13	16.421	16.575	16.734	16.902
14	17.840	18.014	18.191	18.361
15	19.265	19.445	19.635	19.827
16	20.670	20.872	21.076	21.265
17	22.119	22.292	22.510	22.729
18	23.523	23.753	23.985	24.171
19	24.950	25.194	25.416	25.638
20	26.367	26.649	26.857	27.119
21	27.808	28.076	28.326	28.575
22	29.227	29.486	29.778	30.041
23	30.659	30.956	31.254	31.496
24	32.103	32.416	32.683	32.971
25	33.531	33.870	34.134	34.466
26	35.006	35.276	35.612	35.890
27	36.417	36.724	37.038	37.377
28	37.885	38.165	38.530	38.853
29	39.271	39.655	39.962	40.350
30	40.739	41.054	41.421	41.826
31	42.153	42.531	42.864	43.263
32	43.591	43.959	44,326	44.759
33	45.021	45.458	45.809	46.204
34	46.520	46.874	47.277	47.692
35	47.924	48.344	48.742	49.123
36	49.368	49.804	50.193	50.634
37	50.783	51.277	51.648	52.102
38	52.235	52.634	53.091	53.610
39	53.714	54.133	54.551	55.086
40	55.139	55.618	56.046	56.543
41	56.543	57.040	57.541	58.002
42	58.002	58.456	58.972	59.432
43	59.432	59.907	60.492	60.963
44	60.904	61.432	61.913	62.388

Number of ports	Traffic supported in erlangs per port for indicated grade of service			
	0.330	0.335	0.340	0.345
1	0.493	0.505	0.514	0.527
2	1.599	1.629	1.653	1.681
3	2.868	2.907	2.945	2.991
4	4.208	4.258	4.307	4.366
5	5.583	5.649	5.714	5.780
6	6.978	7.053	7.136	7.220

7	8.398	8.483	8.583	8.683
8	9.817	9.932	10.028	10.146
9	11.255	11.385	11.496	11.629
10	12.695	12.844	12.962	13.109
11	14.163	14.301	14.440	14.585
12	15.627	15.778	15.927	16.082
13	17.067	17.233	17.401	17.569
14	18.518	18.719	18.905	19.082
15	20.018	20.175	20.369	20.566
16	21.473	21.673	21.874	22.076
17	22.948	23.169	23.348	23.569
18	24.418	24.635	24.853	25.096
19	25.874	26.117	26.367	26.597
20	27.355	27.596	27.863	28.106
21	28.826	29.114	29.371	29.637
22	30.304	30.600	30.836	31.137
23	31.792	32.072	32.354	32.651
24	33.281	33.562	33.870	34.168
25	34.735	35.070	35.342	35.681
26	36.241	36.523	36.867	37.183
27	37.738	38.033	38.389	38.714
28	39.195	39.501	39.885	40.193
29	40.660	41.054	41.381	41.745
30	42.153	42.531	42.864	43.263
31	43.670	44.042	44.412	44.759
32	45.109	45.541	45.898	46.339
33	46.606	47.001	47.415	47.784
34	48.065	48.505	48.932	49.320
35	49.609	50.000	50.390	50.882
36	51.079	51.497	51.951	52.337
37	52.541	52.988	53.403	53.924
38	54.029	54.448	54.978	55.401
39	55.509	55.939	56.433	56.984
40	56.984	57.485	58.002	58.456
41	58.456	58.972	59.432	60.024
42	60.024	60.492	60.963	61.552
43	61.432	61.973	62.509	62.993
44	62.993	63.461	63.957	64.582

Number of ports	Traffic supported in erlangs per port for indicated grade of service			
	0.350	0.355	0.360	0.365
1	0.538	0.550	0.563	0.575
2	1.707	1.734	1.763	1.791
3	3.034	3.075	3.118	3.161
4	4.426	4.477	4.538	4.599
5	5.858	5.926	5.996	6.068
6	7.306	7.396	7.473	7.561
7	8.767	8.869	8.972	9.060

Number of ports	Traffic supported in erlangs per port for indicated grade of service			
	0.350	0.355	0.360	0.365
8	10.263	10.355	10.476	10.578
9	11.736	11.876	11.992	12.108
10	13.232	13.376	13.507	13.637
11	14.742	14.889	15.035	15.181
12	16.239	16.389	16.575	16.734
13	17.739	17.910	18.085	18.290
14	19.265	19.445	19.635	19.827
15	20.791	20.994	21.158	21.390
16	22.292	22.510	22.729	22.948
17	23.799	24.032	24.275	24.513
18	25.341	25.589	25.824	26.026
19	26.857	27.119	27.329	27.596
20	28.381	28.659	28.881	29.171
21	29.895	30.187	30.423	30.716
22	31.435	31.730	31.978	32.291
23	32.971	33.216	33.531	33.870
24	34.466	34.802	35.070	35.411
25	36.030	36.311	36.652	37.011
26	37.499	37.885	38.202	38.530
28	40.586	40.974	41.340	41.664
29	42.112	42.480	42.864	43.263
30	43.670	44.042	44.412	44.846
31	45.195	45.541	45.988	46.339
32	46.697	47.139	47.508	47.971
33	48.251	48.647	49.123	49.512
34	49.804	50.193	50.634	51.079
35	51.277	51.748	52.153	52.633
36	52.832	53.298	53.714	54.238
37	54.343	54.871	55.300	55.830
38	55.939	56.378	56.874	57.319
39	57.429	57.889	58.456	58.972
40	58.972	59.432	60.024	60.492
41	60.492	60.963	61.552	62.034
42	62.034	62.509	63.113	63.585
43	63.585	64.082	64.645	65.210
44	65.084	65.685	66.199	66.810

Number of ports	Traffic supported in erlangs per port for indicated grade of service			
	0.370	0.375	0.380	0.385
1	0.588	0.599	0.614	0.626
2	1.822	1.848	1.879	1.908
3	3.204	3.246	3.295	3.337

4	4.656	4.716	4.779	4.833
5	6.139	6.213	6.286	6.360
6	7.649	7.738	7.828	7.916
7	9.162	9.277	9.374	9.471
8	10.694	10.815	10.937	11.059
9	12.256	12.377	12.499	12.646
10	13.798	13.931	14.080	14.218
11	15.329	15.508	15.657	15.807
12	16.902	17.067	17.233	17.401
13	18.469	18.627	18.832	19.016
14	20.018	20.214	20.409	20.605
15	21.589	21.795	22.021	22.206
16	23.169	23.392	23.615	23.846
17	24.707	24.950	25.194	25.441
18	26.316	26.545	26.805	27.066
19	27.863	28.106	28.381	28.659
20	29.428	29.702	30.011	30.304
21	31.016	31.315	31.616	31.916
22	32.604	32.906	33.216	33.531
23	34.134	34.466	34.802	35.139
24	35.751	36.100	36.382	36.724
25	37.304	37.664	38.033	38.389
26	38.891	39.271	39.578	39.962
27	40.508	40.819	41.210	41.583
28	42.071	42.398	42.780	43.179
29	43.670	44.042	44.412	44.846
30	45.195	45.630	46.032	46.430
31	46.786	47.231	47.600	48.065
32	48.344	48.837	49.218	49.707
33	49.951	50.390	50.882	51.277
34	51.547	51.951	52.439	52.930
35	53.091	53.610	54.029	54.551
36	54.658	55.193	55.672	56.152
37	56.323	56.763	57.319	57.764
38	57.889	58.342	58.857	59.375
39	59.404	59.965	60.492	61.082
40	61.023	61.552	62.154	62.632
41	62.632	63.113	63.709	64.331
42	64.206	64.708	65.302	65.942
43	65.813	66.304	66.940	67.478
44	67.347	67.937	68.534	69.200

Number of ports	Traffic supported in erlangs per port for indicated grade of service			
	0.390	0.395	0.400	0.405
1	0.638	0.653	0.667	0.680
2	1.938	1.968	1.998	2.029
3	3.389	3.429	3.482	3.526
4	4.899	4.956	5.023	5.082

Number of ports	Traffic supported in erlangs per port for indicated grade of service			
	0.390	0.395	0.400	0.405
5	6.443	6.519	6.591	6.675
6	8.010	8.088	8.194	8.287
7	9.578	9.683	9.798	9.913
8	11.167	11.298	11.407	11.541
9	12.769	12.911	13.038	13.183
10	14.385	14.528	14.685	14.843
11	15.989	16.145	16.302	16.485
12	17.603	17.773	17.945	18.120
13	19.194	19.407	19.597	19.788
14	20.832	21.035	21.239	21.473
15	22.466	22.685	22.904	23.124
16	24.078	24.323	24.561	24.804
17	25.688	25.924	26.168	26.464
18	27.329	27.596	27.863	28.106
19	28.944	29.227	29.486	29.778
20	30.541	30.836	31.137	31.435
21	32.165	32.479	32.778	33.099
22	33.804	34.134	34.466	34.802
23	35.479	35.751	36.100	36.452
24	37.110	37.438	37.811	38.107
25	38.714	39.043	39.424	39.809
26	40.350	40.739	41.132	41.502
27	41.989	42.398	42.780	43.115
28	43.591	44.042	44.412	44.846
29	45.240	45.630	46.077	46.520
30	46.874	47.323	47.692	48.157
31	48.505	48.932	49.416	49.853
32	50.096	50.586	51.079	51.547
33	51.748	52.235	52.735	53.195
34	53.403	53.924	54.343	54.871
35	55.086	55.509	56.046	56.543
36	56.653	57.207	57.652	58.228
37	58.342	58.857	59.375	59.907
38	59.907	60.492	61.082	61.552
39	61.552	62.154	62.693	63.232
40	63.232	63.833	64.331	64.959
41	64.832	65.430	66.070	66.563
42	66.433	67.064	67.675	68.270
43	68.137	68.668	69.335	70.013
44	69.742	70.416	70.958	71.642

INDEX